Talking with Children About Loss

Talking with Children About Loss

*Words, Strategies, and Wisdom
to Help Children Cope with Death, Divorce,
and Other Difficult Times*

MARIA TROZZI
with Kathy Massimini

Foreword by
T. Berry Brazelton, M.D.

A Perigee Book

A Perigee Book
Published by The Berkley Publishing Group
A division of Penguin Putnam Inc.
375 Hudson Street
New York, New York 10014

First edition: October 1999

Published simultaneously in Canada.

The Penguin Putnam Inc. World Wide Web site address is
www.penguinputnam.com

Library of Congress Cataloging-in-Publication Data

Trozzi, Maria.
   Talking with children about loss: words, strategies, and wisdom
to help children cope with death, divorce, and other difficult times
/ Maria Trozzi, with Kathy Massimini; foreword by T. Berry
Brazelton. —1st ed.
      p.   cm.
   Includes bibliographical references and index.
   ISBN 0-399-52543-2
   1. Loss (Psychology) in children. 2. Loss (Psychology) in
children—Case studies. 3. Grief in children. 4. Bereavement in
children. 5. Children and death. 6. Child rearing. I. Massimini,
Kathy. II. Title.
BF723.L68T76 1999
155.9'3—dc21   99-15414
                                                         CIP

Printed in the United States of America

10   9   8   7   6

To my brother, Frank

CONTENTS

FOREWORD

As parents, we would all like to protect our children from sadness or trauma. In our effort to shield them from it, we are probably not wise. This wonderful book offers parents a chance to share grief and loss in an honest way. We have learned that children *do* grieve, and if they can't share their grief with adults around them, youngsters experience loneliness, confusion, and repression, which may cost them enormously. Because they are often overwhelmed or unable to express their devastating feelings of loss, we often ignore or protect them from facing it.

Maria's Good Grief Program has convinced me that helping children to confront tragedy openly amounts to a therapeutic experience. Not only can they share the emotions of important adults around them, but children also can model the coping mechanisms that adults use to face tragedy. Rather than living with a deep wound, which can scar their psychological development, they have the opportunity to develop coping systems for subsequent loss and tragedy. Children also can enhance their future self-assurance as they overcome their wound with our guidance. This approach has come as a revelation to me as a pediatrician, and I'm sure it will to most parents.

In our efforts at Children's Hospital in Boston to prepare youngsters for the stresses of hospital admission, we send out literature to families prior to a child's admission. We urge parents to prepare their children for each step of separation, pain, and recovery during hospitalization. We know that children's ability to face and conquer these experiences are significantly enhanced when parents can share them with the child. Because the parent can be with the child physically in our hospital, we add the importance of sharing emotions as well. From a study conducted at Children's, we learned that when we hospitalized children for prepared admissions, only 15 percent of their parents had followed our urging in the literature. We asked the other 85 percent why they hadn't prepared their children as we had advised them. These parents replied that they had understood that our advice and requests would mitigate their child's reactions to hospitalization, but they ashamedly confessed that they couldn't face the trauma and separation themselves.

We know that parents' participation significantly affects their children's confidence and ability to handle hospital admission and trauma, so we were unwilling to prepare these children ourselves. When we, however, held the hands of frightened parents to support them as they prepared their children, it worked. Children who were undergoing cardiac surgery were significantly more likely to survive and their recovery was significantly shortened if we aided their parents in preparing them ahead of time and if we encouraged these parents to sit by their children during the recovery process.

This seems parallel to Maria's work with other painful experiences that children and their parents face. In this book, she will hold your hand as you share with your children your understanding of a loss, like a death, and your pain of grieving. She also will give you the necessary words to share with your children so that they can understand as well as we do what such a loss means. We can't comprehend death, but we can share it honestly and openly.

Maria's work convinced me of its vital importance from the first. In our often violent school world in Boston, she didn't wait to be asked to join a class in which a member had been hurt or murdered. She called the principal, announcing her conviction that the surviving children "needed" her help. When she went to the class to share these children's terror and their questions, she was able to *interfere* with the inevitable "spread of violence." The terror within the class was significantly reduced. By respecting their need to share suffering with each other and with her, Maria reduced their feelings of hopelessness. They no longer needed to resort to suicide or violence as a reaction. I was convinced that, if she could act as a therapist for communities of grieving children, her approach could be even more valuable for individual children and their families. I have used her thinking and her approach in my own practice. It works!

I urge all parents to read Maria's book and to be ready *themselves* to share their children's grief. If they can be ready and open, they will indeed spare their children some of the scars and distortions of a death or a loss in the family. Parents must prepare themselves for grieving before they can be ready to share their child's pain. This book will surely help in such preparation.

T. Berry Brazelton, M.D.

THIS book embodies the story of every child in that all children experience loss. We can't have life without loss. No one says this more poetically yet to the point than Swami Vivekananda, a great Indian monk and saint, one of the first to introduce Hinduism to the West in the last half of the 1800s.

> *Looking around us, what do we find? A continuous change. The plant comes out of the seed, grows into the tree, completes the circle, and comes back to the seed. The animal comes, lives a certain time, dies, and completes the circle. So does man. The mountains slowly but surely crumble away, the rivers slowly but surely dry up, rains come out of the sea, and go back to the sea. Everywhere circles are being completed, birth, growth, development, and decay following each other with mathematical precision. This is our everyday experience.*

I recalled Vivekananda's words on the day I met Maria, a jewel-like spring day in the Northeast, unusual for mid-March. As I sat in the Boston airport, absorbed in inner silence waiting for my flight to depart from Boston to Atlanta, a vivacious, petite woman began to flip through the pages of a newspaper the second after she seated herself across from me. Casually, as if she knew everyone around her and felt quite comfortable with us, she asked if we knew anything about the fire that had taken place sometime during the night. Nobody said anything.

As I curled myself into a window seat of the plane, to my surprise, the woman with the newspaper sat in the aisle seat next to me. She frantically fingered the newspaper again and spoke, although I couldn't tell whether it was to me, herself, or the world. "I need to find out about the kids in the fire."

I thought, *Is she a pyromaniac?* Having a curious nature, I couldn't resist: "Can I ask what's important about this fire? Not that it isn't a tragic event—but why are you so concerned?"

She smiled and her dark eyes sparkled. "I want to know how the two children died. I'm a grief specialist and I help kids through the mourning process. We might be needed to help in this crisis because these youngsters had siblings. I just want to find out as much information as I can."

When I told Maria that I was a writer, she replied, "I want to write a book and tell the story of bereaved kids. Parents, and some professionals too, don't necessarily understand how loss affects kids. Children are forgotten mourners."

On our flight, Maria's stories tumbled out, one after another. As her rich and vivid tales mesmerized me, she made me realize that kids *don't* say the darndest things. They speak their minds and hearts. We just don't comprehend their language because we think that they don't have a clue about life, so we don't listen to them.

Because I had been a nurse and hospice volunteer many years ago, Maria's words and spirit stirred my own. "Possibly I can help you write this book. You should get your much needed message out there."

For fifteen years, Maria has listened to mourning kids. She has learned to understand what they say and what they *don't* say. Through the myriad stories in this book, she teaches us two dynamic lessons: (1) how to interpret the words, thoughts, and feelings of youngsters and (2) how to relate to kids so that they can survive and grow through losses of any dimension. Authenticity and love are the mainstay of her message.

The stories in each chapter are self-contained and stand on their own. If you read the last chapter first, you'll discover the necessary ingredients to guide your kids through any loss, although this chapter focuses specifically on losses that children encounter in their everyday growth and development. If your child is having a difficult time through a divorce, you'll probably want to check out chapter 14 immediately.

In the five beginning chapters (part 1), Maria's stories focus on how kids process death and other losses, that is, how they think, feel, and react; in chapters 6 through 13 (part 2), her stories highlight how they face the death of loved family members and friends; and in chapters 14 through 17 (part 3), her stories illustrate how they cope with nondeath losses. In every chapter, Maria also details how vital our words and behavior are so that kids can embrace loss without detrimental physical and psychological effects.

Many Westerners don't value death and other losses as one of the profound and wholesome paths of life. These comprehensive stories make us stop to discover the merit of our youngsters' lives and relationships through their losses.

In the last verse of *Song of Myself,* Walt Whitman talks about his legacy to life after his death:

> *I bequeath myself to the dirt to grow from the grass I love,*
> *If you want me again look for me under your boot-soles.*
> *. . . I shall be good health to you*
> *. . . And filter and fibre your blood.*

Death and other losses that kids face can forge good health and strength if, as Maria tells us, "we listen to and walk with children" every step of the way.

Kathy Massimini

ACKNOWLEDGMENTS

I'M most grateful to the countless youngsters and families who have opened their hearts to me and my work. They constantly inspire me as I continue to understand the world of bereaved kids.

This book is a compilation of real stories about children, their families, and their communities. My coauthor, Kathy Massimini, and I have changed their names to respect and protect their privacy. We're indebted to each of them for sharing their pain of loss and trusting us to tell their stories so that others can benefit from their experience. Their honesty, courage, and hope have made this book possible. Through these stories, we also have aspired to honor the spirit and legacy of their deceased loved ones.

Throughout the years, several grief "gurus" have influenced my thinking about mourning youngsters and their families, offering their wisdom and calling attention to issues that require further investigation in research and clinical practice. Sandra Bertman, Myra Bluebond-Langner, John Bolby, Ken Doka, Edna Furman, Robert Kastenbaum, Gerry Koocher, Elisabeth Kübler-Ross, Therese Rando, Beverly Raphael, David Shocnberg, Phyllis Silverman, J. J. Spinetta, Nancy Boyd Webb, and Bill Worden have made important contributions to the world of bereaved children and to helping me expand my thinking.

In particular, I want to acknowledge:

The late Dr. Sandra Fox, my mentor and founder of the

Good Grief Program, who inspired the genesis of my attention to bereavement. I will always be grateful to her for her unfaltering dedication to the task of changing the way in which we think about bereaved children, and for her belief in me to carry on the work she started.

Rabbi Earl Grollman, a pioneer in the field of death education, for his wise teachings and inspired contributions to the bereavement community, and for his continual support of my vision to amplify the effectiveness of the Good Grief Program.

Debbie Dodge, the Dodge family, Dennis Daulton, and the Dodge Institute for Advanced Mortuary Studies for their commitment to the field of death education.

Dr. Stan Turecki, a child and family psychiatrist and author, for his practical and inspirational support of this project early on.

Dr. Barry Zuckerman, chief of pediatrics at Boston University School of Medicine (BUSM), who has been pivotal in my professional development. He has encouraged me and supported the Good Grief Program with his vision and commitment to embrace grief training as a critical aspect of medical education.

Dr. Steven Parker for his invitation to join the Division of Developmental and Behavioral Pediatrics at BUSM three years ago, which has altered my professional life in miraculous ways; for his apparently effortless ability to create a work environment that promotes expansive thinking, nurturing, and good will!

My friends and colleagues in the division, who embody "good works" that benefit children's well-being in Boston and beyond. Thanks to Marilyn Augustyn, Margot Kaplan Sanoff, Betsy McAllister Groves, Tracy Magee, Max Weinreb, Andrea Bernard, Kathleen Fitzgerald Rice, Larry Gray, Carol Hubbard, Remetrious Pena, Sue O'Brien, Naomi Honigsberg, Adrienne Nunley, Margarita Pagan, Cheri Craft, Donna Davenport, Jeanne McCarthy, Margaret LaVoye, Aimee Loiter, Carol Brooks, Holly Newman, Jean Zotter, and Laura Williams.

Professor Tom Clark, who has maintained a powerful place in my life, first as my seventh grade math teacher and later as a willing mentor of my professional development two decades ago. Now

"Clarkie" is my oldest and dearest friend. I will forever be grateful to him for his tireless and unwavering support of every one of my dreams, for his encouragement to think broadly, and for his love and affection toward me and my family.

Dr. T. Berry Brazelton, without whom this book would not have been written. Words fail to express my gratitude to Berry for his belief in me and my life work, for his overwhelming generosity to open professional doors for me, for his teaching without ever lecturing, for his loving encouragement and marvelous joie de vivre, and for his courage to make a difference in children's lives.

Deborah Rivlin for her steadfast loyalty to the Good Grief Program's vision, her invaluable support and patience through our "lean years," her unflagging belief in my ability, her dedicated friendship, and her insight into the world of bereaved kids.

Susan Jennings, writer and colleague of Kathy's, for her keen eye for detail as she patiently offered suggestions to clarify our work.

Steven Callahan, esteemed author as well as Kathy's husband, whose dedication, patience, wisdom, and energy guided this story. We're also indebted to his support over the three years it took us to complete the book.

Stephanie Tade, our literary agent at the Jane Rotrosen Agency, for her optimism about our ideas from the very beginning. She has given us unyielding support and invaluable feedback.

Sheila Curry, our acquisition editor, for wanting to publish a critical message about how we can help kids today face troubled times in their lives. She and her staff at Penguin Putnam Inc. have guided the book's production with astute clarity to the needs of parents and other adults who will benefit from reading it.

Kathy Massimini, my coauthor, for her complete investment in me, personally and professionally, for imagining that we could write this book, for her commitment to perfection and absolute willingness to work for it, for her honesty and intelligence, for her patient understanding of my overwhelming family and professional schedules, and for doing all the worrying.

It was a combination of magical thinking, pure denial, and

strong will that allowed me to consider adding "the book" project to my already overloaded and often overwhelming work and family life. My friends and family have generously buoyed me up through the past three years, offering an abundance of patience and humor as well as occasional snickers.

For all their kindnesses, I'm grateful especially for Nancy, Jane, Gail, Leslie, Lauren, Toni, and my choir group and jazz trio, both of which I temporarily abandoned to take on this project.

And finally, my remarkable family:

My dearest aunt Mimi, who taught me by her example how to love without bounds.

My extraordinary mother and late father, who have cared so much for me and believed that I would care so much about the world.

My sister, Paula Margraf, for her faithful support and love, and for her belief in my vision to share these stories so that other "forgotten mourners" can benefit; for John, Trevor, and Alexandra, whose affection and humor were always present throughout this process.

My beloved daughters, Melissa and Elizabeth, who fill my life with meaning, joy, and pride; for their generous patience with my work; and for their direct and subtle expression of pride in their mom.

My husband, Tom, for offering me his unflinching support and love throughout this project; for joyously assuming a major role in the practical and not so practical chores of our family's life; and, most of all, for believing in my ability to make a difference in the world beyond my doorstep.

Part 1

DANGER AND OPPORTUNITY:
THE MOURNING PROCESS IN CHILDREN

"Danger" and "Opportunity"—
the Chinese Pictograph for Crisis

I Was a Forgotten Mourner

DEATH and loss are vital processes of life. Kids face many losses during the course of their everyday lives. Every fifteen minutes, a baby dies. Every four hours, an adolescent takes his or her life by suicide. Every day, 13 children are victims of homicide. Every minute, an adult with cancer dies. Every hour, 85 adults with heart disease die. Every day, 190 adults die in accidents.

In the early 1980s, I worked with my mentor, the late Dr. Sandra Fox, to create the Good Grief Program. Sandra was the chief of social work at the Judge Baker Children's Center, the mental health facility affiliated with Children's Hospital and Harvard Medical School in Boston. After her untimely death in 1990, I became director of this program. During the workshops I conduct, I talk about how youngsters mourn and how adults are critical to their recovery and healing process. I counsel children and their families privately, work with hospitalized youngsters, and speak nationally to groups of parents, physicians, nurses, psychologists, funeral directors, and law-enforcement officials. In many instances, I'm called to stabilize and manage a community in crisis. Because our society is unable to process children's grief, a tragic death can grind families, schools, and towns to a halt.

People often ask me, "Did you suffer a loss as a child, Maria?" I've always answered with a shrug: "No. At the risk of disappointing you, I have no overt or hidden story lurking in my past. My father died in 1988, which was a deep loss, but I had an Ozzie and Harriet childhood."

In the early 1990s, I interviewed seventeen-year-old Rick for a lecture I was presenting on the psychosocial issues of families living with youngsters who have a disability. Rick's older brother, Luke, was born with Down's syndrome, a genetic disease that impairs a variety of mental and physical capacities. As Rick talked about his nineteen-year-old brother, *I* experienced pain from what Rick *didn't* say about himself. His feelings were missing from his matter-of-fact way of telling me how he could be around Luke for a long time because he was used to him and Luke was a happy person.

Rick always knew that Luke was different and had special needs. "I don't think that anyone told me. My mom did after a while, but I knew already. Mom has to give a lot more attention to him. She does a lot more to try to understand him, like he always gets a second chance—not that I don't—but he gets a lot more attention. It's a lot of work for her, but I don't think it affects me that much." I found myself nodding, not with the empathic gesture of a therapist, but with a gut-wrenching realization that I, like Rick, was a forgotten mourner.

Frankie was my "big brother" and hero. Although I was four years younger, he played with and watched out for me. When I was eight and my younger sister three, Frankie's Boy Scout leader brought him home one day from the Blue Hills, a local hiking area outside of Boston. Evidently Frankie had suffered a seizure. Over the next several years, his physical and mental health spiraled downward. Frankie lost much of his coordination, speech, and muscle movement. When he moved or talked, every part of him shook, often slightly and sometimes vehemently.

After a while, Frankie was unable to catch a ball or play "pickle," a favorite game that he, my dad, and I used to enjoy on the beach during our summer vacations on Cape Cod. He also developed a vacant look and was unable to think clearly because of the medication he took for his "condition," as my parents called it. No one ever gave Frankie's condition a name. I remember being embarrassed by it and wishing that he had something like polio, something with a name that I could tell my friends.

Early one Saturday morning, I heard a huge bang and raced into Frankie's room. He was on the floor, gurgling and flailing his arms, legs, and head in rhythmic movements that looked excruciating. Finally I had witnessed the horror and dread that the word *seizure* implied. That seizure marked the beginning of the end of life as I knew it. In my mind, I divided my life into "before the seizure" and "after the seizure." Frankie didn't die, but I had lost him.

It also seemed as if the world began to revolve around him, which made me jealous for attention. There were *his* pills, *his* erratic behavior, and *his* seizures. My mother constantly hovered over him. By the age of ten, I took on that cause also by becoming his "big sister." Meanwhile, my father minimized Frankie's condition in his efforts to deny it. One Sunday evening, when I was a junior in high school, I couldn't sleep. I went downstairs, sat on Dad's lap, and cried about Frankie. "I feel so sad for him," I said. My father, who was a very gentle and kind person, somehow magically turned my sadness into gratefulness. "Frankie had a good day," he told me, "and we just need to accept this." That was one of the few times I had shared my feelings about my brother with an adult.

Thanks to Rick and the many kids and adults with whom I've had the privilege to work over the past fifteen years, I now can accurately look back on my childhood and adolescence. The significance of *my* loss, like Rick's, was never acknowledged. Frankie lost his physical and mental capacities and my parents lost their promising son, but what did *I* lose? What happened to *my* feelings of sadness, worry, jealousy, embarrassment, and fear? Did they evaporate? No, they were buried—forgotten.

I remember little of my childhood except in relation to my brother. I learned quickly that I was valued and rewarded for acting like a mature adult, for helping out with Frankie, for not complaining about the unfairness of my situation, for not showing pain. I appeared happy, but I harbored a secret. Never did I feel that I was precious to my parents, that my feelings merited expression, that I could ever be "first" in their eyes.

The consequences of my loss didn't end in childhood. As an

adult, I became a first-class "rescuer" (counselor). Seldom did I feel safe to share my vulnerable self with others. I displaced this need by learning how to listen and by trying to become everyone's best friend. Performance equaled acceptance and value to me.

As a child, I never sorted out my feelings about myself, my parents, and my losing Frankie to his disability. Neither did Rick. Luke requires so much more from his mother, and Rick has accepted this by negating his feelings. Luke, Rick says, "gets a lot more attention. . . . but I don't think it affects me that much." Not only do adults fail to acknowledge the significance of their child's loss, but often kids themselves fail to also. For these reasons, I call children the "forgotten mourners."

Rick's story and mine illustrate what I call *nonovert losses*. In this category, I also place such losses that kids face when their parents divorce or when they say good-bye to friends at graduation. Although these losses don't involve death, youngsters undergo the same sense of change, disruption, and mourning.

How does a child of eight or seventeen acknowledge a loss and mourn it? The answer to this question must come from us who love, nurture, and educate our children. How we view death and loss will determine whether or not we allow and encourage a youngster to question any loss and express his feelings about it.

MYTHS ABOUT DEATH, MOURNING, AND PROTECTING CHILDREN

All civilizations create myths to shape reality and address human problems. We pass these myths on to our children and their children. I believe that we, as a culture, have established three mythic beliefs that foster our inability to acknowledge the significance of our kids' losses:

1. Death is not a part of living.

2. Children don't mourn.

3. We can protect children by shielding them from loss.

In *The Tibetan Book of Living and Dying,* Sogyal Rinpoche has said that people in Western society are "taught to deny death, and taught that it means nothing but annihilation and loss. That means that most of the world lives either in denial of death or in terror of it." To ward off death, we spend millions of dollars to develop and use new nonaging creams, pills, surgeries, and the like. The price we pay as we try to capture immortality depicts how we close our minds and hearts to the natural birth-to-death cycle. We dismiss the mourning process as irrelevant to our life cycle and as something that children need not experience.

A few years ago, a couple asked me to see Tommy, their five-year-old son, after his two-year-old brother died accidentally. When his parents would mention his brother's name, Tommy would shut them out or run away. He started wetting the bed and acting unruly in school. What is Tommy telling us by his behavior? He is showing us his grief, his pain, and his anguish from losing his baby brother. Because his parents felt helpless and didn't know how to cope with Tommy's *mourning* behavior, they wanted to sweep it under a rug like many of us want to do. We want to say that Tommy is "resilient," that he'll "get over it soon" and act as he did before. *It* refers to the *death* of his little brother, but we don't want to use the "D" word either. We wait and do nothing until Tommy's unruly behavior evaporates like magic and he bounces back to his "normal" activities.

Earl Grollman, a friend and colleague who has written many enlightening books about mourning, said to me one day: "Maria, what was I doing all those years as a rabbi when I would visit a family who had suffered a death? Where were the *kids?* I never talked with the *children.*" They were probably in a back bedroom crying, but we ignored them. In our need to protect our kids, we prefer to think that they're okay if we leave them alone—we do not share our grief with them or acknowledge theirs.

When Annie's mom, who had cancer, was no longer able to work, nine-year-old Annie had a problem. Her mother's salary had enabled Annie to take ballet lessons. Annie got upset one day because she didn't understand how she could continue dancing without her mom's income. In tears she asked her dad: "Can I still take ballet because Mommy's sick?" Her dad responded, "Come sit next to me, honey. You know Mommy doesn't want you to cry. Big girls don't cry. Don't worry, everything will be fine. We'll make everything fine." I call these words *buck-up therapy.* Although Annie's father loves her dearly and wants to shield her from pain, he hasn't answered her question and has left her alone with her anxieties and fears as well as urged her to repress her emotions. He also has outlawed crying and sadness in their household.

Asking kids to be hypermature is similar to buck-up therapy. When parents die and we tell the oldest boy that he must become "the man of the family" to take his dad's place or when we expect a young girl to pick up where her mom left off, we impose illegitimate responsibilities on children.

If a caring adult, like Annie's father, doesn't allow a child her own unique expression of sadness and anxiety, what effects might she suffer when a parent dies? Although Annie's father took care of her physical needs, he abandoned her emotional needs. After his wife died, he retreated into his own grief-stricken world, unable to assist his daughter or be a role model of grief. As a result, following her mother's death and into adulthood, Annie struggled to find intimacy in her relationships.

By *intimacy,* I mean unconditional love, acceptance, and emotional honesty that all humans require for *security* within a relationship. *Bonding* and *attachment* are words psychologists use synonymously to describe intimate relationships that infants form during their earliest development. Youngsters initially establish such a relationship with their primary caregiver, who is usually their mother. If their mother dies or cannot care for them, they will naturally feel "abandoned." If a subsequent caregiver also abandons them emotionally in their grief, for whatever reason, children might lose their ability to *trust* or turn to adults for security; therefore, they might not be able to develop intimate relationships easily.

In *Motherless Daughters,* Hope Edelman has said that adults who never mourned their mother's death during their childhood often repeat the "loss cycle" in their relationships. This cycle reflects what she has called an "attachment/abandonment pattern." They repeatedly search for a significant person—spouse, boss, or friend—to whom they can become attached in order to obtain the intimate love and acceptance they lost when their mother died. Simultaneously, they worry about and defend themselves against being abandoned by that significant person because they felt abandoned by their mother when she died. As a result, these adults fail to develop feelings of security within their relationships. "Going through an active grief process, mourning the loss . . . and finding peace with it makes the repetition of the [attachment/abandonment] relationship less compelling."

When adults ignore, prevent, or don't encourage kids to express their grief, youngsters can suffer physically as well. Persistent nightmares, sleep or eating disorders, difficulties in completing schoolwork, depression, risk of suicide, and other stress-related disorders don't necessarily suggest a "defined" emotional disorder, but each can indicate that a child, or one who has grown into adulthood, is stuck in the mourning process and has not worked through losses.

Kids also learn behavior from their parents and others who care for them. As role models, adults mold the way in which children mourn. Neither my father nor my mother shared their feelings about Frankie with me, even after I reached adulthood. It's only been since my father's death that my mother has talked about her grief over Frankie. Before this time, she lived in fear, silence, and acceptance. Her fear, her silence, her acceptance were my role models.

Throughout his life, my father denied his grief and ours. In an effort to comfort me on that Sunday evening when I sat on his lap, cried, and reached out to him, he didn't really answer my question. I was actually asking him to help me make sense of *my* sadness and helplessness. But who had helped *him*? And who had shown him how to protect his wife, his son, and his two little girls?

Denial, like other defense mechanisms that we use to avoid the pain of mourning, is a form of protection that appears to work like magic, but it costs us as well. We lose the part of us that yearns for expression, for support, for openness, for honesty. We also never learn the skills we require to achieve what I call *good mourning*. Good mourning promises children a mastery of understanding and a freedom of expression that serves them as they face any loss throughout life.

Is Good Mourning an Oxymoron?

There was next to nothing in the grief literature of the late 1970s and early 1980s about how kids respond to loss. Today, thanks to our ability to look at youngsters with life-challenging illnesses, particularly those with cancer, we know much more about how they perceive, understand, and cope with the death of a loved one or friend. We perform research today that we didn't do fifteen or twenty years ago because kids with cancer didn't live long enough for us to observe how they, their families, and their friends confronted loss. For example, what happens to the siblings and friends of a child who dies from leukemia? What happens to this child's family as a psychosocial unit, and how do they mourn her death?

Dr. Sandra Fox dedicated much of her fifty years to those beset by losses. From her work with children who suffer abuse and deprivation of many kinds, Sandra observed and defined their mourning behavior. She outlined four tasks that they work through as they mourn: *understanding* what caused the loss, *grieving* or experiencing the painful feelings associated with the loss, *commemorating* the value of the loss, and *going on with life* by accepting and integrating the loss psychologically and emotionally within themselves.

Bill Worden, a colleague of Sandra's, has defined mourning as the entire *"process of separating from the person who has died and adapting to the loss."* Sandra stressed that we must assist kids in this process for two reasons: (1) they are not mature enough psychologically to acquire adequate coping skills on their own and (2) they look to us, their caregivers, for help during each developmental stage of childhood. These stages include *preschool, latency, preadolescence,* and *adolescence,* which span the ages between three and young adulthood. To ensure that children develop and master emotional skills as they process an initial loss and then face perhaps more profound ones in the future, caregivers have three major functions:

1. To foster honest and open relationships with children

2. To provide a safe and secure space in which children can mourn

3. To be role models of healthy mourning

Because life doesn't progress in a linear fashion, kids don't first understand and then grieve, commemorate, and go on with life one task at a time. Neither do adults. Rather, our thoughts and emotions surge, ebb, and intersect like waves as the minutes, hours, weeks, and months of mourning progress. A sudden accident, suicide, or murder generates significantly different issues for kids than an anticipated death or a divorce. As they face the pain that a loss generates, youngsters work through the four tasks in small increments, which flow into one another until they have recovered from their loss.

In *Motherless Daughters,* Hope Edelman's message echoes that of Sandra Fox's: The single most important factor that helps mourning kids "become emotionally adjusted, competent adults is the active involvement of at least one stable adult who cares." As Rabbi Grollman says so eloquently, "Grief shared is grief diminished."

We might not always hear our youngsters' cries, but we must be willing to listen and watch for what they say *and* don't say. If we pay attention, we will learn what they need to experience good mourning. Tummy aches, thumb sucking, moodiness, angry outbursts, tearful anxiety, and mature behavior can either mask or reveal their psychic pain and other grief feelings. Our job is difficult because, in many cases, it challenges us to look at our actions and alter our past learning patterns and behavior. If we meet this challenge, we bring families, adults, and children of all ages together. If we deny any loss, conceal it from our kids, or don't value their expressions, they will mirror our unenlightened behavior, possibly suffer one or many emotional problems, and become forgotten mourners.

We need to get into the same lifeboat with our kids, put on our life vests, and have our oars with us. Together, in this survival craft, families can ride out the storm of loss without sinking. The flip side of this metaphor is frightening—to send our children off into unknown, dark waters alone and without survival gear. Ironically, although we would never knowingly do such a thing, our inability to adequately recognize the significance of the many losses that they face, in the normal throes of growing up, isolates them upon unsafe and desolate seas.

The Chinese pictograph for the word *crisis* is composed of two symbols, one that depicts our word for *danger* and the other, our word for *opportunity*. We understand all too well the danger imbedded in the crisis of a loss, but the opportunity is often hidden. This book invites you to seize the opportunity that lies concealed in all losses our kids face. If we charter the boat of mourning with our children, they will realize that only by confronting death and loss and integrating them into their life can they truly embrace living and loving relationships.

WE PUT OLD ROVER TO SLEEP:
The Task of Understanding

WE can't escape loss and death. Every bug, every plant, and every person that is born also dies. Whether we acknowledge it or not, loss surrounds us every day in the news, in our cities and communities, in our schools, or in our own backyards. Kids need to make sense of death or any loss just as much as they need food or warm clothes. We are responsible to help them accomplish this need to understand.

Understanding, the first task of mourning, means knowing what happened to the person who died and why. In the case of nondeath losses, understanding means knowing what situation caused the loss and why it happened. Children can't feel the pain of grief unless they have an honest understanding about what it means to die.

The need to understand is a cognitive and intellectual human need, so it's normal for kids to ask why. "What happened to Grandpa Henry? Why did he die? Where did he go?" Youngsters ask these questions and many others in order to make sense of death at a level appropriate to their age and developmental stage. Their preschool (ages three to five), latency (ages six to eight), preadolescent (ages nine to twelve), and adolescent (ages thirteen to twenty-one) years span the four developmental stages of childhood.

So that kids aren't forgotten, isolated, and left to deal with their confusion and fears on their own as they strive to understand a loss, we must address three issues:

1. The definition of death

2. The way in which children use magical thinking to rationalize death and other losses

3. The cognitive abilities that children possess to understand death and other losses, which depends on their age and developmental stage

DEFINING DEATH

As nurturing adults, we often want to soften our definition of death. This impulse is well intentioned, but it only inhibits our kids' understanding. We cringe and feel inadequate to explain this process of the life cycle. Parents wonder what causes us more anxiety, discussing death or sex—and kids sense our anxiety and discomfort.

Perhaps communicating about death is a painful process because of our experiences as kids. When you were a child, what were you told about death? Some adults remember that no one said anything when, for example, Grandpa Henry died. Sometimes Grandpa Henry went "away" or "to heaven." The veterinarian put our old dog Rover "to sleep." Also, we do a lot of "passing" in this country. As I give workshops around the United States, I hear people talk about "passing on," "passing away," or "passing over." Frequently adults say, "We lost Uncle Sam." A preschool child might reply, "Well, let's go find him." Medical professionals are fond of the word *expire*. When I once asked a group of kids what expires, they said their library cards.

We make *ourselves* uncomfortable, *not our children,* when we use euphemisms and confusing language as we talk with them about death. We need to be direct. Tell kids that Grandpa Henry *died,* that Rover the dog *died.* If Rover was "put to sleep," a child might fear that she too might "go to sleep" one night and never wake up, like Rover.

We also should convey what happens physically to the person who died, by saying that *a dead person's body totally stops working. A dead person can't breathe, eat, talk, walk, or go to the bathroom. A dead person can't do anything.* Preschool and latency-age youngsters might find this definition odd and suggest that it's pretty boring to die! This is, however, an honest explanation of the physical facts of death.

Spirituality in Defining Death

How do our spiritual beliefs fit into this definition? I recall how Hollywood depicted death in a made-for-TV movie in the aftermath of the 1989 San Francisco earthquake, the Loma Prieta. One evening I saw a preview of the upcoming movie. A portion of a bridge had collapsed on top of a car in which a mom and her two kids were riding. Immediately the scene flashed to the hospital and showed Dad coming into the room in which the two children lay. Mom had died and the youngsters, who were maybe six and eight, said: "Daddy, where's Mommy? We want our mommy." Dad told them: "Well, the angels came down and took Mommy." Have you ever heard this response or one similar to it? So the kids said: "Well, just tell the angels to bring her back." Dad looked bewildered momentarily and then said: "Sorry, they are one-way angels. But, we must not feel sad, because Mommy is happier in heaven with God."

That was the end of the clip. Although the father's answers are gentle and kind, they're not truthful facts about death of the body and they might even terrify kids. His youngsters might misunderstand his meaning and blame God or angels for taking their mom from them. They might also be upset because Mommy is happier in heaven with God rather than on earth with them. Honesty about a person's body at death can go hand in hand with our beliefs about the person's spirit. Neither has to negate the other.

Once we explain the physical cause of a death, we can add what our family believes about the spirit or afterlife. Younger children can't understand what they can't concretely "see" or experience in their external world, so sharing our beliefs about the "spirit" can confuse them. However, these beliefs, and the rituals that accompany them, can make children of all ages secure as they open their hearts to their fears of the unknown and to the inexplicable power underlying all life—God, Buddha, Allah, Krishna, their Higher Power, Love.

A few years ago, I worked with five-year-old twins after their older brother died of hemophilia. Because their parents made heaven sound as alluring as Disney World, these little girls wanted to die so that they could be in this dreamy place with their big brother. I remember a child telling me, "Mommy said that because my daddy was so smart, God needed his help with the big Hewlett-Packard in the sky." One four-year-old was told that her mommy was such a good mommy that God asked her to be the special mommy for babies in heaven.

Why would a child be happy knowing that his most cherished person in the world was taken from him to run a computer or care for other kids in heaven? These seemingly protective and comforting explanations might make youngsters (1) blame a higher power for taking their loved ones from them, as the TV movie also illustrated, (2) want to die because death sounds "glamorous" or irresistible, or (3) fear that angels or God will snatch them away too.

Although our spiritual *beliefs* can coexist with the physical *facts* about death, how can we honestly talk about our beliefs? Abstract spiritual reasons are not the *cause* of death. Rather, we should first explain that everyone dies, that "Grandpa Henry's heart was so bad that it caused his body to totally stop working." We can compare it with a machine that can't be fixed. After this factual explanation, we can relate what happens to the person's spirit. A Christian, for example, might say, "In our family, we believe that Grandpa Henry's spirit, the part inside of him that made him laugh and love us and be grumpy with us at times, is now in heaven with God forever." This kind of response is clear, loving, and truthful.

Even with this explanation, young kids might not be able to piece together how the body of a "dead person" can be buried in the ground while the "spirit lives" someplace that they can't see, but don't let this inhibit you from sharing your beliefs about the afterlife. If you say that Grandpa Henry's spirit is in heaven and you take your six-year-old to visit his grave, he will be confused;

but as he grows older, he will learn to make sense of the more abstract concept of spirit.

ADDRESSING MAGICAL THINKING

Because kids live in their own world, they assume responsibility for what happens in that world. Their fears and fantasies also help them to fill in the gaps of a loss that they can't fully understand. Oftentimes, these fears and fantasies about death are unrealistic. *Magical thinking refers to unrealistic reasoning processes that all youngsters use from time to time to explain and make sense of death or another loss.*

For example, a young child created her own magical understanding about the tragic death of Kevin, her five-year-old classmate who choked on a grape. She witnessed Kevin's death in the cafeteria. When I asked her what happened to Kevin, which is always the first question I ask to help children understand a loss, she told me that he died because "he ate his dessert before his sandwich." I clarified this child's unrealistic thinking by telling her that Kevin *didn't* die because he ate his dessert first. I explained that "the grape could have gotten stuck in Kevin's throat whether he ate it *before* or *after* he ate his sandwich. Choking on a grape and dying from this is a very, very rare accident, which doesn't happen to most kids or adults."

Having vivid imaginations, kids also can create a scenario that empowers the person who died with magic or godlike qualities. Very soon after my father died, I was in the kitchen making breakfast one morning when my youngest daughter, Elizabeth, who was eight at the time, called to me from upstairs, "Mommy, look out the window. The sky is gorgeous." It was one of those clear and crisp wintry mornings in January. Then Elizabeth said of her "papa," which she called my father, "He did this for me. Papa made it so beautiful."

In my grief, I cried and said enthusiastically, "Yes, Elizabeth, he did this for you." This answer, however, reinforced an unrealistic view of her grandfather as an omnipotent person who might be able to make all Elizabeth's wishes come true. When I discussed

Elizabeth's magical thinking with Dr. Sandra Fox, I asked Sandra to help me reframe what I said so that it could be a truthful response. Sandra's words were kind but not misleading: "Isn't it wonderful that when you see something as beautiful as a sunrise, it makes you think of your papa?"

Kids also think that they have enormous power to make both good and bad things happen in the world. Because death is one of the most difficult phenomena of life to understand, as youngsters grow and mature, they might attribute it or another loss, like a divorce, to something that *they* said, did, or imagined, often out of guilt.

Fourteen-year-old Brad was convinced that he had killed his grandmother. He was emotionally distraught as he explained to me that he and his friend were playing ball against the side of her apartment, and she kept yelling out the window, "Stop doing that, Brad. You're irritating me." The two adolescents kept throwing the ball against the building anyway. Finally she screamed out, "You fellows will be the death of me," and they stopped playing. The next morning, Brad's grandmother died of a heart attack. She was in her late seventies and had suffered with heart problems for many years. Because of his guilt, Brad was sure that he had caused his grandmother's heart attack. I listened to Brad's recounting of the story, without protesting his assignment of blame, because it's necessary for a caring adult to acknowledge a child's understanding and feelings. I then explained to him that he was using magical thinking to blame himself for something that wasn't his fault.

Although research literature on mourning suggests that children no longer engage in magical thinking by the time they reach preadolescence, which begins around nine years of age, this has not been my experience. I have heard adults say, "If only I had called my father, I could have stopped him from leaving so early in the morning and he wouldn't have gotten killed in that accident."

ADDRESSING CHILDREN'S DEVELOPMENTAL ABILITIES

As I discuss the task of understanding at each developmental stage of childhood, keep in mind that as kids grow and mature so does their perception of death. We also want to remember that every child has a unique temperament and personality, and all youngsters can regress under stress. For these reasons, the four developmental stages represent guidelines, not rigid markers, that define children's understanding.

Grandpa Henry Is Coming Back Tomorrow: Preschool Understanding (Three to Five Years Old)

We know that children under the age of three feel and react to separation, which we detect in their body language and posture. Ask any mother who tries to separate from her two-year-old long enough to take a shower alone! Although infants and toddlers respond to separation, research suggests that they don't have the cognitive capacity to understand the concept of death.

Preschool kids, between three and five years of age, have predictable thinking and behavioral patterns that we can discern as they strive to perceive death. They think that death is temporary and reversible; that is, Grandpa Henry is dead today but he's coming back tomorrow. These children also think that they themselves will never die. The media help to validate their thinking. In "Roadrunner" cartoons, Wile E. Coyote gets flattened repeatedly but always jumps right back up as energized as ever.

To preschool youngsters, death means *living* under different circumstances, like going on a trip from which you *return*. They want to write, call, or fax the person who died in an effort to continue a physical relationship with him. When kids of this age draw "what happens at death," they generally depict one of two classic scenes. Some draw angels and clouds, which form heaven. Just as often, others create underground vertical, not horizontal, boxes that contain people. Sometimes a comic blurb like "help!" emanates from a person's mouth. Tunnels connect the boxes. Inside the tunnels are Burger King, McDonald's, Kentucky Fried Chicken—all their favorite places to eat.

These kids are telling us that life in the body goes on above or below us after death. They want to understand how Daddy will get his newspaper or how Grandpa Henry will get by without his wheelchair. Their concerns are concrete and literal because preschool children think literally, not abstractly.

Marion consulted with me after Timmy, one of her first grade students, died from a brain stem tumor. I advised her to tell his preschool classmates that Timmy died from a sickness in his head, which made his brain and the rest of his body stop working. As Marion took attendance each morning, however, her kids would stop her when she'd skip over Timmy's desk and say, "You forgot Timmy." They thought that Timmy would be coming back.

Marion had already told them that Timmy would never return to class because he died and you can't come back after you die. But these first graders didn't ask whether Timmy would be coming back. Even if they did and Marion had responded truthfully, they still would have continued to look for Timmy to return anyway. Whenever her students told her that she forgot Timmy at role call, I advised Marion to ask them, "Is Timmy here?" Then, despite their daily expectation of Timmy returning, her kids would say, "No, Timmy died."

She wanted to remove Timmy's desk very quickly because it was such a painful memory for her. I felt that it would be best for Marion to leave the desk in place for a while longer so that the class would have a chance to commemorate Timmy's life (see chapter 4). In addition, what message do we give kids if we remove the desk too quickly after their classmate has died? They might think that Timmy wasn't important and that we don't value life. "Hmm . . . Timmy was here yesterday and gone today. If I die, I guess the same thing would happen to me. I'd also be forgotten, just like that."

Despite her youngsters' inability to grasp that Timmy would not come back to life, Marion was clear and truthful with her explanations about why Timmy died and what death means. She helped these preschool kids accept his death as part of their school life, and she taught them to acknowledge and respect all aspects of our life cycle, Timmy's death as well as their own lives.

Will the Worms Get Grandpa Henry? Latency Understanding (Six to Eight Years Old)

Youngsters in latency, between the ages of six and eight, understand that death is permanent and irreversible, but they think this is not a universal phenomenon—that is, they know others will die, but they believe themselves immune, just as preschoolers do. If you ask latency-age kids to draw "death," they often depict a male character covered in black, like Darth Vader. These youngsters want to know if death is contagious and if life is going to be safe for them. Most ask detailed and straightforward questions: "Why is the body cold?" "Why does she look all blue and puffy?" Children at this age want information that will make them feel safe.

Kelly, who is in second grade, came home from school and said at the dinner table, "Billy's dad died. Are you going to die, Dad?" This is a typical question that a latency-age kid might ask because her security is at stake. How can we be direct and truthful and still make our youngsters feel secure? Although the first response might be, "No, I'm not going to die, Kelly," no seven-year-old child worth her salt will believe this.

When I met with a group of pediatric surgeons at grand rounds, I asked these surgeons to respond to Kelly's question. I found their answers to be human—and humorous—in light of the probable responses they could receive from youngsters. "My cholesterol level is quite low. I'm in great shape." "I'm doing well. I eat well, sleep well, and keep busy, so I should live a long life." "I jog and exercise regularly, after all! No need to worry about me dying."

Yes, our kids want to know that we can protect ourselves in order to create a safe environment for them. These surgeons didn't go far enough with their answers, however, because many times the response we'll get from a latency-age youngster is something like, "Well, Billy's father didn't expect to die either, and he jogged every day. Look what happened to him!"

To say to children that *everybody dies someday, but most people live to be very, very, very, very old* (I've added a couple of *verys* since I turned forty) gives them a realistic outlook on life and death. If Billy's father died in an accident, such as a plane crash, we can also say, "There's nothing I can do to protect myself 100 percent, but I certainly try my best because I want to take care of you and live to be very, very old."

Kids just want information, but it must be truthful. I use the word *authenticity* to refer to our honesty and openness throughout the mourning process. Rather than becoming paralyzed by our fear that children might be devastated if we are authentic, we need to realize that, in order for them to feel safe, it's necessary for us to give them the information they seek. Being credible with kids is critical to gaining their trust.

If Kelly lived in one of our inner-city neighborhoods torn apart by random violence, the response to "Will you die, Dad?" would not be the same as if she were a seven-year-old who lived in a middle-class town in which most people die of old age. Unfortunately, children who are the silent victims of domestic and community violence grow up with different assumptions about their world. These assumptions are based on the reality of their daily lives in which their loved ones die at two, twenty-two, and forty-two. A kid living in a neighborhood ruled by gangs realizes that his adolescent brother might be killed at the age of sixteen. A kid whose grandfather molests him or whose mother is beaten regularly by his alcoholic father lives in constant fear of abuse and death. In their homes and on the streets, these youngsters are robbed of the security that they need to develop and thrive. Adults have to help them find and rely on a safe place *within themselves.* Six-year-old Eugene learned from his single mom how to protect himself in their gang-infested apartment complex. When he heard shots, he instantly jumped into the bullet-proof porcelain bathtub, which made him feel secure in the middle of his persistently frightening world.

Latency-age kids who don't have to confront violence as part of their daily lives often criticize the dead, also to ensure their own safety. They place people who die into three categories—the elderly, the handicapped, and the klutzes. Neither of the three can move quickly enough to escape death, but latency-age children are physically competent and can run fast, so they think that death can't catch them.

I talked with eight-year-old Steven and his classmates after his five-year-old brother died in a freak accident. Steven and his family had gone skiing for the weekend. As his parents were packing to leave the condo they had rented, Steven and his younger brother, Mickey, were playing in the snow. All of a sudden, a sheet of heavy ice slid from the condo roof and hit Mickey in the nape, severing his spinal cord and killing him. "Can you tell me what happened?" I asked Steven and his classmates. As they explained the incident with much detail, they laced their stories with how dumb Mickey was to die in this way. "What a stupid way to die! Everybody hears ice when it slides down the roof. He wasn't listening." "Mickey just didn't run fast enough." "His neck was too weak." By criticizing Mickey, these kids found ways to keep themselves safe. Although we want to explain what happened if children don't understand the cause of a death, it is impractical and unnecessary for adults to counter these youngsters' protective thinking. In fact, adults engage in this behavior for the same reason. We call it denial!

Once they reach latency, children also want to know what's predictable and what's going to change following a loss, which relates to security issues as well. "Am I still going to have Honey-Nut Cheerios even though Mommy died?" "After Paul dies, can I have his skates?" Kids are marvelously egocentric at this age and simultaneously fascinated by what makes the world go round.

This fascination makes them interested and curious about the facts surrounding death. They have a need to understand details. By the time they reach six, children might ask if the worms will get Grandpa Henry. This question can repulse adults and conjure visions that we don't want to entertain, but the last thing we should say is, "That's disgusting, we don't talk about such things at the dinner table or *ever*!" The truthful answer to this question is not as disconcerting as we might think. If Grandpa Henry is placed in a heavy metal casket, a container that is sealed, funeral service professionals believe that worms can't get in; therefore, worms don't eat dead bodies buried in caskets underground.

How many details do latency-age kids need? How much detail is too much? Every child's and adult's need for details lies someplace on a continuum. Some kids just need the barest facts.

"Grandma Martha was hit by a truck and died in the ambulance on the way to the hospital." That's what happened and that's all one child might want to know. Other youngsters need a videotape of Grandma Martha being hit by the truck and rushed to the hospital. Adults typically err by assuming that a child, particularly a latency-age child, needs to know *less* than she really wants to know.

You have to walk *with* children of all ages. You can't push them and you can't pull them. In the process of walking with them, you've got to be that safe person who will address what I call the unmentionable thoughts and questions. *If it's unmentionable, it's unmanageable.*

Unless we can talk about what happened with as many details as our kids require, they can't begin to manage the feelings behind their troubling, confusing, or fearful thoughts. The number of details is unimportant. Children need loving adults willing to speak to whatever issues they have. As parents, grandparents, or caregivers, we can make them feel comfortable by saying, "Whatever you're afraid to say or ask, I'll be with you and we'll deal with it together. I might not know the answer, but let's figure it out or find out together." We often overlook the task of understanding because we have such a difficult time facing the unmentionable within ourselves.

What, for instance, is the unmentionable in a situation in which an eight-year-old classmate died in a head-on auto accident? One of his friend's might venture, "Well, I wonder what he looks like now." Five or six other kids might reinforce this question and reflect on it. At this point, they're off and running down the road of healthy mourning because they're able to talk about the unmentionable and not bury it inside.

Most adults have a natural tendency to block terrifying and upsetting images in their mind's eye. If, however, we can't escape them and need to talk to maintain our emotional stability and well-being, we don't want to "unload" our terror on kids. We need the help of an adult friend or therapist.

Talking about the unmentionable with kids is powerful and provides relief. If we allow them to express their mental picture of an accident, complete with horrid details, they learn that their imagination is more powerful than the truth in many situations. Not talking about what we think is unmentionable isolates our children, as well as ourselves, and keeps them stuck in the mourning process. It might be difficult to determine where a latency-age child or any other child will fall on the continuum of what details are important or unimportant to her, but I urge you to be the safe person to whom any youngster can come and ask the unmentionable.

Grandpa Henry Died? You Mean I Have to Wear a Suit and Tie? Preadolescent Understanding (Nine to Twelve Years Old)

Most preadolescents have an adult understanding of death. Nine-, ten-, eleven-, and twelve-year-olds know that death is permanent, irreversible, and universal. They will die someday, and when they do, it's forever, a frightening thought that tends to prevent them from talking or expressing their emotions about a loss. They fear abandonment and want to know how their world will change after someone dies: "Will everything and everybody fall apart, leaving me deserted? The best thing to do is not talk about it, so I don't have to deal with it." Death and loss become intellectual concepts to them.

Because they intellectualize loss, many preadolescents are interested in the biological aspects of death. Medical models, such as the liver, heart, and brain, are important to their understanding of why the body stops working. Rituals at the time of death often fascinate them, and they might be interested in traditional societal and religious practices of commemoration. Students learn about Egyptian mummies, usually in sixth grade, making this a wonderful time to discuss death and dying issues with them.

When my friend's daughter Susan was ten, her pet gerbil, Jekyll, died despite their veterinarian's attempt to save him. When Susan picked up Jekyll's body from the animal hospital, it was frozen and wrapped in a blue face cloth secured with adhesive tape. Once she got Jekyll home, Susan unwrapped the cloth because she wanted to see what Jekyll's dead body looked like. She decided to give him a "proper burial," covering him with a Kleenex and placing him in a Celestial Seasonings tea box. After writing a poem to eulogize him, Susan buried Jekyll beneath a rhododendron bush in front of her home. It was early winter and dark at that time of the evening.

A few months later, Susan and my daughter Elizabeth dug up Jekyll's body on one of those glorious spring days in which you have all your windows open. Susan's mother shared with me their interesting conversation: "Hey, there's the tea box." "Oh, it's all wet and yucky and falling apart." "There's his little leg." Once these preadolescents checked out the state of deterioration of Jekyll's body, they placed it back in the box and reburied it.

Preadolescents also start to think abstractly. Guilt can come into play when they experience a loss because they're beginning to understand the abstract issues of cause and effect. It's not uncommon for them to wonder what they did to cause a person's death or what they failed to do, but unlike latency-age youngsters, they don't want to share these thoughts. Nine-year-old kids, in particular, think that death is a punishment for bad behavior—good people don't die, and bad people do. This "good and bad" kind of thinking changes as they grow further into their preadolescent years.

Unlike latency-age children, preadolescents don't ask many questions about the cause of a death. We might see a callous or "no-big-deal" attitude about a loved family member or friend who has died, an attitude that can be misunderstood. Preadolescents also might say nothing or pretend that they understand what has happened when they don't. If they are behaving in this way, questions might draw them out and provide an opportunity for us to present factual information.

For example, I might say, "You know that Grandpa Henry died of a heart attack. Although Grandma Martha told us that he died without suffering, I'm wondering if you have any questions about his death? Do you understand how heart problems can cause someone to die, and what Grandpa Henry went through?" It's typical for a preadolescent to respond, "Sure, I know all about that. We studied about the heart in school." He might not know all the answers about Grandpa Henry's death, however, which gives me another opportunity to address this young boy's unmentionable thoughts. I would reply, "Well, tell me what you know about heart attacks. Is there anything about Grandpa Henry's death that worries you? You can talk to me about anything."

His answer might very well be, "I want to know . . . you mean I have to wear a suit and tie to Grandpa's funeral?" This seemingly insensitive question, if preadolescents have any, is not uncommon either. Because this kid fears that life, in particular his parents, might fall apart due to Grandpa Henry's death, he wants to "keep it together." His way of doing this is *not* to discuss uncomfortable and painful facts about mortality. Although he doesn't want to express his thoughts, and a parent might feel frustrated at this point in the conversation, the best approach is to answer his question and then share your understanding of why Grandpa Henry died, how you feel about his death, and how life will go on for the family without him.

After the space shuttle *Challenger* exploded in January 1986, some preadolescents in a Midwestern school were absorbed in telling offensive body part jokes about Christa McAuliffe, the teacher who died on that flight. Shortly after this tragic explosion, I spoke with a group of parents, teachers, and psychologists in this Midwestern city and learned that the teacher second in line to replace Christa McAuliffe taught at this particular school. These kids were invested in this tragedy because it could have been *their* teacher who died in the explosion. Their gruesome jokes were a way for them to intellectualize and distance themselves from their feelings about what could have happened to their world had this teacher been on that flight.

How should we respond to these jokes if youngsters share them with us? We can say, "Your jokes offend me, especially now because I'm feeling sad. Please don't say them in front of me." This answer doesn't tell our preadolescents that they are disgusting for saying such things, but it does say that jokes of this nature are hurtful and inappropriate in our presence. We can also share what we think about this tragedy. In this way, we *model* our mourning behavior because we offer them a realistic picture of how we understand this tragic death, which is the most authentic gift we can give them.

Is This War Worth Dying For? Adolescent Understanding (Thirteen Years Old to Adulthood)

At puberty, young people find themselves actively engaged in the issues of adolescence. They are:

1. Separating from their parents

2. Coming to terms with their sexual identity

3. Making sense of their world in a moral way

4. Making vocational choices that will carry them into the adult world

Any one of these issues can be tumultuous for emerging adolescents, but starting to master these four issues also gives them a sense of independence and hope. The impact of a death or other loss can threaten their feelings and dreams of the future.

Although adolescents have an adult understanding of death as final and universal, they're on the threshold of adulthood and see the majesty and power of what lies ahead, a power that makes them tempt fate. Despite their cognitive capacity to *understand* death, adolescents *feel* invincible and immortal. They often engage in high-risk behavior—drinking, smoking, taking drugs, driving at breakneck speeds—and seem to need to live on the edge between life and death in order to make sure that they are alive and living to the fullest.

The death of a friend shatters adolescents' fantasies of immortality and makes them question their behavior, although only for a brief time. Like preadolescents and adults, adolescents also might blame themselves as they look for the cause of a death. "What did I do? What should I have done? Why my friend and not me?" They become philosophical and observe society's attitudes toward issues of life and death. During this stage, adolescents review and revise their ideas and assumptions from childhood and "reconstruct" their world. When they are confronted with the death of a peer, life becomes vulnerable.

During the Gulf War of 1991, I worked with many high school

students to help them explore their issues about their older friends and siblings going off to war halfway around the world to protect Kuwait (see also chapter 11). Most high school teens had never heard of Kuwait, but they had many questions about the war. "My brother is over there. Is this war worth the price of death?" "What are the potential risks of death in this situation?" "What am I living for?"

These questions haunt adults as well. We might not have answers because many of these questions are unanswerable, but we need to ask these tough questions and ponder them with our kids. Although adolescents don't want to be told what to think or do, they want to know why adults do things in a particular way so that they can learn to make their own decisions. We need to express our thoughts and listen to theirs in order to enhance their sense of mastery, purpose, and dignity in life.

Matt was fifteen when his dad, Jack, died after struggling to live with AIDS for three years. Until he contracted AIDS, Jack was a devoted and involved father with two sons. He had a mild form of hemophilia, which didn't hamper him physically or psychologically until he received a contaminated unit of blood. When Jack's HIV status converted into full-blown AIDS, he became a "patient" who was unable to play ball, go to soccer matches, and take family vacations. Finally, he was confined to a hospital bed in a makeshift bedroom on the first floor of his home.

Matt was angry with his dad for "dying on him" one day at a time. He felt helpless and avoided visiting Jack in this bedroom because his dad's personality had completely changed. Jack was often grumpy and disagreeable, refusing to watch any TV shows except those about cooking and fishing, although he had not done either in his lifetime. Sometimes he was mean-spirited and would not talk with Matt or Matt's younger brother. Matt was supposed to understand and tolerate his dad's sickness and resulting behavioral change, but he was incapable of accepting either. He coped by *not* talking about his father, by spending long periods of time with his friends, and by hanging out in his room and listening to music. Although Jack was a victim of poor blood screening, Matt was embarrassed by his dad's diagnosis and didn't want his friends to know that his father had AIDS. Most people in his community were aware of it, but they didn't talk about it with Matt.

When his dad died, Matt was faced with his "differentness" in being fatherless. His old feelings of anger, guilt, and sadness were coupled with relief that his dad's protracted illness was over. During the weeks and months following Jack's death, Matt's mother was able to tolerate her son's withdrawal, moodiness, and occasional hostility toward life and everyone in his path. She remembered my "lifeboat analogy" from one of my workshops that she had attended (see chapter 1). Once a week, she gathered her two sons together for a family meeting, which was a way for them to jump into the same lifeboat together and share their problems. The purpose of these meetings was twofold: to talk about plans for the week ahead and to bring up feelings about the changes that the family members were sorting out. Matt used these planned family meetings to talk about how different life was without his dad. Although he didn't directly discuss his father's diagnosis and illness, these meetings were effective in providing Matt with a safe place to share his feelings when he was ready to do so.

On the one hand, adolescents like Matt can feel invincible, but on the other, they can feel helpless and overwhelmed as they tackle the enormous responsibilities of becoming independent. They also carry their adolescent issues and feelings with them as they face any loss. Adults, however, often dismiss the magnitude of feeling that accompanies adolescent issues and losses. As adolescents learn to mature through the crises of their world and make their own decisions, these youngsters need us to listen carefully so that they can cope with and resolve any difficulty they perceive.

TEACHABLE MOMENTS AND PETS

A kindergarten teacher in an absolute panic called me one Monday after spring holiday. Thumpy, the class bunny had died while this teacher vacationed in St. Martin, leaving Thumpy in the care of a friend. She had thought of buying another bunny, which a colleague of hers had once done, and pretending that he was Thumpy without saying anything to her youngsters. This strategy backfired on her colleague because the replacement bunny, supposedly a male, happened to be a pregnant female who had little ones two and a half months later. Although her colleague escaped educating her kids about death, she was harnessed with lessons on sex education and baby bunny care.

This story offers what I call a *teachable moment*. A teachable moment presents us with the opportunity to communicate truthfully about the meaning of death and its relationship to the natural cycle of life. For many kids, the death of a pet is the first loss they experience in life. Thankfully, the teacher who called me wanted helpful language to share Thumpy's death with her students. I told her to be honest, tell her class exactly what had happened while she was away, and explain the facts of death; that is, "Thumpy's body totally stopped working because he got a terrible infection in his heart. His heart couldn't work, so he stopped breathing."

We have many opportune moments to talk with kids about the meaning of death. Often, preschool kids will point to roadkill (dead animals in the road) and want to know what it is. We can encourage preadolescents and adolescents to share their feelings about death when they dissect frogs in biology. Many animal shows on TV depict the birth and death of birds, tigers, and elephants. In hospitals, we can help youngsters confront their fears about going into surgery and never waking up. I tell them that they will sleep through two or three *Barney* shows instead of saying that they will be "put to sleep." Pets, TV programs, and animals in nature provide us with great stories to help our kids understand death. The following is a true story that you might share with your child one day when the moment arises.

Ten-year-old Jerry had never experienced the death of a person or animal whom he had known. His aging grandparents, who were near and dear to him, had serious health problems, and Jerry's mom wondered whether Fluffy's death would serve him when his grandparents died.

Fluffy was his parents' pet cat even before Jerry was born. She was like a member of the family. Jerry loved her dearly, even as she grew very old. When she was seventeen, which is old for a cat, Fluffy began to forget to use the litter box and had accidents all over the house. Soon she was unable to jump anymore and lost interest in playing with Jerry. These events, coupled with frequent trips to the veterinarian, helped Jerry's mom and dad prepare him for Fluffy's inevitable death. Jerry began to understand that Fluffy might die soon.

One day, Jerry's mom told him that Fluffy was very sick and not going to get better. It was time to take him to Dr. Moses, the veterinarian, to "put Fluffy to sleep." Jerry remembered that his best friend, Samuel, had cried when his parents had Bowser, the family dog, put to sleep without telling Samuel first. Samuel was angry and confused. Jerry knew about *death,* but he wasn't sure what *put to sleep* meant.

The whole family—Mom, Dad, Jerry, his older sister, Penelope, and his older brother, Nick—took Fluffy to Dr. Moses' office. Penelope gently held Fluffy in the backseat of the car. This was a sad and anxious ride for Jerry. He knew that Fluffy wasn't really going to sleep. How would it feel to have her die?

The family waited in another room as Dr. Moses gave Fluffy the shot that caused her to die. A little while later, the doctor came out with their beloved Fluffy wrapped in the blanket in which they had carried her. The ride home was silent, except for the quiet sobbing from each family member, including Jerry's dad.

Dad, Jerry, and Nick dug a hole for Fluffy's grave in their backyard. Jerry chose his favorite spot under a "climbing tree" that he loved. They carefully placed Fluffy's body into the deep hole and covered it with dirt. Jerry asked if the family could say some prayers. Mom and Penelope joined the boys. Holding hands, they each said a little prayer for Fluffy.

The next day, Jerry went to school and told his teacher about Fluffy's death. She shared a story about the cat she had while she was growing up. He was her favorite pet, and he also had to be *euthanized* like Fluffy. She told Jerry that this was the correct term. After lunch, Jerry asked his teacher if he could go home because he just sort of felt sick. Mom came to pick him up and understood that Jerry was probably feeling sad about Fluffy. They spent the rest of the day together. Jerry decided that he wanted to paint a picture of Fluffy, which made him feel better. He hung it on his mirror for several days. One day he decided that he would put it in his treasure box, a special place for prized possessions.

What Rabbi Grollman has referred to as "straight talk" about death, I call authenticity and teachable moments. Authenticity, honestly discussing death, and teachable moments help kids, as well as adults, incorporate the existence of death and other losses into their life. Through these measures, we acknowledge death, not deny it, and we acknowledge that our children have losses and that their losses are significant.

It's difficult to help youngsters accomplish the task of understanding. As we walk with them through the door that houses the pain of mourning, we also help them open other doors. Through these, they find safety as they survive a loss, learn to embrace loss as much as they embrace achievement and gain, and let it nurture them as they go on with living and facing future losses. In the process, we will develop loving and trusting relationships with our kids—relationships in which they will feel free to share whatever in their minds and hearts feels unmanageable.

What Did You Bring Me from Florida?
The Task of Grieving

If children are going to recover and heal from any loss, they must grieve it. *Grieving, the second task of mourning, means experiencing the painful feelings associated with a death or other loss.* Grief is a psychological and physiological response that humans experience as they adapt to the reality of a loss and separate from a person no longer with them or from a situation no longer viable or under their control. *Anger* and *sadness* are the principle feelings of grief in both kids and adults. All humans feel isolated or alone in their pain because grief is idiosyncratic; that is, every person has his or her own style of grieving.

Many people suggest that, as a culture, we tolerate sadness more easily than anger, but I disagree. Sadness, which is usually acute and intense immediately following the death of a loved one or friend, becomes quiet and lingers over the ensuing weeks and months, unlike anger. We feel helpless to ameliorate sadness; therefore, because it makes us uncomfortable, we close our eyes to it and to the grieving child as well.

I'm reminded of a couple whose child was accidentally shot while he and some of his friends were playing with a firearm. The child had four school-aged siblings. The mother of this family worked evenings as a school custodian, so the father got supper together, saw that the kids did their homework, and made sure that they got to bed at a reasonable time. For many weeks after his boy died, the dad spent his evenings in the garage taking apart and putting together the dirt bike that belonged to his son. Out of necessity, the oldest girl, who was sixteen, parented her siblings. As I worked with the father and his family, I learned that he had made himself unavailable to his children, not only because he was grieving but also because he didn't know how to remedy their sadness. By avoiding his kids, he added to their pain and isolated them further. Through our sessions, he learned that he could not take away his children's pain, but he could share his with them. He also came to realize that kids grieve differently from adults.

Although adults might be able to smile, laugh, and carry on conversations about the weather in the midst of their grief, they don't forget their loss. It is, so to speak, a pain in their minds and hearts twenty-four hours a day. Kids experience grief differently. *Unlike adults, children grieve in spurts*. They have a limited capacity for tolerating ambivalent feelings and a lower threshold for psychological pain than adults have; therefore, one minute they can be angry or sad, and the next they can be happy and content, forgetting their grief entirely. We can describe their grief as *sad, mad,* and *bad*. Kids feel sad because they long for their loved one, and they feel mad because she left them. They act out their sadness and anger, making their behavior *appear* bad.

Grieving occurs simultaneously with understanding (the first task of mourning). Adults have two specific functions to help children through the grieving process.

1. We need to recognize and facilitate our kids' grief responses.

2. We need to show them our own grief.

RECOGNIZING AND MANAGING CHILDREN'S GRIEF RESPONSES

Although we should allow kids to lead us as we help them express their feelings, we must be aware of five factors that have an impact on their grief response:

1. Their development stage and cognitive ability to understand death

2. Their necessity to regrieve as they grow and develop

3. Their relationship with the person who died or other loss they experienced

4. The suddenness or anticipatory nature of the death or loss

5. The secondary losses that often accompany a primary loss

Effects of Developmental Stage and Cognitive Ability on Grief

Everything feels out of sync to grieving children because kids don't like change. A disrupted routine is likely to make them feel less safe, especially if a parent or sibling dies.

Preschool and latency-age children can be quite aggressive, obstreperous, and boisterous. They also might exhibit regressive behavior, like bed wetting, thumb sucking, and changes in sleeping patterns. It's not unusual for a seven-year-old youngster who lost her mother three months ago to bug everyone in class, at recess, or at day care following school. She can't keep her hands to herself. When she gets on the school bus, she immediately begins to disturb the kids around her.

When our youngsters become unruly or act out in other disturbing ways, how can we help them? Although aggression and obstreperousness are hard to manage, we need to set the same concrete limits on their behavior as we did before the death; however, we need to do it with more kindness. Specifically, we need to check in with a child very often to ask her how she feels, to comfort her, and to share our grief with her.

Teachers often are confused about what works effectively to miti-gate the disruptive class behavior of a child who has suffered a loss. A paper clip is a very inexpensive tool for this purpose. When a child can't contain his aggressive behavior, ask him to flag you with a paper clip that you have given him for this purpose. Tell him that you realize he might have good and bad days or times in class that might be worse for him than others. When he flags you, give him permis-sion to go to the water fountain or visit the school nurse for a certain length of time. By allowing him to attract your attention and by giv-ing him some "time out," you remind him that you're there for him and that you know life is tough. This simple therapy costs nothing but attention and sensitivity.

Preadolescents and adolescents also grieve in spurts, but they express their grief much differently than younger kids do. Although preadolescents are intellectually curious about medical facts and rituals surrounding death, they are reticent to show or share their painful emotions. Letting their emotions out might tear their safe world apart, so they want to maintain control of the world by not dealing with their feelings.

I believe that they have learned this behavior from adults. Par-ents want to keep their chin up and be "strong" in front of their kids. They then express their anger when their youngsters misbe-have, and anger shows the strength of parental control. To display sadness is "weak," challenging the secure world parents have built for their families. Preadolescents have learned how to cope with their parents' anger and the control it imposes on them, but they are not familiar or comfortable with their parents' sadness. What will happen to them if their parents are sad and out of control?

Sam was eleven when he woke one morning to learn from the babysitter that Vicki, his five-year-old sister, had died in her sleep. His parents were vacationing. When they arrived home, he greeted them at the door: "Hey, what did you bring me from Florida?"

Is Sam an insensitive creep? Of course not. But what is his real-ity after his sister's death? "If Mom goes to pieces, if Dad can't hold himself together, then what?" In confronting his sister's death, Sam feared that his parents' overwhelming sadness would incapacitate them. Who would care for him? His tactless question was sure to illicit an angry response and make this devastating loss more tolerable and safe for him. Sam would rather shield his emotions and make his parents angry than suffer the uncertain consequences of their sadness.

Because Sam fears being abandoned, his parents need to reassure him that he is going to be okay because they're going to take care of him. They also must be authentic in their expression of grief and model it for him: "I can manage it. I'm sad. I may cry a lot. I'll get angry too, but I'm okay; therefore, I will be okay for *you.*"

Adolescents, on the other hand, have powerful emotions as they are learning to shape their independent identity. They want us to be available to them, but they want to grieve and emote with their peers, not with adults. When Christie found out that a close friend hung himself at a college across the country, she called her parents at two in the morning and asked them to come and bring her home from school, which was two hours away. The next morning after nineteen-year-old Christie awakened, she began to bake apple pies and didn't say much about what had happened.

Her mom was concerned about Christie's "odd" behavior, so she kept asking or encouraging her daughter to talk about the suicide: "Why don't you sit down with me instead of baking these pies, Christie?" Finally Christie replied, "Look, Mom, I'm so upset. Can't you see how this is tearing me apart? Life will never be the same without Warren. Please don't bug me. I just want Alan, Susan, and John here. I want to pick Susan up at the train station. She's coming in at noon. Can I borrow the car?"

Christie was baking pies for her other friends who were arriving home from various colleges around the United States so that they could grieve for Warren and remember him together. But she still had to be near her parents during this upsetting crisis in her life. Although adolescents want the prerogative to spill their emotions over onto caring and supportive adults, they want us to respect their need to grieve in their own way and with their peers.

Regrieving

All children regrieve a significant loss through each developmental stage. If a parent dies when a child is four years old, that child will continue to make sense of what it means not to have that parent as she grows and matures, as her needs for love and guidance from that parent change. Marianne, whose mother died when she was a preschooler, will regrieve her mother's death through latency, preadolescence, adolescence, and adulthood. As her "meaning" of growing up without her mother changes, Marianne's grief will reoccur with each change. When she marries, gives birth, and reaches the age at which her mother died, she also will regrieve her mother's death.

I cannot overstate the role that regrieving plays in the developmental life of kids. The child whose parents divorced when he was five, or the child whose mom died when he was eight, needs a caring adult who is mindful of the immense impact of these losses throughout this youngster's childhood and adolescence. Quite often, a pivotal or special event in a child's life, be it happy, sad, or difficult, will engender regrieving behavior.

For example, Ronnie was five when his father died. Both his mom and his dad had always attended his Little League games since Ronnie began playing at the age of three. By the time he was eleven, Ronnie was the pitcher for his team and they had won the playoffs to qualify for the state semifinals. The week before this important match, Ronnie felt a mixture of sadness, anger, confusion, and excitement. Although he was used to his mom coming to his games, along with many other dads and moms, the semifinals were big and important. "Why couldn't Dad be there? Why did he have to die?" It wasn't fair. Because Ronnie needed his dad again, he again mourned his loss. He also needed the sensitive awareness of his mom: "I know you miss Dad now. And I know that he loved you very much and would be so proud of you today. I believe his great spirit is looking down on you and cheering you on."

I often surprise parents and professionals when I say that kids need to regrieve. We don't realize that, because of regrieving, children grieve longer than adults. Knowing that youngsters regrieve significant losses allows us to look at them with more understanding and compassion. Our responsibility is to address their regrieving behavior with the same care, attention, and authenticity as we addressed their initial grief behavior.

Power of Relationships

I regard the power of relationships as anywhere between a delicate piece of sewing thread and a thick lasso that connects two people. How strong the relationship was that a child had with the person who died certainly has an impact on the child's grief. Because kids depend on adult guidance through their growing years, the loss of a primary caregiver is of ultimate significance. The death of an aunt or uncle who lived far away, however, might not have any influential impact on them.

Rabbi Earl Grollman tells a wonderful story about a mother who is a member of his congregation. She was concerned because her ten-year-old's reaction to his grandfather's death was less than emotive. She was sure that her son was "in denial." In the course of a conversation they had together, Rabbi asked the boy to share his feelings about his *zayde*'s (grandfather's) death. The boy said matter-of-factly, "Look, he lives in Arizona. I met him two times in my whole life, and both times he had bad breath!"

A powerful relationship does not necessarily mean a loving one. A child who had a very powerful but antagonistic or ambivalent relationship with the deceased person might find grieving no easier than if her relationship with the person had been loving. When Sara was twelve, her dad, who lived in Los Angeles, was killed in a tragic auto accident. His death filled Sara with horror, relief, sadness, and pain all at once. Sara hadn't seen her father since her parents divorced when she was four and a half. Her mom wasn't emotional as she related the dire news to Sara, and her grandmother offered no support. Neither would anyone in Sara's family on the East Coast go to the memorial service three thousand miles away.

Sara remembered very little of her father's physical looks, and she had clung to the few pictures of him that her mother had given her when she was younger; yet her memories of him were powerful because they had had many conversations on her birthdays and holidays during her early childhood. He also had made and broke many promises—to come and visit her, to send her a plane ticket to visit him, to write letters about his life on the West Coast. The real heartbreak came when he remarried and had a new baby. Sara received fewer calls and letters, while her dad made more promises he never fulfilled.

Mourning this relationship was difficult for Sara, and she required professional support. Her grief was complicated by the ambivalent feelings she felt for her dad. This parent figure had created a stormy relationship with her that helped to define her future relationships, particularly with men. Sara needed to sort through the real person her father was, the idealized image she had of him, and the devastation she had faced so many times because she had felt abandoned by him. His death completed and finalized her feelings of abandonment.

Sudden and Anticipatory Losses

Christie had to face her friend's sudden death by suicide. A sudden death brings on shock and disbelief. Oftentimes, kids initially want to deny the cause of a sudden death, particularly one involving suicide or murder, or project it onto someone or something else to avoid their anger and sadness (see chapter 12).

Children who are challenged with the anticipated death of a loved one, which usually results from a life-challenging illness or a deteriorating condition, might grieve during that person's life, for example, as Grampy shows signs of getting worse with each passing week. A child will notice this and might ask, "Is Grampy going to die?" As you answer, keep in mind that kids rarely will ask a question of this nature if they are unprepared for the answer or outcome. Remember that this child has watched Grampy fail over many months, which helps him make sense of death, but a child who must confront a sudden, unanticipated death has had no preparation. A young boy who has seen Grampy become ill has the advantage of *understanding* his grandfather's final outcome—

death—because he has witnessed a series of deteriorating changes. Allowing a child to cope on his own terms with the inevitable death of a parent, grandparent, or friend is empowering when a caring adult faces the emotional challenge right along with the child (see chapters 6, 7, and 9).

We might not see overt manifestations of grief in survivors of an anticipated death if they have already completely freed themselves from their emotional ties to the person before he died, although this rarely happens. With Alzheimer's disease, however, we are more likely to see this phenomenon. A grandfather, with whom a child had a loving relationship before he went downhill with Alzheimer's, "leaves" his granddaughter long before his death due to the debilitating nature of this disease. This grandchild probably will experience complete mourning while her granddad is alive and will show no signs of grief following his death.

Secondary Losses

Often, the grief reaction of children whose parents are divorced is without resolution because the "death" of their family, as they knew it, presents a number of secondary losses. Adjusting to different houses, living under financial constraints, witnessing the emergence of potential mates for either parent, acquiring half- or stepsiblings, and confronting holidays and birthdays are but a few challenges that also represent losses of their familiar, expected, and secure way of integrated family life. When a family is dismantled, the losses for kids are ongoing and require continuous adaptation and reorganization.

Likewise, kids living with a parent or sibling who has a progressive or protracted illness, such as multiple sclerosis or Down's syndrome, suffer losses that appear without end. These children constantly need to accommodate and reorganize their world around each new health crisis, which requires that they frequently adjust to the needs of the vulnerable parent or sibling. The secondary losses, such as not having a parent participate fully in school events, coach a soccer team, or just be like everybody else's parent, are subtle but without resolution. They become habitual.

In our culture, children suffer many *nonovert losses* that we don't necessarily acknowledge (see part 3).

ADULTS AS ROLE MODELS OF GRIEF

We want to remember that kids learn from our behavior and our relationships with them. On Christmas morning of 1988 my father died. At the time, my daughters were eight and eleven years old. About six weeks later, my husband and I went to a local parent-teacher meeting, and on the bulletin board were essays that little third graders had composed. The students had written about one of two themes, the best day of their lives in 1988 or the worst. My daughter Elizabeth had written: "On Christmas this year, it was the worst day of my life (but I did get Nintendo) because my papa died. And I loved my papa very very much. I was very sad. Mommy is very very very very sad. She's so sad that when she says 'jump,' daddy says we need to say 'how high?' And since papa died, we've been eating a lot of Chinese food and pizza."

What did this little eight-year-old figure out about the grieving process? We can learn from Elizabeth's wisdom if we listen to her. First of all, she saw that she was sad and that I was still extremely sad six weeks after my father's death. Elizabeth also noticed that I was angry, or at the very least irritable, because she and her sister, Melissa, had to jump at my beck and call. In parentheses she indicates how children grieve in spurts and have a limited capacity to tolerate pain. They can be happy with a gift one minute and sad the next as they think of their beloved grandfather.

What was Elizabeth saying in her final sentence? She perceived how life had changed temporarily in our household in one small but noticeable dimension. Although she had to adjust to a new environment in which her papa was missing and her mother wasn't cooking much, she was *not* starving! Mommy was still feeding her and her sister, but with a twist—we were eating more take-out. Elizabeth realized that I was grieving, but I wasn't saying, "Go take care of yourselves, kids, you're on your own." She also taught me something else about families who grieve together. Imagine if she had said, "Six weeks ago on Christmas day my papa died, and since then nothing has changed." Or "Our house was back to normal in two weeks, but I was still sad and my parents didn't know it."

Adults unwilling or unable to show their grief can make kids of all ages feel that it's wrong to express anger and sadness. Youngsters might fear that if they express their feelings, their parents, grandparents, or teachers will get angry. Adults need to exhibit their feelings openly so that kids can see what grief looks like and realize that it's a normal process, one that they don't have to fear. Children also need to see for themselves that our feelings don't incapacitate our ability to care for them. If we can express our grief in front of them while also addressing their needs and concerns, we represent healthy role models whom youngsters can trust and rely on for guidance.

Although adult modeling is ideal, it is atypical in families who confront a severe emotional loss, such as the death of a son or sibling by suicide. For these families, protective behavior often predominates. Parents want to protect their surviving kids from their own pain, and children want to protect their parents from added suffering, which can have the effect of a pressure cooker; that is, their unexpressed feelings have nowhere to go.

Kids who protect their grieving parents block their own feelings and needs. This kind of protection from adults and children might eventually cause one or more family members to withdraw from family life, suffer severe crying bouts and depression, or explode in anger over the least things in daily living, all of which can inhibit effective communication and promote suppression of grief in kids. When families suffer deep traumatic losses, it's a good idea to obtain therapy for siblings, and probably for parents also. In this way, youngsters can work through some of their grief outside the confines of the family and have an outlet to express their sadness.

Hiding our grief is one of the greatest inhibitors we hurl in our kids' path to expressing their grief and mastering healthy coping skills. Youngsters at age four, six, twelve, or eighteen don't realize that the awful feelings of grief finally go away once they have shared and worked through them. As behavioral models, we can help children learn that grief doesn't last forever.

LENGTH OF GRIEVING

Parents and professionals who work with kids always want to know how long children grieve. Many believe from two weeks to six months. How many days can youngsters be absent from classes? Three to five, depending on the school policy. We as a culture don't easily tolerate suffering or support others in their pain, but the reality is that grieving in adults lasts from two to three years. Kids grieve longer, although their grieving process looks shorter, because they grieve in spurts, act out their grief, and regrieve.

We can't rush the grieving process in kids. We can choose to ignore it or skirt around it, but if we do, we jeopardize children's ability to develop sound coping skills and intimate relationships as they face any loss or gain during their lives. Unless we recognize our youngsters' grief behavior, help them manage it, and be role models for them, loss can forever dismantle the secure and comfortable home we earnestly strive to build for ourselves and our kids.

What Happened to Grandpa's Head?

The Task of Commemorating

With a hint of anxiety, parents most frequently ask me, "At what age should a child go to a wake or funeral?" I generally respond, "What do *you* think? What was your experience as a child?" Their colorful childhood memories tumble out. "I saw mean old Uncle Bill lying in the casket, ready to sit up any minute and grab me." "I remember staring and staring at my great-aunt in the casket. I could have sworn she was breathing!" Many adults remember holding their breath as kids when they passed a cemetery. None were quite sure why. It was just one of those "childhood rules."

Kathleen, one of nine children from an Irish Catholic family, proudly told me that when each child in her family turned ten, he or she got "de-waked." Her mother would take the lucky child to a wake in their church parish. It didn't matter whether her family knew the deceased or not. This was a rite of passage, an exercise that prepared Kathleen and her siblings for what was customarily a semiregular family activity. When a relative or friend died, that meant a wake. You might call this an interesting example of anticipatory guidance! Many times, however, our memories of death-related rituals are uncomfortable, scary, and often misinformed.

Commemorating, the third task in the mourning process, is remembering the person who has died. Commemoration confirms the reality of a death, and for this reason alone, it has value in helping children understand what the word dead *means.* When a soldier is labeled "missing in action" or a child is abducted for weeks turned into months and years, the bereaved family and friends have no way to confirm the death of their loved one. There is no physical way to know truly that someone missing has died, which can inhibit a child's ability to mourn completely and freely.

Commemoration is a vehicle for expressing the grief we experience, making it an active and participatory task for adults as well as for kids. This task is powerful in that it also affirms the life that was lived. We commemorate the dead in *formal* and *informal* ways. In general, most kids want the opportunity to decide how they would like to remember their father, aunt, or friend if it is to be meaningful for them. And every bereaved child needs to remember the loved one who has died.

FORMAL COMMEMORATIONS

All the world's religions commemorate death with their own proscriptions and prescriptions. In Western culture, most of us are familiar with Judeo-Christian beliefs and rituals that memorialize the dead. Of course, there are different sects of Judaism and Christianity. Contrast a Roman Catholic funeral in Boston with a Southern Baptist funeral in Memphis. I can't begin to explain the fascinating rituals in Asian and Hispanic cultures. All formal rituals, however, have the same central theme—a belief system about what, if anything, is ahead in an afterlife, which is paramount to helping youngsters accept the reality of life and death.

I think of formal commemorations as a family thing. When adults describe formal rituals, they usually begin, "In our family . . . " In many cases, commemorative rituals not only embody a religious and cultural context but also an individual family context often passed down from one generation to the next.

Many people of my grandparents' generation who died were

waked, or "laid out," in their homes. The front parlor might have seemed less foreign than a funeral home in those days. Where were the kids then? What were they told? Did some caring adult sit with them to describe what they might see, hear, and feel for the first time? I doubt it.

My mother, a second-generation Italian American, was seven when her mother died. She and her two older brothers lived in a large and lovely Victorian home with her parents and her aunt and uncle, who had one child. Today, seventy-three years later, she recalls that she was roller skating when her ten-year-old brother found her and said, "We have to go home. Mama has died."

My mother doesn't remember any further explanation about her mother's death, but her aunt held her and gently scolded her for sobbing too loudly. Although her older brothers were allowed to stay home, my mother was sent immediately to another aunt's house across the street for the next three days. She was not allowed to attend the funeral.

On the following day, she walked back across the street and presented herself at her kitchen door. Her uncle asked, "Would you like to see your mother?" She nodded, and he brought her into a darkened room just off the living room. My mother told me, "I can still vividly remember a profusion of flowers and lit candles surrounding my mother, who looked very pretty and very asleep. Roses were everywhere. I've disliked roses ever since. My uncle walked me into the center of the room and told me to kneel with him on the carpet and say a prayer. I did as I was told and then left."

My maternal grandmother died at the age of forty-one, her illness never explained adequately to my mother or her brothers. It was not discussed, not with kids anyway. After her funeral, my mother went home and life quietly resumed in the household. Her father, aunt, and uncle cared for her and her brothers. Three-quarters of a century later, the attitudes some adults hold about children's participation in the rituals that commemorate death have not changed very much.

I think that the decision for a child's participation is an individual one based on four factors: (1) the child's relationship with the dead loved one, (2) the circumstances of the death, (3) the child's ability to understand the rituals in which he is going to take part, and, most importantly, (4) the child's desire to participate.

Adults need to sit with their youngsters and explain what rituals they will celebrate. Keep in mind a few suggestions that will help you and your kids have a more successful discussion.

- Remember that words like *wake, funeral, coffin,* and *casket* might be unfamiliar.

- Keep explanations short.

- Remember that your language reveals how you feel about these rituals. What you communicate without words or with facial and bodily expressions can be just as important as what you actually say.

- Encourage questions.

- Don't ever coerce kids into participating. If a child resists, find out what he might be worried about by questioning him and sharing your fears concerning wakes and funerals.

Probably no one ever completely discussed with you what actually happens to a loved one's body from the time of death until burial or cremation. Think of all the words that might be a bit difficult for you to talk about with your kids if you had such a conversation.

First, you would have to explain how we care for and prepare the body, which might include autopsy, organ harvesting, embalming, and/or cremation. If I want to watch a noisy group of workshop participants get quiet quickly, I simply ask, "Who would like to explain embalming and cremation?" Unless the group includes funeral professionals, I can hear a pin drop in the room. In the last section of this chapter, I explain what these terms mean so that if kids ask you about them, you will be able to answer with confidence.

Second, you would have to talk about wakes, funerals, graveside burials, memorial services, or whatever formal rituals your family, your culture, and your religion dictate to commemorate the dead. These I discuss next.

Wakes

What is a wake all about? Is it a time when you go to see the dead person "a-wake"? What will happen? What will be the sights, sounds, and smells? I always add the sense of smell because kids tell me that "the flowers smelled so much."

Parents often don't prepare youngsters adequately before taking them to a wake. We leave them to figure things out for themselves, sometimes with amusing or poignant explanations. One mother heard her child tell a friend, "My grammy went to heaven, but her legs went first." Of course, this was the child's reason why she couldn't see her grammy's legs in the casket.

Dr. Sandra Fox told a story that underscores how careful we must be when we use language that is unfamiliar to kids, particularly to very young kids with vivid imaginations and concrete thoughts. Jeff's parents asked Sandra to help prepare their five-year-old son for the anticipated death of his terminally ill grandfather, whom Jeff called "Poppy." In describing the wake, Sandra told Jeff that Poppy's body would be placed in a casket. After his Poppy died, however, Jeff became upset. He said that he couldn't go to the wake no matter what because he didn't want to see Poppy in the casket with his head cut off. Sandra replied, "Head cut off! Who told you this story?" "You did," cried Jeff. Five-year-old Jeff had interpreted Sandra's words literally about Poppy's *body* being placed in the casket. What about his *head*? He didn't want to see his Poppy without a head. Neither would we.

Here's how I would describe a wake to young children, preadolescents, and adolescents. "Mr. Arnold, our funeral director, carefully removed Grandpa Henry from his bedroom. Mr. Arnold and the other funeral professionals placed Grampy's body in a special car called a *hearse* and drove it to the funeral home. They are preparing Grampy for us to see his entire body, head and legs included, at the funeral home tomorrow afternoon. We will attend a ceremony we call a *wake*."

At this point, a child's typical response might be, "What's a funeral home like? Will Mr. Arnold show us around?"

"Well, we can ask him to if you'd like. This is what will happen tomorrow in one room of the home."

If the child asks what I meant by "preparing Grampy," I would continue: "Mr. Arnold is *embalming* Grampy's body today to prepare it for the wake. Because Grampy's heart is no longer working and his blood no longer circulating, the color of his skin won't look very good. Embalming it with special fluids and adding a kind of makeup will make him look like he did when he was alive, so that we can see him one last time at the wake. After Mr. Arnold embalms Grampy's body, he will dress it and place it in a *casket*. A casket is a special box made of steel or wood on the outside with a small bed and a pillow on the inside. Grampy's body will be lying in this casket at the wake. We go to the wake to remember Grampy's life with us on earth. He will be dressed in his favorite suit and tie. Mr. Arnold will also put Grampy's glasses on his face and leave his wedding ring on because this is how we knew Grandpa Henry when he was alive."

A child might interject his thoughts at times. For example, "I know Grampy's favorite tie, the one with the flowers."

"That's right. Now, if you want to touch Grampy's body or kiss him in the casket, that's perfectly fine. But his skin is going to feel cool and hard. It isn't going to feel the same as when he was alive because his body has stopped working and he is dead."

Kids frequently have concerns with the word *wake*. "I don't understand why they call it 'a-wake' if Grampy's dead."

My explanation is, "A *wake* doesn't mean that you're sleeping and then you wake up. It's an old religious custom that we got from England and still use in our family and religion. We go to a funeral home, see Grampy for the last time, and share our grief with others who knew Grampy."

We don't want to give a glossy description like "Grandpa Henry's just sleeping quietly," or "We're going to pay our last respects."

We want to actually and honestly describe the casket, the body, the makeup, the flowers, the people talking softly and loudly, the people crying and laughing, which can be very confusing for kids.

There's the receiving line of the bereaved family and what you say to the family. A simple "I'm sorry" works very well. Once you have discussed everything that will happen at a wake, tell young-sters why you go. It's also a good time to ask them if they have heard stories about wakes from television or from friends. You can correct any misinformation in this way.

Kids are old enough to attend wakes and funerals if they can convince you that they understand what will happen and how they will participate. To evaluate whether your child is ready, after your full discussion, ask her to tell you what she has understood about a wake from your conversation. I have found that very few youngsters under five or six can verbalize their understanding of this ritual; therefore, it would probably not be in a child's best interest to participate if this is the case. Never force your child to go, but encourage her if wakes are part of your family's cultural or religious tradition. For some children, signing the guest book at the funeral home is enough. For others, going with you before vis-iting hours works well. When Bernadette's father died, this was the decision that she and her husband, Gerald, made with their sons, who were seven and twelve at the time.

On the morning of the wake, Gerald took each of the kids sepa-rately for a brief walk around the neighborhood. The family had already talked together about the new experience their sons were about to face later in the day, so Gerald asked each if they had any further questions or thoughts. Seven-year-old Nicholas said, "Susie told me that her grampy had toothpicks holding his eyes open. Will Grampy have toothpicks, too?" Of course, Gerald enlightened Nicholas about this misconception.

A half hour before visiting hours began at the wake, Bernadette and Gerald brought the children into the funeral home after speak-ing with the funeral director. They first took Andrew, their twelve-year-old, to Grampy's casket and knelt together to say a prayer. Andrew stared at him and sobbed quietly for a few minutes. Bernadette and Gerald brought him back into the vestibule where their aunts and uncles were waiting, and then they took Nicholas in to view Grampy's body. He stood in front of the casket and said briefly and matter-of-factly, "Grampy's glasses should be lower on his nose." Much to his parents' surprise, Nicholas confidently reached over and shifted Grampy's glasses. "Now, that's better." He then asked if he could touch Grampy's hand. Bernadette told him that was fine and reminded him that it would feel hard and cool. Nicholas touched it as if to assure that he was doing his own research.

Nicholas and Andrew spent the rest of the day with one of their aunts. They went to the movies, had pizza, and returned home that evening in time for Bernadette and Gerald to tuck them in and review the day. As exhausted as they were, Bernadette and Gerald were grateful that their kids were part of this important life lesson.

Funerals and Graveside Burials

Usually on the morning after the wake, a congregation's clergy member conducts the funeral service. *Pallbearers* carry the closed casket from the funeral home to the hearse, from which they carry it into the church. Sometimes a funeral service takes place at the funeral home or graveside.

Andrew and Nicholas were with their parents at their grandfather's funeral mass. Many caring relatives and friends joined them. Bernadette walked up the steps of the church behind her mother, who had an arm around each of the boys. They never left their grandmother's side. During the mass, both youngsters began to sob. Their wonderful grandmother comforted them and held them tightly.

How do we explain burials to kids? A person's body is usually buried at a cemetery, generally where the bodies of other family members are buried already. The spot chosen is called the cemetery *plot*. Often plots are formed in groups of two or four because families like to think of their members as buried next to each other. According to a federal law enacted following World War II, a casket must be placed in an airtight concrete liner that protects it and the body from water, rodents, and insects. The liner must be buried six feet below the ground, and the family usually selects a cemetery stone to mark the spot. Cemetery groundkeepers customarily assure *perpetual care* of the stone and surrounding grassy area.

Nicholas and Andrew went to the cemetery with their parents following Grampy's funeral service. They stood quietly as the pallbearers placed the casket over the burial ground, the *final resting place* of Grampy's body, and the priest said some prayers. The boys benefited from their participation in this very sad day because it was their first significant lesson in accepting the reality of a loss.

Memorial Services

A memorial service is a celebration to honor the loved one who has died, but no casket with the body or urn of ashes is present. It can be held at church, in the home, or at a place special to the loved one or family. If a wake and funeral take place before the memorial service, they usually are private. If the loved one's body is cremated and there has been no wake or funeral, a memorial service provides kids with an opportunity to acknowledge this person's death even without seeing the body. Oftentimes, the loved one has requested a memorial service instead of a wake and funeral, which parents should tell youngsters and explain the reason behind the request.

Usually family, friends, and clergy gather to say prayers, sing, recite poetry, and/or make speeches in memory of the loved one. Kids can be invited to write a poem or say something in the person's honor as well, which gives them the opportunity to participate in the service and make this form of commemoration their own.

CHILDREN'S UNDERSTANDING OF FORMAL COMMEMORATIVE RITUALS

Whether we tell kids that their *zayde*'s (Yiddish for grandfather) good deeds will live in their hearts forever, or that their grandpa's spirit is in heaven "dancing with Grandma's," or that their Buddhist master attained nirvana, most youngsters also will want to know what has become of that person's body. It amazes me when adults tell their kids that "Daddy went to heaven," but their kids don't demand to know *how* on the spot, especially because they are trying to figure out how Daddy can be in heaven and in the cemetery at the same time. One child's brilliant explanation was that "the insides go up, the outsides go down!"

The questions usually come sooner or later, however, but not as we might expect. Most kids are simply inquisitive and want to know how things happen. "Is there a squirrel heaven, Daddy?" "Can Papa see me from heaven?" "Do bad people go to hell?" "How about angels? Can anyone see them?" Their questions can be infinite and challenging. Many times they come up when you're riding in the car and you have no way of avoiding the questions. But take heart. Your own beliefs and knowledge will guide you. Be sure to consider the age of your child and his ability to understand abstract concepts.

An eight-year-old youngster told me that his grandfather, who had died, was underneath his bed. Bewildered, I waited for his explanation: "My father told me that the Bible says, 'From dust you came, and to dust you shall return.' There's a heap of dust balls under my bed . . . it's gotta be Gramps!"

As you think about your explanations for what happened to Grandpa's body along with your beliefs about an afterlife or not, let this brief summary of children's developmental stages guide your explanations.

Preschoolers (ages three to five) take all explanations literally and can be easily confused and terrified by stories about angels, ghosts, and skeletons. If you were to tell a four-year-old that Grandpa's head and body were placed in a closed casket, he might be frightened that Grandpa couldn't see in the dark or couldn't breathe in a closed container. You need to reassure the youngster that Grandpa is dead, which means that he can't breathe or see. He will forget what you tell him and will ask you where Grandpa went again and again.

Latency-age children (ages six to eight) have a real curiosity about dead people—the bones, the guts, the bugs, the skeletons. Movies and television only broaden their imaginations and curiosity. Ask them what they know. That can help you to frame a discussion. Ask them what they believe and share your beliefs with them.

Preadolescents (ages nine to twelve) are typically interested and curious about rituals of death and dying. They might be less likely to share their fears and fantasies with you for fear of embarrassment. Their sarcastic or caustic remarks belie a curiosity and fear of the uncertain future. They know that the word *dead* means forever, and it *could* happen to them. For them the stakes are higher because they don't want to acknowledge death's permanence.

Adolescents (ages thirteen to adulthood) might have already had an experience with formal rituals or had friends who shared their experiences. Many are much more interested in finding their own informal rituals to commemorate a loved one's death, such as writing a poem or listening to a favorite song. They choose to ritualize with others their own age and apart from their family.

INFORMAL COMMEMORATIONS

Some adults might not recognize the term *informal commemoration,* but we all participate in this activity whenever we bring flowers to a graveside, observe a flag at half-mast, celebrate an anniversary of a death, create a collage of photos of our loved one, or choose to wear a treasured piece of jewelry handed down from a loved one. When we dedicate a building or a book in someone's memory, create a shrine at a tree that was the site of a fatal accident, or sew a square for an AIDS quilt, we are again memorializing someone informally. These informal tasks are of a private and personal nature. Around the immediate time of death or at specific times thereafter, informal rituals can be public and community centered. For example, people of the Jewish faith have a service to unveil a memorial stone one year after the loved one has died. Have you ever walked alongside and touched the black marble Vietnam Veterans Memorial Wall in Washington, D.C., commemorating each soldier whose life was sacrificed in that war?

Whether informal commemorations are private and personal or community centered and open to the public, they are equally powerful for the bereaved. The simplest and perhaps not so obvious way to help kids remember their loved ones is with stories. Children love to hear about Grandpa's farm or about Dad as a teenager.

When I'm asked to address a group of kids who have lost a classmate, I look forward to the moment when I simply say, "I never knew Brian. Can you help me to know him?" Immediately, hands fly in the air and stories begin. Young kids might describe his looks or the kind of ice cream Brian liked. Older kids will talk about his physical attributes and favorite things as well, but they have the capacity to speak about Brian's values, character traits, and experiences. "He was such a hard worker." "He was always friendly to everyone . . . even the geeks." "He used to tell the best ghost stories at camp." I encourage children of all ages to remember their peer honestly and discourage them from idealizing him. Sometimes I accomplish this by saying, "Except for Mother Teresa, everyone has a downside."

Take time to tell your kids stories, to remind them of birthdays or anniversary dates. Don't hesitate to look at albums and videos even though they might engender a tear or two. When he was a child, my dad always had a strawberry shortcake for his birthday, which was in late May when strawberries are plentiful. On May twenty-sixth, I always prepare a strawberry shortcake for dessert. It's a sweet and simple way to remember Papa as we dig into the first delicious bite. "Here's to you, Papa!"

Informal commemorative activities abound in kids' grief groups. Youngsters can make quilts, draw symbols, write poems and songs, design memories with clay, and tell stories. One of my favorite group activities can be repeated with wonderful results. The leader asks youngsters to bring to the group an object that reminds them of the person who has died. One by one, as the kids sit in a circle, a child walks to the center, places his object there, and tells his story. The object might be a fishing rod, a recipe card, or an old worn baseball glove. This activity works miraculously because it gets kids talking about their deceased loved one and their connection with her.

Schools and communities often commemorate a death too quickly in an effort to put sadness behind them, which is understandable but ineffective. Effective school-based commemorative activities should be planned *by the kids with adult guidance*. All youngsters should have the opportunity to participate and all children's deaths should be commemorated.

The death of an unpopular or unknown student challenges adults as they guide kids with school-based commemorations. Although it's impossible to legislate a directive, adults should create an *equal* opportunity for all students' lives to be remembered, not just the popular ones. Adults should attempt to enact a fairness policy that frames the commemoration of any student's death. Communities in which leaders have not carefully legislated such policies have soccer fields named after popular students, sports trophies given in honor of athletic students, and annual banquets commemorating outstanding scholars. There are no icons, banquets, or trophies to honor unpopular students who have died. Only a handful of their classmates will champion them. When these handfuls of kids turn to adults to be fair, to speak for their cause, to amplify their awareness of the unfairness of life and death, we must listen to them.

One day I received a call from a high school guidance counselor who was correct in believing that I would support her. A senior committee, in charge of organizing the school's graduation ceremony, wanted to place a beautiful spray of flowers on the seat in which a young man of the class would have been sitting on graduation day. He had died the previous fall. The teacher who headed the committee resisted the idea, saying, "We commemorated his death. We did it well last fall. Graduation is about hope and the future. It's a time of great happiness and joy. I don't think this would be appropriate."

The guidance counselor, by contrast, looked to me to confirm her standpoint: "It is appropriate. These kids are remembering their friend. He would have sat in a particular place at graduation and they can't forget that." I agreed but cautioned her. "Is this the only kid who isn't graduating because he or she died?" "Oh no!" she said. "I had forgotten. Another young man also died this year, but the entire school never did anything for him somehow. Not many students knew him." I responded, "Well, if you're going to put daisies on one chair at graduation, I suggest that you put daisies on the other."

We need to realize, as this guidance counselor did, that the flowers symbolized the seniors' commemoration, not the faculty's. We need to assist kids with their wishes to remember someone and with being inclusive, but we don't want to do it for them. What they require is our guidance and support so that they won't try to rename a tennis court in someone's honor while they exclude the value of another life in the process.

Think back to Marion, the first grade teacher who had to face Timmy's empty desk with her students (see chapter 2). I told her not to remove it too quickly in order to give Timmy's classmates time to remember him. A couple of weeks after Timmy's death, Marion asked me, "When and how should I remove Timmy's desk?" I told her to ask the students because it's *their* commemoration and a powerful outlet for their grief. They should be asked, "What do you suppose we should do with Timmy's desk? What would you like to do with it?"

Marion's students knew that Timmy was crazy about dinosaurs, so they decided to raise some money in order to buy books about dinosaurs. After the kids pooled their collection, they bought three books and asked Marion to inscribe in the front of each, "To Our Friend Timmy, Who Loved Dinosaurs." Then they decided to decorate Timmy's desk with dinosaur stickers, leave the books on top of it, and place the desk in a back corner of the classroom. Some parents brought in a rug to put under the desk and a few pillows to put around it, and Timmy's corner was created. The kids used Timmy's corner during free reading time.

Toward the end of the school year, Marion asked me what to do with Timmy's desk then. Of course, I told her to ask the children. They said that they wouldn't be a group next year because they had to go into three different second grade classes, so they decided that the desk should go back to where it was before. After cleaning it, the kids placed the books in the school's library, a spot where they could go to find these dinosaur books and remember Timmy throughout their grade school years. I also suggested to Marion that the kids have some "Timmy time" on the day they dismantled the corner in order to affirm Timmy's life and use his name. We all need to hear the name of the child or adult in our life who has died. For years bereaved parents have told me that they just want people around them to use their child's name. Youngsters feel likewise. Hearing a loved one's name brings them joy, not pain.

What would happen if we did not help our kids find acceptable ways to remember loved ones? Would youngsters have or retain memories? Possibly, but possibly not. My simple gesture of baking a strawberry shortcake on my deceased father's birthday amplifies for my two daughters the value of remembering our loved ones. Photographs, story telling, revisiting old neighborhoods and cemeteries are not necessarily accessible tasks for kids without our guidance. We can create these commemorative opportunities if we understand their powerful significance. I believe that our role is pivotal to children's ability to remember.

My mother has very few memories of her mother. She assumed that her father, aunt, and uncle thought it best not to talk about her. She learned quickly that when she brought her mother's name up, everyone around her became silent. The subject was off limits. The only physical memory my mother has of her is a few formally posed photo portraits. Interestingly, our daughter Elizabeth shares a similar likeness and beauty to my grandmother, which is immediately noticeable in these old sepia photographs.

Commemoration can also serve a powerful need in an anticipated death. How my mother would have cherished a journal written by her mother. I encourage parents who are HIV positive or who are living through the end stages of cancer to deal with their fear of leaving their children before they are "raised." Meaningful ways of facing this fear include writing journals, creating memory books of photos and letters, sharing family histories and stories on tape, composing timely letters for a child to read when she graduates from high school or has her first date. Letters are wonderful means of helping kids through all rites of passage that mark their future.

What You Need to Know About Caring for the Dead

Depending on the circumstances surrounding a death, a physician might require or request an autopsy or ask for organs to be donated to save other lives. A funeral director will need to know whether a body will be embalmed, cremated, or buried directly. How should we explain these terms and practices to kids and overcome our own fears about them?

Autopsies

An autopsy refers to a medical examination of our dead loved one's entire body. Autopsies are performed to determine the cause of death. They give detailed information that can be useful to researchers looking for cures, police investigating a death, or loved ones needing to know more about how a person died. This explanation is usually sufficient for most youngsters.

Keep in mind that autopsies are complicated and involved, the specifics of which can be confusing to adults and kids. If youngsters have questions, however, listen and answer honestly, especially regarding a traumatic and violent death. Offer as brief and simple answers as possible. For example, if Susie asks, "Will the doctor cut Walter open?" we can reply, "The doctor has to make a cut down Walter's chest and tummy to find out exactly how he died, which will help the police. After this, the doctor will sew this cut back up. What's really important for you to know is that an autopsy can't hurt Walter because he is dead and can feel no pain. It won't make him look any different from how we knew him."

If your child is interested in the detailed procedure of an autopsy and you feel that he can handle explicit writings and photos of human anatomy without being traumatized, you can find more facts in encyclopedias and on the Internet. I suggest that you review any written information and photos before you share them with a child.

Organ Harvesting

Organ donation by a loved one before his death or by his family following his death can significantly aid in our treatment and cure of a person desperately needing a kidney, liver, or heart transplant to stay alive. In 1996, there were 34,550 people waiting for kidney donations, 7,460 waiting for liver transplants, and 3,700 waiting for donor hearts.

Some adults who are dying might consent or request to have their organs *donated* and *harvested*. Others, like myself, carry cards to this effect and have indicated this on their drivers' licenses to signify their intent.

How do we explain organ harvesting to a child when the first thing we must tell her is that her dead loved one will look like he is breathing and has a heartbeat until a doctor can remove all organs for preparation, shipping, and transplant to suitable, waiting recipients? What if Walter died of an accidental blow to his head, but the rest of his body remained perfectly intact? The doctor would run a series of brain tests to establish that Walter was *brain dead*. This means that he has no brain function—he can't eat, talk, or walk. Only machines keep the body working.

Kids wishing to view the dead person's body before organ harvesting will see their father, grandma, brother, or sister on a breathing machine that forces the body to breathe and the heart to beat. There also will be a heart monitor with wires connected to the chest, which makes sure that the heart keeps beating until it and other organs, like the kidneys, are removed in the operating room and preserved carefully. Fluids will run into the veins to help keep all organs working until they can be harvested for transporting and transplanting. It's important to stress, "But your brother's body has stopped working and can never begin again on its own."

The National Donor Family Council, a Gift of Life program of the National Kidney Foundation, has outlined a "Bill of Rights for Families" for those who wish, or who are asked, to donate their loved one's organs. For example, as part of this bill, the attending physician or transplant surgeon should give the family the right to view the dead person's body following organ harvesting. If a youngster asks, "What happens to Walter after the doctors take all his organs?" we should ask if she would like to see his body before Mr. Arnold, the funeral director, takes it to Watson's Funeral Home to prepare it for the wake.

I would explain that "the transplant surgeon will treat Walter's body very respectfully and carefully and clean all his wounds. When you see his body, there will no longer be any machines attached to it. Although Walter might look like he's sleeping then, he won't be because he's dead. If you want to touch his body, his skin will feel cool and soft."

The National Donor Family Council offers a free newsletter, *For Those Who Give and Grieve,* that donor families can receive quarterly. Donor families can share their stories in this newsletter and be in touch with others who have experienced losses and given the gift of love and life to donor recipients. There is also a National Donor Family quilt project dedicated to the memory of loved ones who were organ donors. Each quilt square commemorates the life of the loved one. Families are encouraged to share their feelings about making the square and include comments about the square's design. The council is compiling these words into a book, *Stories from the Quilt.* If kids choose to do so, designing and creating a quilt square, as well as writing about it, would be a powerful way for them to accept the reality of a death and make a commemoration of their own.

Cremation

Many older kids would be interested to know that cremation of the dead probably began during the early Stone Age, around 3000 B.C. In Greece, cremation became a large part of the elaborate Grecian burial custom. The Greeks were great warriors then, and cremation was the way in which they cared for their dead in their war-torn country. It was encouraged for health reasons and quick burial of slain warriors.

Cremation spread to England and North America in the 1800s because of hazardous health conditions, such as plagues and cemeteries fostering contagious diseases. According to the Cremation

Association of North America, there were 425 crematories and 150,000 cremations in the United States and Canada in 1975. These numbers have grown to 1,100 and 470,915, respectively, in 1994.

This history can allay your fears as well as your kids' about the reasons for cremation. It's not so mysterious after all, and its interesting history can be found in some encyclopedias or on the Internet. How do funeral directors or cremation providers perform present-day cremations?

I asked Dennis Daulton, a licensed funeral director, how he talks with kids about the cremation procedure. He feels that parents should use simple language but speak in specific terms, the same terms that we would use with adults. "Cremation does in a matter of hours what nature does in years. Instead of going to the cemetery with the body, we go to the *crematory*," Dennis explained. This is a good way to begin our discussion with children. Your family or your deceased loved one might have certain beliefs about wanting to be cremated, which you also should explain.

Kids might ask whether the body is set on fire or burned, and this might be a frightening concept to them. You want to allay these fears immediately by saying no. Instead, tell them that there is no open flame or fire, only intense heat, lots and lots of heat. Remind them that their loved one feels no pain because the body is dead. The body is enclosed in a wooden or cardboard container and placed in a *retort*. A retort is similar to a kiln, a furnace used to bake pottery with the same amount of intense heat (1,800 degrees Fahrenheit). Most of the body evaporates under this intense heat. What remains are *ashes*. These are small bones fragments *pulverized*, or ground into very tiny particles resembling fine gray or white sand. The ashes are this color because this is the color of our bones. They aren't the same gray as cigarette ashes.

The ashes are placed in a container called an *urn* and returned to the family. Your kids might be curious about the ashes. If they request it, you might want to show them. View them first yourself so that you can describe more fully what they look like.

What happens to the ashes following cremation? Depending on

the desire and age of your kids, you might want to include them in planning what your family will do with the ashes. Families can choose to bury the urn with the ashes in a family burial plot; inter it in an urn garden, which many cemeteries have; place it in a glass-enclosed niche called a *columbarium*; or spread the ashes in particular places meaningful to the family or loved one. Although some younger children might not completely understand these options for memorialization or burial, being involved in the planning comforts them and helps them understand that life goes on even though their loved one has died.

Embalming

It can be a very delicate situation for funeral professionals to go into a family's home and take a cherished loved one from them. This occurred in my family when my father died at home one Christmas morning. Mr. Dolan, our funeral director, was very kind as he gently and respectfully moved my father's body to the funeral home for embalming. We appreciated that Mr. Dolan left his family early Christmas morning.

I vividly recall, in my grief, asking my husband to distract the girls so that they wouldn't see my father's body removed from his home in a black plastic shroud. Tom reminded me that the kids would be fine and we were both available to answer any questions. Of course, we didn't want to hide the truth from them.

How do we explain the embalming procedure? Many kids think of Egyptian mummies when we talk about embalmed bodies. Simply put, the funeral director drains blood from the entire body and replaces it with a special fluid to keep the head and body looking like it did when the person was alive. Embalming *preserves* the person's body so that we can see it one last time at the wake. Dennis Daulton told me that some youngsters are curious about the process and want to "look around" a funeral home. He shows them the embalming room and explains the equipment he uses for this purpose. This allays a child's anxieties and fears.

Many kids and adults want to know how long an embalmed body is preserved. Once all living things die, their bodies eventually *decompose* into dust or soil. This goes for squirrels, dogs, carrots, and people. We don't know how long it takes for an embalmed human body to decompose. It depends on the embalming fluids, the type of casket, and the cemetery in which the body is interred. Decomposition might take hundreds of years, but it will eventually happen.

Is Commemoration Overwhelming?

Although we and our kids might engage in many formal and informal rituals to remember and celebrate the life of a loved one who has died, our purpose should be to help children *process* the impact of this person on their lives and *bridge* a relationship between life and death. We don't want to bombard them just with "facts" about a ceremony, procedure, or lifestyle that reflects a person's life and death. When we allow kids space and time to ask their questions, they will let us know how simple or detailed our answers need be so that their commemorations can come from the heart. If we listen to children and are honest in our commemoration, their acceptance of the reality of death and life will comfort their grief, not overwhelm them with pain. It will also have a dynamic impact on their ability to integrate the memory of their loved one within themselves as they go on living.

MEMORY EMBRACES:

The Task of Going On

DEATHS and other losses influence and alter the course of our lives. As we attempt to pick up the pieces, it's helpful to share with our kids how a loved one remains in our memories and lives. It's also important to encourage kids and give them space to express how this person has touched and continues to affect their lives. How can they experience and reach out to him now that he is no longer living? How do their thoughts and memories of a deceased person change over time? How does a parent's behavior affect youngsters' ability to go on, the fourth task of mourning?

Going on involves a transformation over time in which bereaved children learn that the pain of grief subsides and the legacy of their loved one lies within themselves. Kids maintain an inner connection with and representation of the deceased as they develop other friendships, attend school, play, and perform all the things that shape their daily lives. The strength and longevity of this connection is proportionate to the severity of the loss. Their connection to and memory of the deceased person also hinge on our willingness to help children integrate this loss within themselves.

Going On Without a Parent

The loss of a parent has the deepest and most profound impact on a child's future. One dimension that psychologists have studied over time is a child's *attachment* to a deceased parent. Years ago, some researchers contended that as grief diminished in kids, they no longer remained attached to the parent whom they loved and lost. Those who maintained a deep involvement were considered unresolved in their grief. More recently, bereavement specialists have learned through subsequent studies and interviews with children who have lost a parent that the final task of mourning a beloved caregiver involves a shifting of attachments, not a severing of them.

When she was seventeen, Valerie's father died suddenly of a heart complication. At nineteen, Valerie had many vivid and happy memories of her dad. She enjoyed talking about him and his impact on her decision to major in occupational therapy. Her values and attitudes toward life are, in her words, "like his." This sort of representational attachment makes Valerie's dad immortal within her heart and mind. Her inner representation of her father, or how she views his spirit, changed over time and comforted Valerie. Her father's spirit became not only a memory but an inner guide for the way in which Valerie lives.

Along with her colleagues, Phyllis Silverman has outlined five mourning characteristics that evolve and change within kids as they grow, develop, and regrieve a parental loss:

1. They locate and relocate the deceased parent.

2. They experience the parent's presence.

3. They reach out to the parent.

4. They preserve memories of the parent.

5. They keep and cherish mementos, like necklaces and baseball caps, that the parent liked to wear or gave them as a special gift.

Youngsters can display these characteristics in four different ways that might or might not evolve over time.

My Mother Is a Ghost!

Some children conceive of their deceased parent as a *frightening ghost* or an *emotionally intrusive presence* that dominates them and their world, usually for the first year after the death. They imagine this ghost right beside them instead of in heaven or some uncertain place. In many cases, these kids have had ambivalent or untoward relationships with their parent when the parent was alive.

Although it's not uncommon for kids to dream about or talk with a deceased parent initially after a death, those who see this parent as a ghost usually have scary and upsetting dreams. Unless they are forced to do so, however, they don't talk about the dead parent nor do they cry. When a well-intentioned adult forces a child to talk, the child either expresses anger or wishes that his parent had not died. If he doesn't work through the mourning process and receive meaningful help from adults, he might continue to be angry or depressed much of his life.

When Judy was ten, her mother died after many years of living with cancer. Now, in her early fifties, Judy remembers her mom as "not really being a mother to me because she would spend six months at a time in the hospital, and we weren't allowed to visit her there." From the time Judy was a year old, her mother spent more time in the hospital than at home. Judy's older sister, who is twelve years her senior, cared for Judy. "She was my real mother."

Although she had not seen her mom for six months before her mother died in the hospital, Judy had to attend the wake. "It was awful to see someone who didn't even resemble my mother lying there." Neither her father nor her three older sisters spoke about her mom's death or life. Death wasn't talked about in Judy's home, and she had no wish to talk about her mother's life or death. "It was as though she fell off the edge of the earth."

Judy was *emotionally detached* from her mother, feeling cut off from any relationship with her. Her mother became a ghost who had vanished from Judy's memory until Judy was in her twenties and finally grieved this loss. Before then, Judy never cried, nor did she want to remember her mother; it was too painful. She said, "I only knew my mother as sick, so this was life to me as a child. I was neither happy nor sad about her long illness and death. But after she died, I dreaded that I would dream about her." The principal announced her mother's death over the loudspeaker at school, which terrified Judy and made her angry. She didn't want her teacher or classmates to talk about it because she didn't want "to become upset."

Judy's future husband "helped me work through my grief and remember my mother. We sought help and I grieved for her for the first time. My grief process took me many years. Experiencing this grief helped me to bond with our oldest daughter when she was born."

Even during her young adulthood, Judy needed assistance to grieve her mother's death. Without help, kids rarely can resolve their grief and go on. Those who envision a deceased parent as a frightening ghost not only have had problems in their relationship with this parent before she died, but they also have had difficulty in their relationship with the surviving parent. Judy's father was "strong" in front of his four girls and never showed his grief. "He lived as if nothing happened and so did I," Judy related.

Nine-year-old Annie, whose mother had breast cancer that metastasized, had some real concerns about how she was going to continue ballet when her mom could no longer work (see chapter 1). As Mommy's health deteriorated, Annie saw that she was bedridden and required care, but neither her mother nor her father told Annie about Mommy's impending death. After her mom died, Annie's dad could not share his intense emotions with his little girl. He believed that men and "big girls" shouldn't cry. Because neither parent talked with Annie, shared their sadness, nor prepared Annie for her mother's death, she wouldn't talk about her mother for nearly a year after her death. Mom had become a frightening ghost and an *emotionally intrusive presence* in Annie's life. This nine-year-old girl had terrifying nightmares about Mommy coming to take her away.

My Mom and I Used to Have Fun

Immediately following a parent's death, some kids are able to talk about and remember specific events in their life with this parent. It took Annie almost a year to accomplish this task. Soon after her mom died, she became disruptive in school, was unable to concentrate on her homework or tests, and avoided conversations about her mother. This prompted her dad to seek professional counseling, which allowed ten-year-old Annie to express herself. She felt angry and misunderstood. As she learned to trust that her world would not fall apart and that her father would not abandon her if she voiced her anger, sadness, and questions, Annie began to reminisce about her past with her mom, and her mother's ghost vanished.

Some kids who reminisce about the past are uncertain about where to locate the dead parent. Many, however, believe that she is in heaven, as Annie did once her frightening visions of her mother subsided. Their memories don't cause fear. On the contrary, these youngsters feel as if their parent is watching over them. When asked, they reveal that they don't talk, pray, or dream about her. They don't hear her voice or want to visit her grave. Their connection centers around their memories of the past and their preservation of things that used to belong to the parent, linking their world with and their world without that parent.

For example, once Annie began talking about Mommy, she liked to think about the time her parents took her to Disney World. Annie had numerous stuffed animals that her mom had bought for her. A year after her mom's death, Annie's conversations revolved around what she and her mother "used to do." These conversations comforted Annie because she then felt sad about her mother's death and expressed her sadness as well as her anger. She cried and said that "I never said 'I love you' before Mommy died. Maybe she didn't know this. . . . It [life] didn't get easier right away, and I'm sad, but now it's better."

In this way, Annie began her mourning process, and her relationship with the spirit of her deceased mother evolved toward one in which she found more peace and contentment. Hopefully, this relationship will endure and progress as Annie grows older and she and her dad continue to talk about her mom, visit her grave, and celebrate special events that had an impact on Annie's life with both parents.

My Dad's in Heaven and I Talk to Him

Other kids experience an intense interactive relationship with their deceased parent immediately after the death. Their parent is an active spirit in their lives. They believe that their parent is in heaven, or in another good place, and they visit the grave, talk with this parent, and *maintain an ongoing relationship with the spirit* of this parent.

Seventeen-year-old Valerie, about whom I talked at the beginning of the chapter, located the spirit of her father in heaven right after he died. She derived great comfort from thinking about him and believed that he watched over her all the time. The daily presence of his spirit in her life motivated her to act in ways that would please him. Although she prayed to him, requesting his guidance when she had any kind of problem at home or school, Valerie understood that her dad's spirit didn't and couldn't make things happen like magic. Some younger kids, however, engage in magical thinking if they think they hear a deceased parent tell them that he will make a wish come true. If children believe this will occur and if they share this belief, we want to assure them that Dad's spirit watches over them and lives in their hearts, but he doesn't have an earthly power to make wishes come true.

Youngsters who maintain an interactive relationship with the spirit of their deceased parent talk often about the parent, cry because they miss him, and think that they are most like him. Valerie said that "everyone loved my dad. He was a great person." However, she didn't believe that her father was still "alive" somewhere. She realized the finality of his death but valued and welcomed the nearness of his spirit and its watchful presence.

Experiencing the presence of their dead parent's spirit and reaching out to it mitigate children's pain. More often than not, as these kids grow, they come to see themselves as a living legacy of this parent.

I Look and Act Just Like Him

Two years following her father's death, nineteen-year-old Valerie began to internalize and immortalize his values, goals, personality, and behavior to remain connected with his spirit. These qualities were a *legacy* from her dad, and Valerie cherished them within herself. "I look and act just like him." She said that she still thought of him as much as she ever did, but she didn't buy him a Father's Day card this year, as she did last year. She also didn't go to the cemetery or talk about him as much as she once did, but she still loved to remember him with her family and friends.

Valerie had what I call *memory embraces* of her dad. For example, she and her sister enjoyed teasing their younger brother about Dad buying him a bowling trophy when he was eight. At that time, Valerie's brother would become upset because she and her sister had many soccer trophies, but he had none. The three siblings embraced this memory and enjoyed laughing about it and many things that Dad did to help ease their growing pains and show them his love. At nineteen, Valerie regularly wore a white-gold necklace that her father gave her, and she cherished the many photos of him around her bedroom mirror.

Valerie also understood the nature of her personality and attitudes. They are "deep but light and playful, like my father's." She valued this in herself above all because her mother was just the opposite—somber and stern. Although Valerie didn't "make myself this way," she was proud to be like her father (see also chapter 6).

Kathy's father became a legacy in her life as well, although she felt somewhat differently from Valerie. When she was nineteen, her father had a massive heart attack. Because she was in nursing school at the time, she realized that he would probably die due to heart failure. Knowing this, Kathy cried profusely the day before he died, but she understood and accepted his death. Although she was sad and her mother was shocked and overcome with grief, she felt that her father would have been miserable had he lived. "He was very active and would not have wanted to temper his lifestyle. Unfortunately, people who had heart attacks during the late 1960s weren't allowed to lead a very physical life." Now fifty, Kathy says that her father "is one in spirit with me." She possesses his extensive curiosity about what makes things tick, she enjoys nature, and she has a passion for constant growth and development, which were all dynamic qualities of her father's. Kathy also believes that her personality and ideals mirror her father's and immortalize his great spirit.

Kathy remembers his death "as if it happened yesterday," but she has felt *emotionally detached* from her father since the day he died. She respects the life they shared together, has mementos of him that she keeps close at hand, and appreciates the ways in which she is like him, but she did not develop any kind of ongoing inner relationship with his spirit after his death. Although Kathy has positive feelings about her father, she has never entertained the idea that their father-daughter relationship continued or grew following his death. Valerie, on the other hand, has very much welcomed the presence of her father in her life and is *emotionally attached* to maintaining an ongoing relationship with his spirit. She realizes that her dad can't take care of her in the world, but she prays to him, believes he watches out for her, and reflects on how he would want her to approach adulthood.

Mourning As an Understood Force and Experience

In summary, it is not unhealthy for kids to feel attached or detached from their deceased parent. More importantly, they must work through the first three tasks of mourning—understanding, grieving, and commemorating—in such a way that their memory and the spirit of this parent become an *understood force and experience* in their life. This is what happened for Valerie and Kathy; throughout their lives, this force will continue to assert its presence and evolve within these women.

If kids regard the deceased parent as a ghost about whom they can't speak, they will be less able to grieve the death, accept its reality, and go on with life in positive ways, whether they feel an intrusive attachment or respectful detachment from this parent. Youngsters like Judy and Annie, who had a troubled or difficult relationship with their parent when the parent was alive, will need to work through the same first three tasks—of *remourning*, in this case—in order to find an acceptable and understood place within themselves for this parent. This place within might be attached with positive meaning or detached and distant. Of course, if the parent-child relationship was complicated or abrasive, the child probably will require the assistance of a counselor to process and resolve ambivalent feelings.

Remember, however, that with the help of at least one loving adult who can share his understanding, grief, and memories, a bereaved child will be able to find an "inner place" for a primary caretaker whom they have lost.

GOING ON WITHOUT A SIBLING

The death of a sibling can also have a deep and abiding impact on youngsters depending on (1) their age and awareness of the loss, (2) their relationship with the sibling, and (3) their parents' ability to support the surviving children as they mourn this severe loss.

When Chelsea was six, her premature sister, Lorie, died within twenty-four hours of birth. At twelve, Chelsea knew Lorie only from a photo in which Lorie looks "about twelve inches long and very gray." Unless her parents talked about Lorie, however, Chelsea didn't think about her sister or recall much about her death. When I reminded her, she remembered how the family celebrated Lorie's birth and death for the following two years. They would send balloons flying up to the sky to honor Lorie's spirit in heaven. Chelsea believed that Lorie was in heaven with her dog, Maggie, who had also died. When I asked Chelsea if she was ever jealous of Lorie because of her parents' grief, she replied, "No, never."

Chelsea was so young and never had an opportunity to "know" or develop any relationship with her sister who died; therefore, her grief was minimal and the only legacy of Lorie that lives within her is the one that Chelsea's parents have created (see also chapter 8). For siblings who knew and developed relationships with their brothers or sisters who subsequently died, two divergent paths can emerge to complicate their task of going on.

Behaving Like an Adult

Some kids learn to "act like an adult" as a coping strategy during a sibling's prolonged illness. This form of behavior might give them enough *secondary gain*—praise for acting mature or for never griping about getting a parent's attention last—that they continue functioning in this role throughout their remaining development.

Twelve-year-old Josie felt that it was "only right" to put off her needs for attention or help during her younger sister's fight with leukemia. "After all," she reasoned, "Susan could die." When neither her mom nor her dad was in the soccer stands to watch Josie play game after game, she felt disappointed but rarely complained. She got carpooled by every other mom in town, but her own mother hardly ever had time to take Josie anywhere. Although she felt abandoned by both parents, she often took solace from hearing how mature she was acting and how much they valued her sensitivity toward Susan's "situation." This praise made Josie feel good inside and almost made up for her feelings of being left out so often.

All kids learn that they must occasionally make extra room for a sibling and her needs. However, with a chronic crisis brought on by a sibling's life-challenging illness, occasions turn into the norm, usually lasting years not just weeks or months. Although we might look on this situation as unfair to the healthy sibling, it is probably unrealistic to expect parents to equalize their attention and time. Often, it is utterly impossible to do so (see also chapters 8 and 9).

Susan died when Josie was fourteen. After this time, Josie felt more grown up and serious than her peers. In a way she was, because she could never shrug off her serious outlook toward life. Despite all the efforts that her mom and dad made for Josie after Susan's death, there was an emptiness in the house that never went away for her. As an adult, Josie recognized that she had paid a real emotional price for the way in which she responded to her sister's illness and death, although she always felt lovingly toward her sister. Her emotional costs were the legacy young Josie had from her sister, which were twofold: Josie "lost" two years of her childhood and she "lost" her parents as she had known them before Susan's illness. Neither Josie nor her parents would ever be the same. The family unit that Josie had known when Susan was healthy died with Susan and her illness.

Placing a Sibling on a Pedestal

Keith was injured but recovered fully from a car accident in which his older brother, Joseph, died. At that time, Keith was eight and his brother ten. Joseph had been a great student and known widely throughout the community as a star pitcher in Little League. Keith, who was a good student and usually made the team cuts in soccer and football, never distinguished himself in scholarship or sports, as Joseph had.

Ten years following his brother's death, Keith felt "like I was constantly in Joseph's shadow, which was larger than life. I never felt quite good enough, not as a student or an athlete. It's hard to know, if Joseph had lived, whether I would have felt the same feelings of sibling rivalry."

Comparing oneself to a sibling, especially an older one, is part of the territory of growing up. One real difference in a situation in which a sibling has died is that this sibling never grows older. The story of James Barrie, author of *Peter Pan,* marvelously illustrates this form of sibling rivalry. At the turn of the century in England, James was heartbroken when his older brother died in a skating accident at the age of thirteen. To comfort his mother, young James took on his brother's ways, his clothing, his habits, his hobbies. His mother always reminded James that his brother would forever be a child. He would never grow up. James did and had no children, but his constant reflection on the boy who never grew up, coupled with the wonderful tales of fantasy his mother told him when he was a child, became the catalyst for the beloved character of Peter Pan.

Unlike Keith but like Peter Pan, Joseph would never grow old enough to go through adolescence with all its ups and downs. He would never challenge his parents to have his ear pierced, nor would he ever get caught drinking beer on a Friday night with the guys. Who knows what kind of adolescent Joseph would have been? For Keith, Joseph could do no wrong because Keith placed his brother on a pedestal. "Somehow, going through the past ten years was even harder because Joseph never disappointed Mom or Dad—he never brought home a *D* on his report card. He never did anything bad enough to get grounded. He didn't live long enough."

Most of us resolve our sibling rivalry as adults. Keith had to do this as well. As an adult, he understood the impossible task he took on, that is, living in the shadow of an icon. His grief resolution was incomplete until he was able to stop comparing himself to an impossible legacy, bigger than life, that he had created in his imagination.

Some kids and adults are able to resolve their rivalry feelings with the help of counseling. Others compete with their sibling's legacy throughout their adult life. With therapy, Keith realized that he had created a false icon of Joseph and that this icon partially defined the way in which he grew up. As he entered adulthood, he effectively worked through the mourning process by acknowledging and valuing the bright and sensitive qualities that defined who he was.

Going On Without a Friend

Over one Christmas holiday, a young college junior died of a cardiac problem of which no one, not even the student, had been aware. The college sent out a letter to the homes of all students, informing them of Sam's shocking death. After the students returned to school, I met with the resident assistants in Sam's dorm to talk about his death. Some of his friends from the dorm wandered into the room, one being a freshman who had lived next door to Sam. The pain on Neil's face touched me deeply. He didn't talk, so at the end of our meeting, I asked him, "What would you like to say? What do you need from your resident assistants?" I'll never forget his response. "No one ever talks about Sam. He died three weeks ago and now everybody's on to writing papers and having keg parties. I need to talk about Sam. I need to use his name."

Neil wanted to preserve his memories of Sam, which would enable him to grieve and commemorate his loss. With my questions, he was able to reach out to his resident assistants and friends to help him accomplish this. When Neil had started college in the fall, Sam had helped him adjust and not feel out of place on campus. Neil told the group that "Sam was a great person, someone I'll never forget. I felt like a geek, but he showed me I was okay. His humor was awesome. . . . I think he's in a good place now and sending us good vibes. But I miss him."

I took this opportunity to speak with Neil's resident assistant. "I suspect that many people on your floor need to reminisce about Sam. How can you help them?" He was unsure, so I suggested what he should do: "If you tell your residents that it's okay for them to come to you and talk about Sam, I doubt that any will come. But I challenge you to knock on some doors one evening and say, '*I* need some time with you to talk about Sam. Come on down to my room.' I think you'll find standing room only. You need to take the lead and use Sam's name."

Most adolescents want the help of their peers to go on with life and remember a friend who has died. Through peer groups, adolescents experience a loved one's presence and cherish songs, poems, and mementos meaningful to themselves and their dead friend. Depending on the intensity of a relationship, an adolescent might emulate a loved friend's ideals and want to integrate these within himself. For example, many of Sam's values resonated within Neil. Although Neil will go on to develop other friendships, he probably won't forget the impact of Sam's legacy on his life. From time to time throughout his adulthood, Neil will possibly identify within himself what values he learned from Sam and speak about him.

Younger kids who lose a friend usually require adult assistance in remembering their friend as they go on with daily activities. David was eight when his best friend, Ryan, died. They had been friends since infancy and played together every day. At eleven, David said that he didn't really think about Ryan. He has gone on to make other friendships that have replaced this relationship, although he will never forget the legacy that their friendship had on his life (see also chapter 9). For the past three years, David's mom, Connie, has reminded him of the anniversary of Ryan's death, on which day they plan something special to celebrate Ryan's life. Photos of Ryan on the refrigerator also help David and his family remember their lives with him. David doesn't know where Ryan's spirit is now. He isn't sure whether he believes in a heaven or afterlife.

Ben, a cousin of Ryan's, kept a photo of Ryan above his bunk. After Ryan's death, Ben would talk with Ryan every evening before he went to sleep. Ben said that Ryan would answer him and talk with him about all kinds of things. This brought Ben much comfort and peace. He knew that Ryan was in heaven and looking out for him.

It's not uncommon for kids to replace a friendship with other friendships. In fact, it's necessary for youngsters to bring what they reap from one relationship to others. If a friendship is meaningful, adolescents will do this among themselves and in some way memorialize the legacy of their lost friend throughout adulthood.

The Healthy but Painful Path

When kids experience the pain, anger, and sadness accompanying a loss, particularly a profound loss, they are apt to face many psychological pitfalls as they pick up the pieces of their lives and carry on. As a result of their work, however, they can develop an inner strength to boost their coping skills and prevent psychological problems as they survive the loss and confront future ones. When kids block or inhibit the heartache accompanying a loss, they are more likely to endure persistent psychological or physical symptoms through which they aren't able to work and grow. We want to be patient and gentle advocates as we assist these children to overcome their fear of being crushed forever by intense grief, to open their hearts, and to release the tears that relieve and exhaust their pent-up pain.

We must help all youngsters realize that mourning is not about forgetting their loved ones. Margaret Wise Brown wrote a poignant children's book entitled *The Dead Bird,* in which some youngsters found a dead bird and they "came and visited the dead bird every day, 'till they forgot." I'd like to add a sentence to this story: "But whenever the children saw a beautiful sparrow flying or nesting, they thought of their beloved dead bird." Kids, and adults as well, need to shift their attachment to the deceased by making an inner connection with the spirit of the loved one, which has nothing to do with forgetting. Valerie did this by allowing her memories of her father to become an inner guide for the way in which she lives. Talking about the person, praying to him, embracing his memory, and cherishing mementos of him are all effective ways that children develop healthy skills to survive loss and go on with life.

Part 2

WHEN SOMEONE DIES

Don't Hug Me:

When Children Lose a Parent

WHEN he created the main characters in his novels *Lie Down in Darkness* and *Sophie's Choice,* William Styron didn't realize why he depicted them as mentally depressed. Since Styron discovered that he suffers with depression, he has candidly attributed it to his "incomplete grief" over his mother, who died when he was fifteen. In his nonfiction memoir, on television, and during writing workshops, he has linked chronic depression and grief: "So many people who suffer depression in their lives are people who suffered a bereavement, especially of a parent, in their early life." Until he uncovered the root of his sadness, Styron endured profound mental anguish, used alcohol to excess as "medication," and contemplated suicide. It took William Styron many years to understand the basis of his depression. Once he did, he was able to work through his grief and manage his feelings in positive ways, which has included sharing his experience with us.

A parent's death is unlikely during the majority of kids' childhood and adolescence in the Western world; however, if a parent dies, it is probably the most severe loss any child will have to face. Without a caring adult who can assist children as they mourn for a primary caregiver, they might not be able to attain trust and intimacy in other relationships or survive associated psychological symptoms, which can be serious and varied.

Five-and-a-half-year-old Monica and her parents vacationed in the White Mountains of New Hampshire one year. While Monica's mom was crossing a beautiful country road at dusk, she was hit by a car and died immediately. After witnessing her mom's death, Monica was afraid to cross all streets. To "protect" Monica, her father, grandparents, and friends did whatever was necessary so that Monica didn't need to cross a street for almost three months.

When I conducted a workshop for the faculty at Monica's elementary school the day before classes began in September, Monica's teachers were concerned about how to approach this problem. All the kids at the school had to cross a busy street in order to gain access to the playground. These teachers felt that they wanted to honor Monica's wishes. Should she get to choose each time recess came around? Should she stay with the school nurse and miss recess? Or should she confront a reenactment of a very recent trauma?

I told these compassionate adults that Monica's grief was isolating enough; therefore, staying with the nurse during recess was one more isolating experience and not a good solution to help her address this fear. I suggested that her first grade teacher *normalize* the fear and involve Monica's entire class in the solution.

On the first day of school, Monica's teacher talked with her class about "road safety precautions." To practice the procedure they would use before they crossed the street, she asked her students to get into groups of three, hold hands, and look to their left and right. Outside, the teacher then took Monica's hand and her best friend's. After they practiced, they made sure that all traffic had stopped at the crosswalk, and each group crossed together.

The following week, I spoke with Monica's teachers again. Monica had successfully crossed the street numerous times. In fact, on the second day of school, she held out her hand and stopped traffic. She had become "the crossing guard!" Since that time, she was consistently "in charge" of halting traffic so that she and other kids could cross safely. I suspect that she will need to repeat her strategy of stopping traffic many more times to help herself work through the intense horror of being on the scene when her mother was struck and killed. She found an *internal locus of control* for overcoming her fear, a tremendous boon to her coping skills.

Monica's father was relieved to see that his daughter no longer avoided street crossings. Although her dad and his family hadn't known how to confront Monica's problem with her, he agreed with the school's strategy and also engaged in crossing streets hand-in-hand with Monica. Had Monica not had a father and other concerned caregivers who were willing to help her discover a healthy inner strength to combat this fear, Monica could have been debilitated by a lifelong phobia, resulting in an inability to leave home to accomplish even simple chores like shopping. Possibly she might have developed this extreme fear, called agoraphobia, without realizing why.

Sudden deaths, such as Monica's mother's, are instantly shocking and overwhelming. The death of a parent who has lived with a prolonged and life-threatening illness affects a child differently over the course of the illness; however, despite the circumstances of a death, kids suffer an intense range of feelings as they confront the loss of a primary caregiver. Surviving parents need to keep the following in mind as they help youngsters mourn their deep loss.

1. Don't deny the truth when you explain a parent's illness or death. Honesty is the foundation of trust, which kids need in order to build healthy coping skills.

2. Don't evade youngsters' questions concerning their parent's illness or death, but don't inundate them with details for which they haven't asked. Answer truthfully and remember that avoidance keeps kids and you in pain.

3. Don't *gatekeep*; that is, don't allow other well-intentioned caregivers, family members, and friends to keep kids away from a dying parent or from discussions that they fear might upset children. You know your child. Together you, your child, and your spouse can make decisions and choices about what's best for the child and the dying parent.

4. Don't overwhelm kids with your grief. As you express your anger and sadness, assure them that you'll care for them and that you will survive this loss together.

5. Don't ask kids to take on the role of their deceased parent, that is, to act like an adult.

TAKING ON A CHILD'S ROLE

Often when I meet with a small group of health-care professionals, we set up a scenario or two in which they can "become kids again" by acting and conversing as they think youngsters would. Once, when I conducted a workshop for pediatric nurses who care for critically ill homebound infants and children, I asked them to role-play a dad and his eight-year-old son. How would they, as a father, explain Mom's anticipated death? In the following scenario, notice how the two nurses felt awkward and tongue-tied.

DAD: *You know Mom has cancer. It's important that we talk about this because Mommy's not going to be with us much longer. How does that make you feel?*

SON: *OK. Can I go watch TV?*

DAD: *It's real important that we talk about this because Mommy's not going to be with us much longer.*

SON: *Why not?*

DAD: *She has a serious disease that we've talked about before.*

SON: *Yeah, I know.*

DAD: *And she's going to go up to heaven. She's not going to be with us anymore. She's not going to be able to cook or have supper with us.*

SON: *Well, why not? The doctor has been helping her all this time, so why won't she be all right?*

The nurse who took on the role of the father was frustrated with the son and didn't know how to go on with their conversation. What would be honest and more meaningful for a parent to say in this situation? Although it's terribly difficult, we need to relate that *"Mom is living with cancer, but she isn't expected to live much longer, so she's going to die. We all die someday."*

Don't wait until the very last moment to talk about a parent's anticipated death. Prepare a child all along as the parent's health declines. When and if death appears imminent, explain how you physically *see* why Mom won't live much longer. "She used to work, remember? But she hasn't worked in two years. Now she's very ill and can't even eat her meals anymore. She loves lemon meringue pie, but she can't eat that anymore because she can't digest it. She came home from the hospital this time with a feeding tube."

I asked another nurse to take on the role of the eight-year-old son while I played his dad.

DAD: *You know, so many times in the past, Mom has been in the hospital and she's come home and she's been okay. Sometimes she's even gotten better. Remember when we went to Disneyland because Mommy got better? This time she's not going to get better. From everything that the doctor tells me—and Mommy knows too—she's not going to get better. She's going to get sicker and sicker. You know that Mommy's cancer has spread to her brain and her liver. Her body can't work the way it's supposed to, the way yours and mine do. Lots of things that Mom has done has helped her, but there is nothing else that can help. She's been trying to get better like crazy, but this time it hasn't worked. Mommy may die soon.*

SON: *How will I talk to her?*

DAD: *You can't talk with Mom after she dies because a dead person's body totally stops working. It can't talk, listen, think, or go to the bathroom. We don't know for sure whether Mommy will die next week or next month. We can still hope, and I still pray that she won't die, but we need to face the real possibility of Mommy's death together with her. We'll help you to help Mom when she comes home tomorrow. She really wants to be home. Know why?*

SON: *Why?*

DAD: *Because she wants to be with you and me. She wants to be with the people who love her the most and whom she loves the most. That's us. We're going to get a lot of help too. Nurses are coming in, and they're going to help us take care of Mom because there's lots of stuff we can't do for her. But let's think about what we can do for Mommy.*

SON: *Well, I can read to her and draw pictures for her and sit with her.*

DAD: *You sure can. And you know how she loves it when you rub her feet. Her best time is in the morning, so what if we ask your teacher if you can stay home until eleven whenever you want so you can rub Mommy's feet and watch that favorite show you both like? How would that be?*

SON: *Great! I don't want her to die, though.*

DAD: *I know. I've been holding on and holding on and holding on, not ever wanting to think that she could die. But we have to face the fact that she is going to die. Mommy feels it's true and so does her doctor.*

This is quite a heavy conversation and longer than most younger kids would endure at one time. A four-year-old would probably say, "Sure, I understand. Sounds like Mom's going to die. I'm going to be sad when it happens. Will I be able to watch Barney on TV?" I would say, "Sure you can." An eight-year-old would likely want to know, "What's going to happen to me? Who will take care of me? Will the nurses make soup the way I like it and take care of me too? Are you going to stay home until eleven every day too, Dad?" Adolescents would have more philosophical concerns. "It isn't fair. I'm mad. Why does this have to happen to Mom? She's such a good person." These are all universal questions and concerns that require our attention and support.

Openness and honesty in explaining a parent's death provide children with strength to accept their loss. In the process, we want to encourage them to express their feelings, assure them that we can mitigate their concerns, and help them confront whatever emotions they have in anticipating or accepting the death.

JANIE'S STORY: DADDY'S GONE

One of the most challenging consultations I've ever faced involved three-year-old Janie and her dad's death. I had been asked to speak with the staff of a preschool because Janie's father, Robert, was dying. He had been living with cancer for sixteen months, and his doctors told him and his wife that his death was imminent. Anne, Janie's mom, shared this information with her teachers, which prompted them to call me.

The family enjoyed a weeklong trip to Disney World a month before Robert died. A week following their trip, he and Anne attended an open house at Janie's school. To Anne and Janie, Robert's activity level belied the seriousness of his illness. When I arrived at the preschool, I was surprised to learn that Robert had died three days earlier. The school administrator pointed out a woman who was seated and ready for my consultation with the staff. This was Janie's mother.

I went over to Anne, introduced myself, and offered my condolences. She was a young woman in her early thirties and Janie was her only child. She immediately told me about her husband and Janie. "Robert worked very hard and was hardly ever home, due to his work. On the day he was hospitalized, I told little Janie that Daddy had gone to work. Robert died two days later in the hospital. Now, Janie still thinks he's at work. I don't plan to tell her that he's gone. . . . I'm an adult, and even I still sort of expect him to come through the kitchen door."

What was I going to say? Anne required a therapeutic response. She had buried her husband the day before. Her pain was raw and her exhaustion telling on her face. She needed consolation more than advice at this time; yet, the preschool teachers sought psychoeducational assistance to help Janie and their other preschoolers. My mind raced through their inevitable questions. "What can we expect from Janie in the weeks to come?" "Would the other kids know about her dad's death?" "If they did, would they inform Janie, who didn't know?"

I took a deep breath and suggested to Anne that she try to sit through my two-hour discussion with the teachers and listen to my experience with death and young children. I told her that we could face this together. She nodded and reached for my hand.

Initially I explained to the group that Anne's hiding the truth from Janie was understandable and protective, particularly because Janie was only three. However, in my judgment, keeping this vital information from Janie was a mistake and would ultimately create more difficulty for the child and Anne.

As our training session unfolded, the staff wanted to know how they should react to Janie's constant need to use the bathroom. For the past three weeks, she had been asking her favorite teacher to take her down the hall to the bathroom at least *fifteen* times every morning. On most occasions, Janie would get to the bathroom and say that she didn't need to go. Anne shared other physical and psychological signs, indicating that Janie was upset and under stress. She had begun to awaken during the night, to burst into tears, and to crawl into bed with her mother. Each subsequent morning, Janie didn't remember her sleepless fits or tearful outbursts.

When Robert was hospitalized for the last time, Janie "caught" her mother and grandmother crying. On the afternoon of his death, Janie had awakened from her nap and pointed to her dad's truck parked in the driveway. She said, "Daddy's gone."

What is Janie saying by her behavior? Although no one had told her that her dad had died, she was clearly reacting to his final days of illness and to his death. I felt sure that Janie *did* know that Daddy was gone and life was changed. Her mom needed to tell her. I reassured Anne that Janie's grief would be minimal because she was three. She was already reacting to the emotional chaos of the family's grief and that would continue because young kids act out their pain and sadness. Consistency of routine, love, and telling her that her feelings are okay would serve Janie well.

Anne wanted to know how to undo her story about Robert being at work. First, I told her to expect that Janie, even after she learned that her father had died, would ask on and off when Daddy would be coming home, because preschoolers think that their loved ones who die will come back. I then suggested that Anne honestly and simply say to Janie: "I told you last week that Daddy was at work. Actually, he went to the hospital because he was so sick. Even though his doctors tried and tried to make him all better, he didn't get better. He got sicker and on Saturday, Daddy died."

Once Anne arrived home, she and her daughter went to visit one of Janie's aunts. During the car ride, Anne told Janie about Robert's death in the way that I had suggested. Janie cried and responded, "He died." Minutes later, they arrived at their destination. Janie ran to her aunt and matter-of-factly told her, "My daddy died." Janie's aunt cried, Anne cried, and Janie looked at them both and hugged them.

With ongoing love, attention, and honesty from her mother and caregivers, Janie would act out her grief for a period of time because she had a safe environment in which to do so. As she grows, her father's death will take on new and different meanings and she will regrieve for him at each developmental stage. I advised Anne to help Janie always remember her dad and their relationship together as they created a new life without him.

SALLY'S STORY: IS MOM GOING TO DIE?

At ten, Sally was tall and stately like her mom, Gloria. Her face beamed with a radiant smile when Tim, her father, said that she had her mother's genes rather than his, but Sally rarely initiated a conversation about her mom, who died of Lou Gehrig's disease (ALS) when Sally was nine. A friend of Tim's astutely compared ALS with Alzheimer's, saying that a person with Alzheimer's doesn't know anything but can do everything, whereas a person with ALS can't do anything but knows everything. Always terminal, ALS slowly and eventually paralyzes all body muscles while sparing the brain. Gloria was diagnosed with ALS when Sally was six. Sally remembered her mother as living in a wheelchair. She had no recollection of a "normal" mom. Only photos showed her that her mom was healthy once.

Gloria was a school psychologist. Her friends described her as charismatic. Everyone who knew her loved her and admired her courage. Staying in control of her environment was critical to Gloria as she declined physically during the course of her three-year battle with ALS. Although Tim held on to every routine that represented "ordinary daily living" for his daughter while he became the sole breadwinner, the errand doer, the soccer coach, the taxi service, and eventually the principal caregiver, Sally remained emotionally attached primarily to her mom throughout most of Gloria's illness.

No one talked about Gloria's debilitating illness, not even when she started using a cane and then a walker. When she could no longer climb stairs, Tim had an electric lift installed on the banister to transport her upstairs. This was the first and only time Sally asked the unmentionable, "Is Mom going to die?" Tim's response was brief: "Yes, Mom will die." Sally cried but said nothing. Gloria was furious that he had released the "bomb," but he didn't regret it. "My daughter can count on my honesty, and I will always be honest with her."

As Gloria's illness progressed, resulting in her need to have more physical care, her family and friends rallied. Tim recalled that it sounded as if a continual party filled their spacious home nestled in a lush river valley. Gloria's colleagues often dropped in after school with games and treats for Sally and dinner for the whole family.

I had worked with Gloria's colleagues at her school but was surprised when I learned that Gloria and Tim wanted to talk with me. Our meeting occurred just days before her death, and both seemed in extreme mental pain. Although neither Tim nor I could decipher Gloria's speech, her best friend and colleague interpreted for us. The only other person who could still understand Gloria was Sally. Gloria wanted my assurance that Sally would be "okay" following her imminent death. She asked predictable questions. "Should Sally be with me when I die? If I die at night, should Tim wake her?" There are no right answers to her questions. She and Tim needed to decide what was best for their daughter. Tim tried to reassure her that he would do his best to help Sally through this most difficult event in her life and raise her well.

On the morning of her death, Gloria sensed that this day was different. Although she had all but lost her ability to move, speak, or swallow, she was still in charge of her life. She had planned her memorial services, outlined what she wanted at her death and how Sally would be told, and made a list of people whom she wanted to see on her last day. She also had created a link with Sally and other important people in her life with letters that she wished for them to read after her death.

On the afternoon of Gloria's death, when Sally jumped from the school bus at the end of her driveway, she saw many cars surrounding the house. Tim was waiting for her. "Mommy is much worse. She is having a very hard time breathing now."

On the evening of her death, Gloria was in and out of consciousness but requested that Sally sit on her lap. Tim noticed how scared and awkward Sally looked sitting with her mom. "Gloria was not like herself or how we knew her." When he tucked Sally into bed, however, they didn't talk about her feelings.

Gloria died around midnight. She and Tim had decided not to wake Sally if her mom died during the night. In the morning, Gloria's body had already been removed to the funeral home. Sally cried when Tim told her that Mom had died, but her overt reaction was minimal.

Neither Gloria nor Tim was able to make it safe for Sally to share the normal feelings of a nine-year-old child whose life was turned upside down by a deadly illness called ALS. Although Gloria was a psychologist trained to help people acknowledge and express emotions, she had intellectualized her death and was unable to help her daughter with the very real feelings of being abandoned by her mother. Each family member felt angry and sad, but no expression of anger or sadness was allowed in the home.

It's not surprising that Sally refused to participate in Gloria's

commemorative services and insisted on playing soccer in a tour-
nament the day of the funeral. Tim told her that she must at least
attend the funeral service in church, and Sally did so in her own
way. She covered her ears throughout the service, which included
informal eulogies made by family members and friends. At the
commemorative celebration following the funeral and burial, Sally
wore a sign on her chest that said *Don't Touch Me*. She couldn't
let in the pain of losing her mother, and she suppressed the tears.

In their heartfelt effort to protect their little girl from their pain
and hers, Gloria and Tim had worked fiercely, both in their own
way, to make Sally's life normal during the three years of Gloria's
illness. Following her death, Sally held on to the one thing she had
learned from her parents—to go on with her life as if nothing had
happened.

A year and a half after Gloria's death, I met with Tim in his
home. He spoke of Gloria's photos around the house, but I saw
none. He said that he talked about Gloria and encouraged his ten-
year-old daughter to do so, but she rarely did. She wouldn't visit
her mother's grave. Right after Gloria's death, Sally's only concern
was that her dad not date. He assured her that he didn't want to
and wouldn't.

Sally's main worries were for her dad's well-being and their
financial stability. Tim addressed these concerns truthfully: "We
have a very good life insurance policy that Mom left us. With my
income and this, we are doing fine financially and can get everything that we need. You know that I'm healthy and we have regular checkups, but everyone dies someday. The likelihood of my
dying soon is very remote." Sally also asked what would happen to
her if he died. Tim had made a provision in his will that entrusted
her care to Gloria's brother and his family in the event that something did happen to him. Sally's concerns were common and
understandable worries for a child, and Tim's answers were
healthy assurances that the family would survive.

At the time, Tim was happy to work freelance because he felt
that it was important for kids to have a parent who is "just simply
around all the time." He believed that his being home for Sally
made a difference in her life and ability to cope without a mother.

Like any preadolescent, Sally had many fears about growing up. She talked with her dad about puberty and wearing a bra, things that most young girls would discuss with their mother. This pleased Tim because "it's my responsibility to discuss all things with my daughter, even the ones that she would normally share only with Gloria." Single-parent families, whether due to death or divorce, should create the bond that Sally and Tim have of talking about all of a daughter's or son's growing concerns.

Both Tim and Sally had their routines and did their best to make a home with each other. There was no sign, however, that Tim had begun to sort out the painful feelings he had experienced over the past four and a half years. Neither had Sally, nor will she until Dad gives them both permission. As Tim said to me, "I haven't grieved and neither has she."

When families are confronted with a tragic disease that will eventuate in death, it's understandable why they would cling to the sacred routines of life before the disease and not welcome the realities of this overwhelming life event. Herein lie the benefits of ongoing family counseling. At the least, it regularly reminds family members that they *are* affected in their own particular ways by this chronic life-threatening disease. At best, counseling creates a safe haven for each family member to adapt new processes of coping with difficult and devastating feelings. Most of all, therapy helps each change "overwhelming" feelings to "more manageable" ones.

Even today I would recommend counseling for Tim and Sally. As they continue to pick up the pieces of life and establish a new norm, they will need a safe place to acknowledge and express their grief without fearing that their life together will fall apart.

Gloria left two letters for Sally to read, one following her death and one a year later. Although Sally read the first, she said nothing about it to Tim or anyone else. She refused to accept the second letter on the first anniversary of Gloria's death. Both were much too difficult for her to bear at age ten.

Tim's capacity to sort out and realize his feelings associated with Gloria's care and his role as husband and single father will largely determine Sally's bereavement outcome. Because of his genuine love and care for his daughter, Gloria's desire to have her daughter know her as Sally grows up, and the devoted friends who continue to surround Sally, she has the support to help her face many painful feelings, along with her dad. In her own time and at her own pace, hopefully this preadolescent will.

VALERIE'S STORY: YOUR DAD IS GONE AND WHAT ARE WE GOING TO DO ABOUT EVERYTHING?

Valerie's father died when she was seventeen. At nineteen, she had matured through a painful adolescence of living without the most important person in her life. "His death was a totally sudden thing. My sister, brother, and I were getting ready for school one Monday morning when my sister found Dad collapsed on the bathroom floor. He was forty-seven and overweight, but he was strong, healthy, and active. At the hospital, he kept going in and out of episodes that the doctors called 'irregular heartbeats.' On Thursday, he went into a coma, but the doctors were optimistic. Dad loved this Sheryl Crow song, 'All I Wanna Do.' When it came on the radio, he would move his toes. He would squeeze my hand when I asked him, so I thought, like everyone else, that he would come out of it.

"Over the weekend, he went drastically downhill. His dark hair had turned almost totally gray. His skin was jaundiced. He looked very bloated. It was just sad. The priest prayed over him. He just couldn't get enough air to breathe. The doctors said that he died of ARDS—adult respiratory distress syndrome—which means that he stopped breathing. He had a virus in his heart, so there was nothing they could have done. From the coma, he would have had brain damage. So his death was kind of a blessing for him."

Three years after her dad died, Valerie felt that his death was a blessing for him, but when the doctors initially told her, she screamed at them. "What did you do wrong? Why couldn't you help him?" During the first couple of days after this, "When my friends came to console me, I would lose it." But Valerie took comfort in her father's commemorative services. The police blocked off all roads to the funeral because there was a tremendous line of cars going to the church and cemetery. Her dad was a public servant, soccer coach, and Eucharist minister, so he knew everyone in the community. The outpouring of people at his memorial service made Valerie proud to have had such a father.

Valerie was the oldest of three children and felt that her dad was closest to her. She could talk with him about anything, from sports to morals. "He knew what went on with teenagers, and if I got into a bad situation, he said, 'Use your head.' He told me he knew he could trust me. He was protective but not overprotective. My father was the center of our family, and everyone else was around him. All my friends got along with him. Everybody loved him. My father would discipline us, but my mother was the bad guy. I favored my father over her."

Nine months following her dad's death, Valerie went away to college, as she had planned with her father, who helped her choose both the school and her occupational therapy major. When September came, she had mixed feelings about leaving home because she wouldn't be able to help her mom, who "had so many problems." During her first semester away, Valerie suffered with migraines. One was so severe that it landed her in the hospital. Her mom went to the college, took care of her, and brought her home.

Once Valerie returned home, "I resented the fact that my father wasn't there and that she was in charge. Everything was falling apart. She would say, 'I'm all alone. You kids go out, but I have nothing to do.' The things she said would make me feel so guilty, and I tried to understand because she was upset all the time. She would walk into my room and start crying hysterically. She hardly had any friends. Friends that my parents had together were very sympathetic at first but that stopped. She wasn't very understanding. It was like the whole structure of our family, the whole bond was gone. My mom was totally destroyed."

Because her mother was overcome with her own grief and overwhelmed by demanding new roles for which she was unprepared, she was unable to provide an environment in which her kids could feel safe and secure, an environment in which they felt they could survive. Paying the bills on one part-time income, coping with her own enormous sense of loss, and taking on her husband's job as major decision maker and disciplinarian took all this mother's energy. Valerie explained the household in this way: "My mom was hysterical all the time, my sister just kept everything in and quiet, and my brother pretended that he was a tough guy who wasn't affected by my father's death. Everyone was feeling differently."

Whenever Valerie had a conversation with her mom about her dad's death, a constant theme surfaced for her mother: "He's gone and what are we going to do about everything? If something happens to me, you'll have the guardianship of your sister and brother. Your aunt [who was seventy-five] isn't well enough to take care of you kids." This mother asked her daughter to take on an adult burden, one that a seventeen-year-old shouldn't be made to take on. Valerie rebelled. "I left the house and totally separated myself from it."

Determined to be responsible for herself, Valerie moved into her own apartment, struggled to attend a local college, and worked fifty to sixty hours every week as a waitress to pay her bills. She developed intestinal pain, for which she sought medical help and was successful in overcoming, and she received medication for insomnia. "I hadn't had a good night's sleep since my father's death. Ativan [a minor tranquilizer that relieves anxiety and fatigue] helped me when I needed it. Now I rarely need it."

After six months on her own, Valerie reached a new understanding with her mom. "At first, my mom was distraught that I moved out. She said, 'What are you doing? You can't do this. Valerie, I don't agree with what you and Tommy [Valerie's boyfriend] are doing, nor would your father approve.' Later on, Mom came around and said, 'You can make your own decisions. I just want to help you and work with you.' " This last statement from her mom was "great and relieving."

For the first year and a half following her dad's death, both Valerie and her mother tried to create new lives in the midst of their grief and an emotionally unstable household. Both were exhausted by long hours of work, by scraping together enough money to live, by feeling totally isolated and misunderstood. While Valerie's mother was forced to take on a new role as head of the household, her daughter took on an equally overwhelming task of living independently. Their roles were parallel in that they were full of struggle and strife; yet neither could empathize with the other. With time and distance, however, Valerie's mom was able to put aside her own grief in order to help her daughter. After another six months of struggling, Valerie talked over her problems with her mom and decided to move back home once her lease on her apartment expired.

"My relationship with my mom is better. We still have our differences, especially regarding my boyfriend and sex, but I've stopped worrying about it. Now I know I can deal with her because I've done it for so long and can take care of myself. She called to remind me about a doctor's appointment, but I told her I knew because I've been on my own and have to be responsible. It makes me feel good that she cares and is there for me now."

Two years following her dad's death, home was more stable for Valerie. Her mom had found full-time employment, developed some social life, and realized that she couldn't control Valerie's decisions. When I asked nineteen-year-old Valerie how she felt about her father's death at this time in her life, she said, "My mom, sister, brother, and I now talk about fun things, like funny things that happened or funny things he said. It's so much easier. It's not painful to talk about him, not at all. I still think of him every day and pray to him. I know he's there. My mom has had weird dreams about him, like he comes to her when he was young. I tell her that things are okay. She has a life now too."

I met weekly with Valerie for six months following her dad's death. Her father had been the central figure in her family's life. His commitment to his wife and kids, his stable but easygoing style, his energy for the kids' sports and activities, and his public persona that was "bigger than life" all left an enormous imbalance in the family dynamics. After three years, the family learned to come together in their grief.

Valerie's mom said that she looked her husband right in the face every day when she looked at Valerie, a compliment that made a mature nineteen-year-old going on twenty respond, "Wow, that's awesome!"

ATTAINING INNER STRENGTH TO COPE WITH LOSS

All of us probably know or know of a child or two who has lost a mom or dad. As Sally's father said, "Sally and I are a different family, but I guess not that different. The kids who live across the street lost their mom a few years ago, and a colleague of mine with two daughters died with ALS three months before Sally's mom did."

What have we learned from Janie, Sally, and Valerie?

- Parents need to talk about an anticipated death and address all their kids' questions, because this empowers youngsters with strength to accept the death when it occurs. It also keeps the family together in that parents and kids share their sadness and concerns, realizing that they can solve any problem in the process although they can't "prevent" death.

- Whether a spouse's death is anticipated or sudden, the surviving partner certainly needs to grieve, express her grief with her children, and find nurturing people and ways to gain support for the difficult work ahead. This, in turn, will mitigate the family's suffering and enable kids to develop healthy emotional skills to confront future losses.

- Once a parent has died, the surviving parent needs to provide a routine and home in which kids can feel safe to express their grief and go on with life. If emotional chaos reigns or if a parent wants a child to act like an adult, it will inhibit the child's grief work.

From what many kids have shared with me, I've composed a list of Top Five Do's that all parents should keep in mind as they relate to their children, not only surrounding the death of a parent but during the course of their daily lives together:

1. Do set the stage for questions and open communication. Be the safe person to whom your kids can come to ask the "unmentionable."

2. Do be watchful for any physical or psychological signs of stress in your kids, and seek professional assistance if necessary.

3. Do address and talk about all your kids' growing needs—for example, their concerns about puberty—as your new family unit goes on with life.

4. Do be open about your sadness and sensitive toward your kids' when celebrating holidays, like Father's Day, Christmas, and anniversaries, and when celebrating milestones in their lives, like graduation and going off to college.

5. Do encourage your kids to talk and write about their deceased parent, which helps them to find an inner place for this loss in their daily lives.

As you review this list, remind yourself that living without this important family member, grieving his loss, and making life-size adjustments in routines, dreams, and goals take *time*.

A Care Bear for Mamaw:

When Children Lose a Grandparent

Our grandparents link us to our past. Their very presence tells the story of where we came from. Representing our ethnic roots, grandparents pass on their ways of doing things, ways that they learned from their grandparents. Family recipes, Great Depression or war stories, and religious beliefs are just a few legacies we inherit from them.

For many kids, grammys and grampys are active and engaging extended family. They babysit, take kids for ice cream and pizza, and attend birthday parties, recitals, and soccer games. Other youngsters, whose grandparents live far away, develop relationships through telephone conversations, cards, packages, and vacation or holiday visits. Regardless of the distance or nature of the grandparent-child interaction, Grammy or Grampy's death is likely to be the *first* important loss that a lot of kids face.

Because my mother was so young (seven years old) when her mother died, and because her family didn't talk about my grandmother after her death, I have virtually no link or connection to her. Although my mother told my sister and me what little she remembers about my grandmother, these precious memories of my maternal inheritance are too few.

In addition to a grandparent's legacy, how you face your parent's death and model this experience for your children also has a great impact on their ability to cope with this loss and future ones. Although we can't nor would we want to transfer our relationship with our parents to our kids, our feelings before, during, and after our parents' deaths; our grief behavior; our religious beliefs; and our family traditions all undoubtably influence our kids' response to their grandparent's death.

A Grandparent's Opportunity to Pass On Memories

In the last year of my father's life, with each hospitalization and "monthly tune-up," as he liked to call it, it became more obvious that his body could no longer withstand the battle it had waged against congestive heart disease for over two decades. About four months before he died, my father's hospital tune-ups came every two weeks.

Knowing that his time was short, he quietly began to record on audiotapes his famous "jungle stories," with characters like Eagie the eagle, Allie the alligator, and Molly the elephant. Because these were precious days and weeks for me and my children, we made a conscious effort to spend more time with my parents. The girls could repeat their grandfather's stories by heart. They delighted in the loving memories that they were, in fact, creating with him. A week before his death, I snuck the girls, dressed in their Christmas best, into the intensive care unit to see their "Papa" before we went to a *Nutcracker* performance. Years later, they remember how pleased Papa was to see them and how they giggled when his heart monitor fluctuated as they kissed him hello.

My sister, who lives out of state, made more frequent visits home with her baby daughter and five-year-old son, Trevor, in order to spend as much quality time with him as they could before he died. Papa gave Trevor some of his cherished treasures—his World War II medals, his Navy insignia, and his special coins. Trevor knew that these mementos were precious because of the way Papa talked about them. His mom reinforced their specialness by saving them meticulously in boxes. Now Trevor is thirteen and has a young adolescent's understanding of the sentimentality and pricelessness of his gifts from Papa. When he sees a TV or feature film story about World War II, he makes the connection to his Papa. My sister has transferred Papa's memorabilia to Trevor's care.

Someday Papa's granddaughters and grandson will tell their own kids about their great-grandfather who took the time to create and pass on meaningful mementos, which affected their lives. In this way, Papa's gifts not only helped his grandchildren cope with his death, but they also might keep "giving," perhaps for generations to come.

A Parent's Opportunity for Teaching and Modeling

It's difficult to think of our parents' dying. Naturally, this thought conjures up all sorts of emotions. No matter our age or relationship with our parents, when they die, we face the world without them for the first time. Their deaths also bring into focus the reality of our own mortality. Hopefully, we will seize the opportunity to share our grief with our siblings and review our unique relationship with our parents. Many of us, however, don't have the luxury of facing our profound loss without simultaneously having to help our kids mourn theirs. It's no wonder that parents often ask me, "How can I prepare my kids for the eventual death of their grandparents now that they are aging and so am I?"

My blueprint for what you *should* do is simple:

- *Include your children in the preparatory process.* Let them know that their grandparents are aging and that a grandparent's death might very well be the first serious loss they experience.

- *Describe the declining health of a grandparent.* I'm always amazed when parents think that their kids don't pay attention to their grandmother's failing memory or their grandfather's inability to drive anymore. As you talk about how Grammy can't do what she used to do, invite your youngsters' questions, even the difficult ones. "Is Grammy going to die someday? When? What will we do? What will happen to Grandpa? Will he still live in his house or will he come to live with us?" These questions will come in spurts when you least expect them, and they present wonderful teachable moments.

- *Find other teachable moments from your friends' experiences with the illness and/or death of their parents.* As each opportunity presents itself, point out how your friends and their kids (1) go on with life as a grandparent declines, (2) change a routine to accommodate the illness of a grandparent, and (3) return to normal routines after a grandparent's death.

- *Find ways for your youngsters to help as a grandparent declines or is hospitalized.* Kids like to feel a part of the caring and giving process. They can choose to read to Grampy, watch a TV show with him, or help cook for him. When your life's routine has been interrupted with frequent visits to Grampy, your kids can pitch in and do some household chores for which they aren't normally responsible.

- *Recognize that youngsters of different ages, stages, and temperaments will respond differently to the same situation that involves the decline or death of a grandparent.* Respect these differences.

- *Express your grief for your parent in front of your kids.* I can't emphasize this statement enough. You are the model from whom they learn to mourn. Remind them, particularly when you are out of sorts, exhausted, short-fused, or weepy, that you are missing their grandmother or grandfather. And be sure to tell them that you are still able to care for them.

- *Invite your children to participate in the commemorative rituals that are part of your religion and culture.* If they are interested, share with them the history of these rituals. Remember that kids need to be old enough to understand your explanations if they want to participate. Don't forget to ask them if anything worries or concerns them about the preparation of the body after death, the memorial service, or the burial.

- *Talk about a grandparent and use her name frequently*. Share stories about Grammy and display photos of her in order for kids to understand that they will always have memories of their grandmother even though she has died.

My blueprint for what you *shouldn't* do is also simple:

- *Don't hide information pertinent to the declining health of your kids' grandparents*. Use simple, direct, and age-appropriate language as you explain a grandparent's illness or disease. Youngsters learn that they can or can't trust you to tell them the truth.

- *Don't overload your kids with information*. This might sound like a contradiction to the previous advice; however, it's always a good idea to let your kids lead your discussions. When a child has had enough, she or he will let you know!

- *Don't assume that very young children aren't affected by their grandparent's illness or death*. Often, parents talk in front of their three- and four-year-olds, oblivious to these youngsters' interest. Kids then hear bits and snatches, become anxious, and can reach incorrect conclusions.

- *Don't be a superdad or supermom*. When your parent is dying, you automatically become their son or daughter again. Find support for yourself and find someone who can support and comfort your kids at times. You probably cannot be the "best" daughter and mother at the same time. Ask for help!

EMPTYING A BUCKET OF TEARS

Daniel and Ian were at a neighborhood birthday party with their mom when their dad arrived unexpectedly and took his wife aside. Five-and-a-half-year-old Daniel announced, "Mom's crying real loud!" The couple then told their sons that Grampy was very, very sick and had been taken to the hospital. That evening, Grammy, Mom, and Dad were quiet, sad, and teary as they told the boys that "Grampy died. He is not alive anymore and has gone to heaven to be with God."

Grampy, a young sixty-seven-year-old executive who had just retired, was raking leaves in his backyard when he apparently died instantly from a ruptured abdominal aneurysm. His wife discovered his still body in a bed of leaves. Emergency medics took him to the hospital, where he was pronounced dead.

This marvelous gentleman's world revolved around his wife, three daughters, and grandchildren, but he also touched the lives of all who knew him. He spoke with Daniel and Ian every day by phone and visited them at least twice a week. The boys loved spending time with Grampy. He taught them how to fish and canoe in the pond behind his home. Every visit with Grampy became a celebration—picking apples, choosing pumpkins, visiting Santa, and camping overnight in the backyard.

Nancy, their mother, felt that her father was robbed of his retirement years and that her family was robbed of him. Her husband was enormously supportive and took over the boys' care as much as possible because she cried every day and found her busy life with two little boys nearly impossible. When Nancy voiced that she worried about crying so much in front of her sons, I suggested that she give them a concrete analogy to explain why she cried every day. Tell them that "everybody has a pretend bucket of tears inside. Every time I cry because I miss Grampy, the bucket empties a little. Someday, the bucket will be completely empty and I won't cry anymore. But I will always love Grampy and miss our good times with him."

Once Nancy explained this to Daniel and Ian, they would speak with confidence about the "bucket emptying again" when they saw their mother or grandmother crying. This analogy helped her sons understand that their mom was okay and would not mourn forever.

The family had many photos and videos of happy times with Grampy, which the boys enjoyed viewing and remembering. When they visited Grammy in her home, they often expressed how sad they were that Grampy wasn't there to show them his tools in his workshop or take walks with the red wagon he had built for them.

The boys also created art journals depicting the fun times they had shared with Grampy. Their parents and grandmother gave them wonderful opportunities to embrace Grampy's legacy and master coping skills that would serve them as they faced future losses.

A CARE BEAR FOR MAMAW

Josie was a loving woman devoted to her daughters and grandkids. Her parents, both born in Sicily, had taught her "family togetherness." She spent just about every day with her two younger granddaughters during their infant and toddler years. Jessica, Josie's youngest granddaughter, was eight when her "Mamaw" began to show signs of senile dementia, characterized by progressive mental deterioration with loss of memory and attacks of excitement or depression.

Because Josie was anxious and easily excited, she would sometimes make unreasonable and illogical demands on Jessica's mom, JoAnn. Although JoAnn had many of her own feelings about her mother to deal with over the years, she explained to Jessica and her older sister why Mamaw would become a different person as her mental faculties gradually went downhill. She included the girls in their grandmother's care but never burdened them with her concerns about her mother.

As Mamaw's condition continued to deteriorate, Jessica understood and tried to help ease Mamaw's tension and anxiety. Sometimes Jessica was the only family member who could cheer her grandmother or subdue her anger about simple things, like why she needed to visit her physician. When she was twelve, Jessica began to give some of her things—Shirley Temple movies and stuffed animals—to Mamaw, knowing that they would please her grandmother. Mamaw also loved angels, so with her mom's guidance, Jessica gave Mamaw angel pins, candles, and statuettes for birthdays and holidays.

Jessica remained sensitive to her Mamaw's needs. The family would watch in awe how she was able to make Mamaw laugh when no one else could, how she would shower Mamaw with affection, how she would watch Shirley Temple movies with

Mamaw over and over again. Because of her mother's constant explanations as Mamaw continued to go downhill mentally, Jessica was able to observe, accept, and adjust to her grandmother's failing mental health without difficulty.

Josie became more and more mentally disabled until, at the age of eighty-two, she refused to eat or drink. She had already made her funeral arrangements with JoAnn and told her four daughters that she wanted to die at home. With around-the-clock help at home and regular visits from a community health nurse, Josie's daughters made sure that she was comfortable and didn't suffer. Jessica was fourteen at this time. She realized what was happening because her mom had explained Mamaw's behavior and wishes.

Ordinarily, Jessica and her mom visited Mamaw two or three times a week and talked with her often over the telephone. When the family knew that Mamaw was dying, Jessica and JoAnn visited Mamaw every day after school. Mamaw had become bedridden and could no longer speak, but Jessica sat by her bedside and told Mamaw funny stories. One day she brought Mamaw her favorite stuffed animal, a Care Bear. She placed it in Mamaw's arms. And Mamaw smiled.

A few days later, Mamaw lapsed into a coma. Jessica knew that her Mamaw would not live much longer. On the day she died, Jessica came to visit her after school. She placed her Care Bear in Mamaw's arms and sat with her, just as she did almost every day. About an hour after Jessica and her mom left, Mamaw died peacefully with the Care Bear in her arms.

When Jessica returned with both her parents to see her grandmother for the last time at home, she sat in a corner of Mamaw's bedroom and sobbed. When the funeral director and his assistant came to take Mamaw's body to the funeral home, Jessica asked for her Care Bear and held it to her heart for hours as Josie's daughters and their families, her sister and brother-in-law, and her caregiver sat around her home and shared wonderful "Josie stories" into the night.

Many of Jessica's friends also knew and loved Mamaw, who was kind, warm, and generous toward them. They attended Mamaw's funeral and burial service and were a great comfort and support to

Jessica. So were the many photos and videos of her grandmother and the family that Jessica's dad had taken on special occasions like birthdays, dance recitals, and holidays. Jessica would always have these, her Shirley Temple movies, Mamaw's angels, and her Care Bear as a legacy of her loving Mamaw.

A CHILD'S OWN REMEMBRANCE

In addition to cherishing mementos from grandparents and sharing memories about them, kids also can commemorate the life of a beloved grandparent and remember their ethnic roots if we encourage them to create a "remembering page" (see following page).

Many kids would love to remember their grandparent by creating something of their own. I urge you to present them with this opportunity.

CARRYING MEMORIES INTO ADULTHOOD AND BEYOND

If we assist our youngsters through the death of a grandparent, their experience will strengthen their ability to cope effectively with other losses they will encounter at different stages in their lives.

My daughters retain loving and active memories of their grandfather, who died in 1988. At a recent Thanksgiving weekend, my family gathered for a bountiful meal with all the trimmings and then watched old family videos. My girls, both teenagers now, laughed at their games and antics with Papa. Papa also left his legacy through his jungle stories. I expect that my children will embrace his memory and talk about their Papa to their children someday. More importantly, when their beloved aging "Nonni" (grandmother) dies someday, their prior experience of facing Papa's death will provide a solid perspective on mourning that will, undoubtedly, serve them well. What more can we ask for our kids?

A Kids' Remembering Page

This is a story about (grandparent's name) _____ .

My grand_____ was born on _____ .

Her (his) parents' names were _____ ,

and she (he) grew up in (town/state/country) _____ .

She (he) had _____ sisters and _____ brothers.

She (he) married _____ , my grandfather (grandmother),

and lived in (town/state/country) _____ .

My mother (father) was one of _____ children.

My grand _____ loved to _____ .

She (he) didn't like _____ .

When I visited her (him), I particularly liked to _____

_____

_____ .

My favorite thing that my grandparent gave me is _____

_____

_____ .

What I will miss most about my grandparent is _____

_____

_____ .

If I am a grandparent someday, I would like to _____

_____

_____ .

On the back of this page, I have drawn a picture of me and my grand_____ (doing) _____ .

Angels Don't
Have Headlights:
When Children Lose a Sibling

WHEN Brian's baby sister died of sudden infant death syndrome (SIDS) during the Christmas holidays, his parents told him, "The angels came down and took your baby sister." Five-year-old Brian either couldn't sleep or had fitful nights for six weeks after his sister died. The first time he met with Dr. Sandra Fox, she asked him if he wanted to talk about his sister. Brian said, "No, I want to talk about angels. I have two things to tell you about angels. First, there are lots of them out there, and they're on the loose at Christmas. The other thing about angels is they don't have headlights"—so Brian couldn't see them coming.

Brian had to stay awake at night so that the angels couldn't sneak up and take him away too. His grieving parents wanted to protect their bright little boy by telling him this soft angel story; however, this story terrorized Brian. At his young age, Brian's *literal understanding* about his parents' explanation left him with *unmanageable feelings* (see chapter 2).

No matter how old kids are, they don't automatically know that they can survive death once their brother or sister has died, either suddenly or following a lengthy battle with a disease. Surviving siblings don't have the psychological skills to confront this loss without being immersed in confusion and turmoil.

For example, a fire took the lives of three young children near my home. A twelve-year-old girl escaped with her six-month-old baby brother. She was on all the TV news channels the following evening. Many adults who saw the interview thought that she was holding court with the reporters, as she told her story with a brilliant smile on her face. "Three of my brothers and sisters died, and my baby brother, Mom, Dad, and I are living with my grandmother. Our babysitter helped me and the baby jump from the window."

This twelve-year-old dealt intellectually with the trauma of her siblings being burnt to death, not allowing her emotions to surface and take control. She didn't want to "fall apart" in front of the world.

Another example involves a ten-year-old boy and his seventeen-year-old sister who start out in their beds at night, but both are out of them by morning. The boy sleeps in the hallway and his sister racks out on the living room sofa. Sometimes they end up in their parents' bedroom sleeping on the floor. Their younger brother had recently died after living with leukemia for five years. Why can't these two kids sleep? They managed to stay healthy, but their brother didn't, and not without first turning their lives and their family life upside down for many years. Now their guilt interrupts their sleep.

The fact that kids are afraid to die, that they seem totally unaffected by the loss of a brother or sister, or that they can't sleep tells us that they need our assistance to sort through a variety of stress-provoking issues that can complicate or inhibit a youngster's anger and sadness. Dominant among these issues are (1) denial, (2) isolation, (3) bewilderment, (4) jealousy, (5) fear of dying also, (6) guilt for surviving, and/or (7) resentment because their lives were disrupted by the lengthy illness of a sibling who required inordinate attention from their parents.

How can parents guide surviving siblings when they themselves are grieving what is surely one of the most severe losses in their lives?

Some communication and behavioral techniques that they can employ to help the family share their grief and survive without detrimental psychological effects are these:

1. Provide an honest explanation of how a sibling died. Don't confuse spiritual beliefs with physical facts of death.

2. Be willing to talk about the changes a vulnerable sibling endures as his illness progresses. Healthy siblings notice these changes. If they ask, "Will he die?" answer with honesty, hope, and sensitivity. Kids want to know if their brother or sister will or did suffer following an anticipated or sudden death.

3. Don't ask healthy siblings to be adults, and be sensitive to their stresses and individual coping styles as the family faces a child's death.

4. Acknowledge that mourning for surviving siblings is complicated and lengthy.

5. Provide social and psychological support for surviving siblings and the entire family.

Support and care outside the home can boost surviving youngsters' ability to sort through their complex feelings and enlighten grieving parents with healthy strategies to keep the family going. Nurturing adults from a school, church, or support group can identify stresses that might plague kids, unknown to their parents. Extended family and friends can lighten household sadness by engaging in fun-filled activities, like going to the zoo or movies, with surviving youngsters. Mental health professionals can help to reduce family stress, enhance the security and self-esteem of surviving kids, and assist families in coming together in their grief.

Although kids have the same grief feelings as adults, remember that youngsters understand death and express their grief differently. Family dynamics and relationships prior to a sibling's death also can have an impact on surviving siblings' ability to mourn effectively.

CHELSEA'S STORY: I WAS A MIRACLE BABY, BUT MY SISTER DIED

Chelsea didn't get to see her baby sister, Lorie, who died a day after she was born due to complications of her prematurity. Emily and Len, Chelsea's parents, were devastated, but this loss minimally affected six-year-old Chelsea (see also chapter 5). Young Chelsea was not capable of a relationship with a sister whom she had never met.

What did have a great impact on Chelsea's behavior, however, was her parents' grief. Emily described Chelsea's reactions following Lorie's death: "Chelsea acted out and was naughty to get my attention. She was pretty irritating. That's when family and friends pitched in to keep her busy and occupied. We also had bought a small stuffed squirrel for Lorie while I was pregnant. Around a year after Lorie died, Chelsea asked to take the squirrel to bed with her sometimes. I told her that I thought her sister would love the fact that she played with the squirrel and that she was welcome to take it to bed anytime she wanted to."

Emily also discussed her grief with her daughter. "Chelsea never asked any questions about Lorie, but I would be driving with her and just start crying. I would tell her that it had nothing to do with her, that Mommy was sad because Lorie died. I also reassured her that I wouldn't be sad forever. At night I told her that I wouldn't always cry. I would always miss Lorie and talk about her because she was a part of our lives. We couldn't see her now, but I believed that we would be with her and see her one day. My family and wonderful friends from church helped with Chelsea so that she didn't have to be around me and my grief all the time. It also gave my husband and me some space to grieve."

Chelsea's mom said and did all the right things to help her surviving six-year-old child feel safe. She recognized her daughter's untoward behavior as a reaction to the family's upset and grief. She reached out for support and established a network of assistance through extended family and church.

When Chelsea was twelve, I talked with her about what issues, if any, affected her concerning the sister she had never known.

Although she remembered very little about Lorie's death or how she felt about it when she was six, Chelsea compared her sister's birth to her own. "Lorie was born premature, like me. I always knew what *premature* meant because, ever since I can remember, my family told me how I was born premature. I weighed one and a half pounds, but Lorie weighed a little less. We have a picture of her. She looked the same as me. She's gray and scary because she has lots of tubes in her picture. I lived in the hospital for four months on many machines that kept me alive. My parents were afraid that I would die too, but I made it. Everyone told me that I was a miracle baby."

Chelsea could relate to Lorie's "gray and scary" photo because it helped her to understand what a premature infant, like herself, looks like at birth.

I asked her if she thought that you could miss someone whom you never got to know. She replied: "Well, I don't think about Lorie, unless someone like you asks me about her, but I miss her because I wonder what she would look like now—whether she would look like my dad or my mom. I'd like to play and do other stuff with her. I think she's in heaven and probably knows what's going on down here. I think she looks out and over me. I think of her as a guardian angel, but I don't talk or pray to her. I tell Mom all the time that I wish she and Dad would have another kid. She says, 'No, I'm too old and it's too dangerous.' I don't ask Dad because he's not the one who gets pregnant."

Chelsea wanted a sister with whom she could grow up. Emily said of her daughter: "She hates being an only child. Even though she has stepsiblings, they don't live at home and are much older than her. All Chelsea's cousins and friends have siblings. When she was ten, she came to Len and me and asked if we could adopt a baby. She saw a boy on TV who needed a home. Chelsea said, 'Call right now. I want him. Please, Mom and Dad.' She sobbed her eyes out."

As Chelsea has grown, she has understood and accepted that it wouldn't be wise or healthy for her mom to risk having another premature infant with unsurmountable problems. She now has a baby niece who "doesn't remind me of Lorie. I don't think of her as a replacement for Lorie, but I think of Vicky as my sister. I'm too young to be an aunt, but I'm old enough to be a sister to her even though she doesn't live with me." The pain of not having a sibling has subsided for Chelsea as she has learned that another loving youngster can be a "sister" in heart and spirit.

SARA'S STORY: I LAUGHED AT HIS FUNERAL

Sara turned fifteen the day before her older brother, Michael, hit a telephone pole as he was driving home at about three in the morning from a party at which he had been drinking. Michael had just graduated from the prep school where Sara was a freshman. They had hung out and played sports together. Michael had also included his younger sister in his social life, occasionally inviting her to join him and his friends.

When a police officer came to Sara's home to deliver the terrible news, he hesitated to tell her and her mother of Michael's death because her father, who traveled extensively on business, was away. As her aunt pulled into their driveway, the officer finally told her mom that Michael had died. Sara was in the hallway but heard. She couldn't believe that her brother was dead and thought that he had to be in a hospital somewhere. "I said, 'Mom, it's all right.' My mom was crying and screaming with my aunt at the kitchen table. I went into the living room, where nobody really goes. I sat in one of those chairs by myself and just thought. I still don't know whether my brother died right away or not, or if he suffered."

Michael's death fractured precious family bonds that were once intact and strong. Initially, Sara met with me once, visited a psychiatrist once, and then refused therapy of any kind. Her father, Richard, who was unable to eat or sleep, refused counseling. I counseled her mother, Rachael, regularly for a year. A year and a half after Michael died, when Sara was sixteen, she agreed to meet with me for an interview, because she wanted to "help other kids and their parents understand how losing a sibling totally changes your relationship with yourself, your parents, and your friends."

It was difficult for Sara to express her sadness. The family held a wake, but "I didn't stand by my parents because I didn't want to be hugged by other people. I had never been to a wake before." At Michael's funeral mass on the following day, "my mom said I could sit with my friends. I didn't want to be in the front with all the emotional people. I wanted to be hidden. I didn't cry once through the whole thing. Michael would have never cried. I laughed actually. My friends hit me because that wasn't the right thing to do. I don't know what made me laugh. It was so silent. I couldn't just sit there. I had to do something."

Silence at her brother's remembrance service invited painful feelings to surface. Laughing was a way of running from the pain, of "bucking up," as Sara felt that her brother would have done and wished that her parents were able to do.

Rachael and Richard did not suppress their grief, which irritated and angered Sara, particularly because Richard "wore" his anger and sadness. "Dad has placed photos of Michael all around the house like he's trying to keep my brother alive. I see pictures of him everywhere I go. It's annoying. Dad can't face the fact of it, and everything has gone downhill for him. He seems like he has aged. He talks a lot about Michael and says, 'I'm doing this because Michael told me to.' He bought Michael a card on his birthday and he wrote a poem about him that he put up on Michael's grave." Rachael didn't talk on and on about Michael as Richard did, but Sara heard her mom cry many nights. "I guess that's the way she has to do it. I would slam my bedroom door."

It is no wonder that Sara blocked her sad feelings. Her parents had slipped away from her, just as her brother had been taken away, and she didn't feel safe to express her sadness because her parents' grief overwhelmed her. In addition, Sara rationalized that Michael would not have wanted her to be sad. "I feel like, even my parents, they don't know what it's like for me and my brother's friends, so why are they crying? Why can't they just go on without carrying on the way they do? Michael would not have acted like they do."

Although Sara blocked her sadness successfully, she expressed her anger vividly. Right after Michael's death, Rachael said: "Everything makes my daughter angry. Sara flies off the handle in an instant, slams doors, and stays in her room. She often has night-mares and turbulent episodes of sleepwalking." Sara couldn't tol-erate her parents' continual outbursts of anger and sadness, but Rachael comforted and cared for her daughter during Sara's angry outbursts, frightening nights, silent car rides, and poor academic performance.

The most stressful and insurmountable issue for this adolescent, however, revolved around her feelings about her brother. Right before he died, "I was angry with myself and him because, after the last time we talked, I was in a really bad mood. I said, 'Bye, don't talk to me.' I never cry. For the first week, I didn't share any-thing with anybody. But then I showed my emotions to my friends for a little while. Now I don't show them to anyone. They tell me that, if I want to talk, they are here for me. But I just think by myself. I want to be strong like my brother and not show emo-tions."

Because Sara blocked her sadness and wanted to be "strong," she was not able to feel the presence of her brother's spirit in her life. "Some of my family says that he's still here, watching over us. Once, my grandmother said that he touched her elbow in church. I'm the only one who doesn't feel that he's around. I believe that his spirit is up in heaven, but I don't feel this. My friends tell me that he came down here to do something, and he did it, so then he left. I do believe this because he did so much when he was alive. He accomplished everything he wanted to do in life. He wanted to work in the Army or Navy and fly planes. He already had his pilot's license. He sailed boats, scuba dived, and played all the sports he wanted. Whenever my brother wanted to do something, he did it. He did it all while he was going to school too."

Sara also made an idol of her brother, an idol to which she could never live up. "I try to be like him. Sometimes this makes me feel good, but sometimes not. He was so nice and I'm mean. He was always friends with everyone in his grade, even if he didn't like the person. I can't do that. It's hard. Michael always accomplished what he wanted, and it's just hard for me to do that."

Believing that her brother had done the impossible, Sara was tormented by the memory she created of him. How could she live up to his can-do-no-wrong life? She "tried to forget about him and go on," but she couldn't. Sara imprisoned herself behind bars from which she didn't know how to escape. In her mind and heart, Michael towered on a pedestal so high above her that she would never be able to reach him. Until she can feel the pain of his death and accept his drinking and driving and any other mistakes he made, which have shattered her life, Sara will never learn that grief subsides over time and that the legacy of his great spirit lies within herself.

Sara also chose not to involve herself with the circumstances surrounding her brother's death. Michael had attended a party at which he and his friends drank heavily. After his death, Richard and Rachael sued the parents of the boy who gave the party. Suing the parents and preventing teens from drinking and driving became Richard's "cause."

During the criminal trial, Sara attended a horse show. "My parents asked me if I wanted to go to the trial and I said no. They didn't push me. I didn't want to know about it because I didn't have much to say about it. I'm not angry with the parents. I understand that kids try to hide from parents to have fun. My dad wants to show the world that what happened to Michael and what these parents did was wrong. But you can't do that. It's too difficult. Dad is in overdrive and obsessed about the whole thing." Although we can empathize with this dad, he didn't realize how his actions affected his only surviving child. Unknowingly, he has forgotten his daughter, isolated her with her pain, and enhanced her feelings about her brother being greater than life, something that she could never attain.

As she grieved for her son, Rachael cried openly and often while trying to respect her daughter's needs to grieve on her own timetable and in her unique way. She also fought her natural urge to be overprotective. Despite Rachael's efforts, Sara has refused to talk with her mother. "I used to be close with my mom, but not since Michael died. I can't share with her how I feel because, if I cry to her, she'll want to cry to me. I don't think it would make it better for us to cry together."

Some of my work with Rachael helped her to realize that her

continual expression of sadness and the constant turmoil that she and her husband generated as they prepared for the court trial made Sara feel too vulnerable to share her feelings, not only because Sara grieved differently from her parents but also because she needed a consistent and inclusive family dynamic before she could go on securely with life without Michael. To Sara, her parents' emotions were in constant chaos and disarray.

At sixteen, Sara felt that the hardest thing about Michael's death was not having her brother see her accomplish things, like riding horses, her favorite pastime. She said, "I want to get better in everything that I do. I should have better grades than last year. I should be better. I put this pressure on myself, my parents don't." Taking responsibility for pressuring herself and not projecting it as coming from her parents is a wise observation for an adolescent.

Although Sara stoically shared her thoughts about Michael and her parents, it was clear that she was unable to open her heart or emote feelings. Despite my presence and care, it was also clear that Sara continued to isolate herself from others because her parents had isolated her from themselves in their overwhelming grief. This adolescent was not yet ready to embrace her sadness, which she felt might kill her too.

When I asked Sara what worried her most about going on without Michael, she said, "I still miss my brother today as much as ever. I worry if things will get harder when I get older and past this age. I don't know if I'll get past the age of eighteen because he didn't. I don't know if other teenagers feel the same in this situation. I don't know what I'm going to do in my senior year or at graduation. I'm afraid that I'm going to freak out. I just want to skip my junior, senior, and college years."

It's natural for adults and kids of all ages to feel that they can't or won't live past the age at which a loving brother or sister died. In what way could I let Sara know that my door was never closed and my hand always extended to her? I told her that if she needed strategies to help her get through her junior year, she should meet with me. We didn't have to discuss her brother, her parents, or how she chose to deal with his death.

The criminal trial, which was behind the family a year and a half after Michael died, helped Richard to begin to accept his son's death, even though the defendant parents were found innocent. With the court case finalized, possibly family life would return to an even keel, Sara would share her immense sadness, and her parents would dedicate their time and energy to their only surviving child, a bright and talented person in her own right. Most importantly, if Sara and her parents could come together in their loss, she would realize that she doesn't have to live up to her fabricated legacy of Michael, that her parents love her, and that she is worthy of love. I have great hope for this outcome in time.

DeeDee's Story: I Will Never Be an Only Child

DeeDee was a fledgling preadolescent when her younger brother, Paul, died at age five from a heart complication precipitated by the chicken pox virus. Paulie, as DeeDee called him, was born with complex congenital heart disease when she was three and a half. Many cardiac specialists said that they could surgically repair Paul's heart anomaly and he would be fine. These physicians didn't minimize the severity of Paul's condition, but they assured DeeDee's parents that they could "fix it," as Marsha, DeeDee's mom, said.

Paul spent most of the first two years of his life in the hospital. DeeDee didn't see Paulie or her parents very much because his illness disrupted family life. She spent much of her time with her maternal grandparents. Being a toddler, DeeDee was not aware of the critical realities of Paul's disease and surgeries.

At fourteen, DeeDee's memory of her feelings about Paul, his surgeries, and family life were vague, but she warmly recalled eating Chips Ahoy chocolate chip cookies and Smartfood with her grandparents. From ages three to five, "I missed my parents a little bit, and I think I was always a little jealous of Paulie during his surgeries. 'Oh, look at all the attention he's getting,' I'd say to myself. I didn't really have a bond with him when he was that young, and I didn't have a clue about what was wrong with him other than he was sick. It bothered me a little that he got presents, but I didn't mind being at my grandparents' house. I went to preschool and had some friends already."

Paul received cards on all occasions from some "strangers" who were in the hospital with him, which didn't seem fair to DeeDee. She wanted cards too. Otherwise, between three and five years of age, she accepted without question Paul's numerous health-care regimes, visiting nurses, and continual trips to the hospital. This was how DeeDee knew her brother, and this was reality for the first two years of his life.

Following Paul's surgeries, the family moved to another home. After the move, DeeDee saw her brother as "normal and healthy in every way." In the evenings, they would read stories at bedtime. Sometimes Paul, being afraid to sleep, would go into DeeDee's room. She would make up stories and songs for him. One evening, she remembered singing him to sleep and feeling "so satisfied. I thought I could really be a mother someday."

DeeDee had just turned nine when Paul died. "He must have been so sick during the first two years of his life and when he died, so why didn't I know about that and all the pain he went through? I should have been more concerned for him. I always ask: Was I good to him? Was I nice to him? Was I a good sister? Why did I and a million other children survive the chicken pox but Paulie died because of it? Why didn't I do a better job of comforting him when he underwent his surgeries and got so sick from the chicken pox?"

At fourteen DeeDee intellectually understood that there was no way for a four- or five-year-old, no matter how bright she was, to understand the severity of a brother's health problems and the meaning of being a sister. Intellect is one thing and emotions are another. DeeDee was trying to reconcile her feelings of guilt for surviving when Paulie didn't. She was regrieving his death and searching for answers to many overwhelming questions.

Unlike Sara, DeeDee didn't place her deceased brother on a pedestal. In fact, she could recall Paulie's ability to get on her nerves. "I had lots of fun with him, but we fought too. He always wanted me to know what was up. It was annoying sometimes, but he looked up to me, I think. As a third grader, that made me feel important and content. After he got well, I never felt that my parents gave him more attention."

DeeDee's dad, Herb, told her about Paul's death when her parents came home from the hospital without him. Her grandmother became hysterical after hearing the news, which frightened DeeDee and made her wonder what was going on. She felt as if "I was out of my mind. And then I wet my pants. I thought it was a dream. Dad cried. It was weird because I had never seen him cry. I just hugged him."

Paul's wake was scary. DeeDee knew the meaning of a funeral, but she hadn't heard of a wake. Her grandmother explained this term as the family drove to the funeral home: "It's when people who loved him come to see him, say a prayer for him, and say good-bye. He's just going to look like he's sleeping. We'll be fine." Dad took her to view her brother's body in the coffin. "I remember Paulie being so discolored and sunken looking. It definitely wasn't like he was sleeping. It scared me. I looked at him for a couple of seconds and just walked away. I told my grandmother that it didn't look like Paulie and that he didn't look like he was sleeping." DeeDee had confronted her grandmother with a true fact about death, something that her grandmother wanted to deny in order to protect DeeDee and herself.

At the funeral, DeeDee expected her dad to talk about Paul and Paul's best friend. Instead, "He said that I was the best sister Paulie could have had, and I started to cry. Dad really cried too. My grandparents cried, but Mom held it in. She didn't ball her eyes out but her eyes would water. I could tell she was really upset, but she tried to stay brave."

DeeDee not only witnessed how everyone grieves differently, but she then experienced what mourning after the formal commemoration celebration was like. "About a month after Paulie died, our house felt quiet. There was nothing to do. I had friends who would come over and I got gifts—now *I'm* getting them because he died. That felt weird. We did a lot of things to remember Paulie too, but my parents have never been the same. I lost my parents as they were when he was alive. I'm not mad about this, nor do I hold it against them, but how they feel about life is totally different, particularly how my father feels. He's very quiet."

When Paul was alive, Herb would play catch, for instance, and do many other activities on the spur of the moment with his kids. "Since Paulie's death, Dad has not been spontaneous. Mom and I make fun of him sometimes because he's grouchy and moody. I would say he is depressed, but sometimes when Mom and I say something about Paulie, he will speak up, 'Oh, I remember that.' He'll get into the conversation and laugh. Then I tell myself that Dad is okay. Paulie mostly gets him animated, but not much else does . . . maybe golf."

At fourteen, DeeDee could not bare her soul to her father because her dad walled himself off from the family and allowed sadness to overshadow his life. On the one hand, DeeDee felt responsible to protect him from falling apart, while on the other, she felt isolated from him and wanted a father with whom she could identify and relate. With her mom, she could talk about anything, even if she knew her feelings might upset her mother, because Mom was willing to share her understanding and grief with DeeDee.

Marsha and Herb considered filing a litigation suit against the hospital, whose emergency staff, in their judgment, recognized Paul's cardiac infection too late to treat it successfully, despite Marsha's plea for them to be more aggressive. Although DeeDee understood what the word *litigation* meant, she tried to get a handle on why many lawyers told her parents that her brother's life wasn't as valuable as an adult's. I explained to her that *value* in the case of litigation has to do only with *financial worth*. Our culture doesn't say that kids aren't as important as adults, but legally they don't earn money and support a family as parents do; therefore, parents are given more financial value in a legal suit. DeeDee had misunderstood her mom's explanation. I encouraged her to sit down with both parents and share her confusion, as she had done with Marsha many times in the past, so that she would not be misinformed, unsure, perplexed, or anxious about this for the rest of her life.

As an adolescent, DeeDee struggled to come to terms with the following question: "What does it mean to be a sister, and how can I carry on my brother's memory? I always tell people that my brother has died. I can't sit and pretend I'm this only child because that's not who I am. I'll talk with kids who have been only children all their lives, and I have a totally different experience. Some kids have told me things like, 'Well, you only had a brother for five years, so it wasn't a big deal. I had my grandparents for a really long time and it was more of a big deal for me.' How can you say that my situation was less? Most people try to compare and you shouldn't."

DeeDee learned a wonderful lesson about *competitive grief*, that is, our desire to measure our grief feelings against other people's. Competitive grief says that "my pain is worse than yours." A friend of her mother's helped her understand what a person's life means to the world despite his age and accomplishments. "Your brother did what he had to do. He made the world a better place and he did what he was supposed to do. That's why God brought him up there already." DeeDee agreed: "I thought her response was great. It's a cool way to think of it."

When DeeDee thought and talked about her brother or prayed for him in church, she "connected with his essence. I also think about him when I see the TV show *Full House* because we used to watch that together and he loved it. I'm still not used to being by myself. It's tough on a rainy day. I'm all alone."

Marsha's mission is to have all kids vaccinated against the chicken pox so that her son's death would not be in vain, but DeeDee's is to carry on her brother's legacy. For Spanish class, she created a family tree and proudly placed Paul in it. "I never want to pretend that I didn't have a brother and that I was an only child. I wonder if my kids will care that I had a brother who died when he was five. That's part of who I am."

Paulie's death greatly influenced how DeeDee viewed herself and her future, which forced her to grow up much too early. Would she have been such a serious adolescent had Paul not died? "Sometimes I feel like I have to pursue my life thinking for two people. I used to feel that I have to do everything doubly well just to make my parents happy. I feel that I have to do that for both of us now. I have to make up for him. This term might be the first time I won't make the honor roll. I'm in high school now, and classes are hard. My mom seemed to want more. It annoyed me.

She told me I could do better. I said, 'Hold on, don't do this. No, I can't do better. I hate it when you tell me this.' I've never said that if Paulie was alive, you wouldn't be pushing me so hard, but I kind of feel this way sometimes."

DeeDee's counselor, whom she has been seeing since Paul's death, helped her to understand her feelings and her parents' mourning behavior. She also helped DeeDee learn how to talk with her mom about many tough issues surrounding life without Paul. At fourteen, DeeDee had gained remarkable insight into her jealousy, confusion, and guilt-ridden feelings. I believe that she will eventually free herself from survivor's guilt and carry on her brother's legacy just by being herself and valuing *her* qualities as well as his, while realizing that she can never compensate for the loss of her brother or her parents' loss of a son.

LESSONS THAT SURVIVORS CAN TEACH PARENTS

Over 100,000 youngsters, from birth through age twenty-four, die yearly from cancer, heart disease, accidents, suicide, and homicide. Countless siblings survive to mourn these losses and go on with their lives. Although the circumstances surrounding a sibling's death are always unique, most kids who have lost a brother or sister experience many of the feelings that Chelsea, Sara, and DeeDee have. Here are some ways we can help children who have lost a sibling:

1. Don't overwhelm surviving siblings with parental grief, which blocks their ability to mourn and realize that you are a safe person who can help them work through their loss.

2. Recognize that survivors might experience guilt and think of themselves as inadequate brothers or sisters.

3. Encourage survivors to share their confusion, jealousy, and fears, although these feelings might hurt or distress you.

4. Don't expect or encourage survivors to compare themselves with, live up to, or replace a brother or sister who has died.

5. Encourage survivors to be the unique youngsters they are, and value them for who they are.

6. Recognize that survivors have suffered a double loss; that is, they have lost a sibling *and* their parents as they knew them before.

These lessons might not be easy for parents to hear or learn because their grief and remorse are great. Remember, however, that we aren't alone as parents. Extended family, friends, clergy, and mental health professionals will reach out to us if we open our hearts to them and to our surviving youngsters.

A Video Connection with a Dying Child:

Anticipatory Loss

RYAN Andrews McCormick was a tall and energetic kid whose zest for life never ceased during his two-year battle with cancer. When he was seven, his parents, Beth and Scott, observed his unusual lack of energy on the baseball field. Specialists diagnosed Ryan with hepatic cell carcinoma, a diffuse and inoperable form of liver cancer in children. Beth said that only sixteen youngsters in the United States were diagnosed with this disease during the same year that Ryan was. The rarity of this type of cancer in kids made Ryan a candidate for a liver transplant.

During the summer between second and third grades, Ryan received chemotherapy and radiation. Having suffered severe side effects from these treatments, he was hospitalized many times. However, his excellent response to treatment made him eligible for a transplant, which he received a couple of months into his third grade school year. Within a month following successful transplant surgery, Ryan was back in class and able to complete third grade without major problems.

During the summer between third and fourth grades, the McCormicks learned that Ryan's cancer had spread to his brain. He suffered a stroke and then multiple seizures. Following surgery associated with a brain hemorrhage, he went from one crisis to the next until he lapsed into a coma and died peacefully at home.

Life changes dramatically for a newly diagnosed youngster, and his illness precipitates a long-term *chronic crisis* in his life and in the lives of all who know him. The course of the child's illness, his personality and coping skills, and his family's and friends' behavior toward him in part determine his response to this life-threatening situation. In turn, the affected youngster's behavior, outlook, and medical care have an impact on his family and friends.

THE CHILD WITH A LIFE-THREATENING ILLNESS

Ryan's life revolved around play and story telling. Beth, Scott, and Ryan's sisters, Amanda and Jodie, used to call him Ferdinand, after the happy bull who loved flowers and could be absorbed by little else. Ryan was a happy child absorbed by play, which came before schoolwork and studies. He had a heartwarming laugh and sense of humor and liked to create scary stories.

David, his best friend since infancy, didn't attend the same school as Ryan, but they played endlessly after school and during summer vacations. Play was paramount in their lives as they acted out feelings and solved problems through it, which is not atypical for young kids. They enjoyed power-enhancing characters and games. Ryan's favorites were Power Rangers and Nintendo, but he also loved baseball, karate, and swimming. Not surprisingly, Ryan confronted his illness through play. By masking and dressing as invincible characters, he felt empowered to overcome and conquer any battle that life presented. This was an adaptive coping strategy for him.

Children with life-challenging diseases more often act out their sad and happy feelings in indirect ways, as Ryan did through play. Remember, however, that all kids have unique temperaments and personalities. For example, Joey, a nine-year-old boy with a malignant brain tumor, wrote and talked about his cancer with his family and friends. He tackled a large project of writing a book entitled *Joey, You've Got a Brain Tumor,* which explores his feelings and ideas about his illness and impending death. Joey's classmates in fourth grade provided the artwork for the book.

In it, Joey has detailed the procedures and treatments he underwent to combat his cancer, along with his feelings about his illness, family, friends, and doctors. At the end of his book, Joey has written: "I try my best. If I don't do my best in the world at least I will have tried. I have tried my best on everything. I have tried everything that I had on this book because other people need to know what it is like to have a brain tumor. . . . Since I've had cancer, I have felt good to this day and I am working hard. Let me tell you the things that have really helped me—my family and my friends. The thing about cancer is I know I have it and I know I have to deal with it. My family has helped me more than the doctors, and Tyler [a friend] has helped me more than the doctors—because they know me. . . . Finally, I got to go into the classroom I had in fourth grade and I said, 'Hey, busters, what's up?' That was the happiest day I ever had in this past half year of all these medical times!"

Not many nine-year-old kids are as candid and articulate as Joey was about his up-and-down battles and his hope for healing. Because Joey was eager to talk about the struggles he underwent to heal and keep a positive attitude about his cancer, his aunt encouraged him to write this book in order to help himself and other kids.

From Diagnosis to Liver Transplant

Ryan and his family lived in a well-educated, middle-class community. His parents, Beth and Scott, had grown up in the 1960s. They took parenting seriously and, when their oldest daughter was born, both consciously decided to work part-time so that they could equally coparent their children. When their son's diagnosis came, they had to decide what was the best way to disclose the disease to him and his two sisters.

Disclosing a Dire Diagnosis

Research literature and empirical evidence from thirty years ago suggested that parents should protect their child from the knowledge of his life-threatening illness. Today, professionals and researchers who work with terminally ill youngsters have learned that protecting the child from his diagnosis can isolate him with unmentionable fears and anxieties.

From the very beginning, Beth and Scott were honest with their son and daughters about the nature and course of his illness. Months before the call for transplant surgery came, they explained the procedure to Ryan and shared their hopes for a successful outcome. Beth and Scott also revealed to their eight-year-old son that if the transplant failed someday, he would probably die. Although it's understandable that these parents wanted to be truthful and help Ryan make sense of his illness, I would not advise parents to divulge a possible dire outcome to a child unless the child specifically asked.

Ryan never questioned his parents, sisters, friends, or any caregiver directly about his dying someday, nor did he talk about his fears or anxieties. His reaction to the frightening news that he probably would die if his transplant failed was one of bravado. "I'll be fine," he reassured his parents. According to Beth, Ryan remained cheerful, positive, and powerful as he underwent chemotherapy, radiation, and liver transplant surgery. He used play to act out and work through scary feelings.

Although Ryan's school psychologist and teacher attended one of my daylong workshops and then consulted with me, I didn't counsel him or his family. Each family member received psychological therapy during Ryan's illness and following his death, but I was not privy to the nature of their therapy. I can only wonder if Ryan's refusal to talk about his fears and anxieties was linked to protecting his parents and sisters. Kids with life-challenging illnesses typically worry about abandoning their parents, suffering a painful death, and facing the uncertainty of an afterlife. There is also the inevitable question—When?

Family Life in Chronic Crisis

Siblings suffer a special burden when a brother's illness demands that they put their needs aside for his sake. Altruism over a long period of time is not part of a youngster's normal way of life; therefore, the emotional costs that healthy siblings can face are dear.

At the time of Ryan's diagnosis, his oldest sister, Amanda, was almost sixteen and his other sister, Jodie, who was very close to Ryan and shared a bedroom with him when they were younger, was eleven. Jodie threw herself into school and schoolwork, which was her way of responding to the stresses of her brother's chronic crisis and disruption in daily family life. For many years, Amanda suffered with depression. She learned to cope with Ryan's ups and downs and lack of family routine through her adolescent friendships. Her friends were her greatest support on a daily basis.

Throughout Ryan's illness, Amanda remained upbeat with Ryan and made him laugh. He was her best audience. Jodie was very affectionate and warm to him. The girls faced Ryan's illness in their own individual style. Their unique relationship with him, their ages and stages of development, their temperaments, their needs, and their coping skills dictated their responses and behavior toward him.

Financial pressures on a family are not uncommon if one parent works less or not at all to keep the family going and to care for the sick child. Marriages suffer as "free time" becomes rare and normal pleasures seem a commodity of the past. Because they both worked part-time, Beth and Scott were able to care for Ryan and maintain their jobs simultaneously without undo burden on one or the other. Neither had to give up work or their normal weekly income to stay with him in the hospital or care for him at home during his chemoradiation therapy and transplant surgery, which lifted their anxieties about providing for their family's daily needs. The family also had excellent health benefits that ensured the best of care for Ryan and weekly counseling for Beth, Scott, and their daughters.

However, routine and normal family relationships were secondary to Ryan's survival, his treatments, his surgeries, and his care. The family lived without knowing their future from day to day. Yearly vacations, season tickets to hockey games, and summer baseball practice were on hold and possibly would not happen. This is the reality that most families face in fighting a child's chronic battle with a life-challenging illness.

Community and Friends' Reactions and Support

Ryan's loyal and best friend, David, visited him daily at home or in the hospital. David never minded playing with toys that required little exertion or watching videos when Ryan wasn't able to dress in costumes or engage in karate or other strenuous play. He even was fitted with a radiation mask like Ryan's because he accompanied his friend to these grueling treatments. As a reward for Ryan's bravery and David's faithful friendship throughout this summer, Make-A-Wish Foundation invited Ryan, his family, and David to Disney World. Make-A-Wish is a nonprofit, volunteer organization created in 1980 in order to fulfill the special wishes of kids who suffer life-threatening illnesses.

Ryan's teacher and school friends also rallied around him. Judi, who was his teacher in second and third grades, felt that Ryan was a "superspecial little boy." Because she kept in continual contact with him and his family, Judi was aware of his diagnosis and intensive treatments. In order to complete his treatment regime, Ryan wasn't able to begin third grade on time. Judi took the opportunity to explain to her other third grade students that Ryan had liver cancer and had undergone chemo and radiation all summer long. She also prepared them for his altered physical condition once he returned to school. They would notice that he was thinner and that his head was shaved because he had lost most of his hair. Many kids in her class had known Ryan from previous years, so they expressed their sadness and said they wanted him to get well soon. Judi and the class decided to be his avid supporters.

Although Ryan had no hair and wore a Ben and Jerry's multicolored beanie when he came back to school, he continued to energize his old school buddies and his new ones with his creative stories, his laughter, his fondness for play. His fun-loving spirit made it easy for them to relate to him.

Ryan got the call for transplant surgery on New Year's Day, so he missed school for a month following. When he returned, his third grade class welcomed him back with a song and dance they had composed and choreographed with the help of their music teacher.

Judi made a video of the party they held. Some students danced and all sang what they entitled "A Song for Ryan."

> *Ryan likes lollipops, Genesis, and airplanes.*
> *He likes to play baseball and Super Nintendo games.*
> *Ryan collects baseball cards and Batman toys.*
> *When he went to Florida, he made a lot of noise.*
>
> *We all miss you, Ryan.*
> *We all miss you, Ryan.*

Jules, a school friend, gave Ryan a Cal Ripken, Jr., baseball card because he knew Ryan loved baseball but wasn't able to play. Ryan discovered that it was worth fifty dollars, much to Jules' surprise. He told Jules how great the gift was and that he was a real friend. Jules said, "I didn't know how much the card was worth, but I would have given it to Ryan anyway. I wanted him to have it. We weren't best friends, but I enjoyed playing with him. He had so much energy and I liked him a lot."

Ryan's teacher, guidance counselor, and school nurse worked with his parents and helped him complete his studies while encouraging his playful demeanor throughout third grade. They also assisted and encouraged his classmates to get in the same boat with Ryan and be his friend during his high and low times.

FROM LIVER TRANSPLANT TO CEREBRAL METASTASIS

Although Ryan had an arduous medication regime following transplant surgery, he recovered well and finished third grade without major complications. Shortly after school was out, however, he had a seizure and was diagnosed with brain metastasis. By the end of the summer, Ryan underwent surgery to control cerebral hemorrhage. Following this surgery, his physicians told Beth and Scott that their son probably would die within a month. Due to hemorrhage and surgery, Ryan suffered right-sided paralysis, confining him to bed and making it impossible for him to start fourth grade. He also had to work hard to speak, laugh, and make himself understood. At this time, Beth and Scott brought him home from the hospital, and hospice nurses and volunteers came to assist with his care. Ryan's parents not only worked around the clock to care for their son, but they also struggled to face his imminent death.

Do We Have a Future with Him?

Beth and Scott clung to Ryan's survival. Because his disease seemed to be in remission following his successful transplant, Scott was sure that Ryan was cured. In an interview I conducted with Beth, she said, "I guess you could say we were in denial and never gave up hope for his cure until his brain surgery." After that, Beth and Scott were able to accept that Ryan would die soon. They talked about it together and tried to prepare themselves and their girls for this inevitable trauma.

Denial is a defense mechanism that serves a child and his parents throughout the course of his illness. However, parents, as well as a child's caregivers, usually give up their denial at different times and in different ways than sick children do.

What's Going to Happen?

Ryan's best friend, David, didn't abandon Ryan because he was bedridden following his brain surgery. David said, "I didn't mind that he was in bed at all. We watched videos and movies together every day and played with our toys in his bed." Both kids were content to be with each other and create play that suited Ryan's needs.

Judi, who requested to have Ryan in her fourth grade class also, began to bring him videos that his classmates made for him once school started in September because Ryan couldn't attend class. After Judi delivered the third video and visited with Ryan, he began watching it but stopped abruptly and started to cry. He told his mom, "Turn it off. I just want to go to school. I want to go to school now." Beth responded that he couldn't because he was too sick. Following this he asked, "What's going to happen?" This mother wanted to be truthful with her son no matter what he asked. Finally she said, "You're going to die."

Scott, who overheard this conversation from the kitchen, rushed into the living room, where he had created a new bedroom for Ryan. Ryan began to cry, "I don't want to die. I don't want to go to heaven." He cried this out repeatedly and called on his sisters, "Amanda and Jodie, Amanda and Jodie, I don't want to die." His dog became upset and jumped on his bed, licking him all over his hands and face. Following this, Ryan suffered a seizure.

When his mom spoke frankly about his death, Ryan was apparently overwhelmed, which precipitated his seizure. Ryan had asked, "What's going to happen?" For almost two years, he had never broached this question. This was the most upsetting moment Beth encountered in her relationship with her sick and dying son.

In my speaking engagements and workshops, I advise parents to use the operative word *wish* when a child doesn't ask or talk about his possible death directly. If a dying child wants to do something but is frustrated and upset because he can't, we can say, *"I know that you wish you could go to school, but you can't walk or move the right side of your body and you can hardly talk. This makes it impossible for you to go."* Point out specific reasons and remember that kids ask only what they are prepared to hear. Our job, a difficult one, is to listen carefully in order to make sure that we understand what they're asking. Such an answer that I provided is truthful and will usually suffice when a child asks indirect questions about his life and death. We need to let the child lead us!

If and when youngsters ask "Am I going to die?" my answer would be: *"I don't want you to die because I love you so very much. We are doing and will continue to do everything we can to help you get better, but everyone dies someday. Why don't we talk about death and our fears about it?"* Never isolate your child with his fears or questions. Be in the same boat with him and assure him that you'll never abandon him. Observe his play, his behavior, and his words to understand and acknowledge his concerns about his life and death.

ANTICIPATORY COMMEMORATION AND RYAN'S DEATH

When a person's death is imminent, she and her family have the opportunity to deal with "unfinished business," for example, talking over problems never resolved and coming to terms with ambivalent feelings. Generally, kids don't have unfinished business; however, a child might pull back or withdraw from family and friends. Ryan's insistence that the videos should end might have been his way of withdrawing from life and saying that his courageous battle was nearly over. Behaviors that signal finality, such as saying good-byes, divulging last wishes, or withdrawing from daily life, can prompt family and friends to celebrate a dying child's life with him, if at all possible. Such life-affirming events I call *anticipatory commemoration*.

Nature of Anticipatory Commemoration

Two days after Beth told Ryan that he was going to die, he asked his parents to take him to the mall. "If I'm going to die, I want to spend all the money in my bank account." Although Ryan barely had the muscle strength to hold himself erect in a wheelchair, his parents took him shopping. He had a difficult time getting around and cried because he couldn't make up his mind what was the best thing to purchase. In the end, he bought a "crazy mask" that blew up when he put it on, enabling him to wear it only once. Ryan might have realized that he would have the chance to wear it only once; therefore, he chose a fitting toy.

The fact that Ryan's parents supported their son with his dying wish is remarkable because they knew that the chances of his shopping spree being successful was almost nil in the face of his deteriorated physical condition. Because play was meaningful to Ryan until he died, Beth and Scott were willing to help him in this endeavor. The lesson here is that they did it together despite the hardship, sadness, or outcome. They were able to share with Ryan one last thing that meant the most to him in his life. I can't think of a better way for a child and his parents to commemorate his life at the end.

Ryan's teacher, Judi, and her fourth grade class also remembered Ryan during his final days. In order to make him feel part of the class, the students made videos for him on Fridays and entitled them "The News of the Week from Room 209." They displayed and explained their projects about rockets and the solar system, fortune-telling and monsters, and estimations of acorns in a sac, among other things. At the end of each news video, his classmates greeted Ryan in various ways: "Hi, Ryan, I miss you." "Hi, Ryan, I'm Jules. We were in third grade together and loved to play." "Hi, Ryan, hurry back."

Every Friday for three weeks, Judi delivered these videos to Ryan. She also gave him a letter that his classmates wrote. They told him how much they missed him and looked forward to his return. As best he could, Ryan dictated a return letter with Scott's help and said that he hoped to see them for Halloween. He also asked them to tell him about their brothers, sisters, and pets.

Ryan's teacher and classmates were telling him, "We are not abandoning you as you die. We will continue to be by your side now and forever." This is the most powerful and loving gift any friend can bestow on a dying friend. With these videos, Judi also helped her students prepare for Ryan's impending death.

Ryan's Death

Two days after his shopping spree, Ryan lapsed into a coma. Connie, David's mother, prepared him for his visit with Ryan and his probable death at any moment. She explained that Ryan was unconscious and couldn't talk or play. When David saw Ryan, he commented that his best friend was "sleeping." He got some toys and began to play at Ryan's bedside but said nothing else throughout this visit.

Six days after Ryan went into a coma, he died peacefully at home, one month before his ninth birthday and a week and a half before Halloween, his favorite holiday. His parents knew that the end was near and remained by his side, along with Ryan's dog. His sisters, who were at school, asked not to be notified there of Ryan's death. They might have felt that the information would be too hard to handle at school. Even when death is imminent, the dreaded phone call or final moments are painful and can still shock youngsters.

Amanda, who was seventeen, called from a friend's house and learned of her brother's death. She and some friends later came to her home and knelt by Ryan's bed in silent prayer. His twelve-year-old sister, Jodie, looked in the living room window before she entered the house after walking home from school. Beth motioned to her that Ryan had died. She went to his bed and cried. Both siblings continued to receive counseling after their brother's death. Often, healthy siblings require professional assistance in the aftermath of an anticipated death to help them sort through ambivalent feelings toward their deceased brother or sister (see chapter 8).

When Connie told David of Ryan's death, he cried but didn't want to see Ryan's body. David said that he was sad and just wanted to do something to take his mind off Ryan. "When something bothers me, Mom tells me to watch TV. Watching TV helped."

Judi, Ryan's teacher, had explained to her fourth graders that Ryan was very sick. She encouraged them to talk about their feelings. One of his classmates asked if Ryan was going to die soon. Judi said, "Yes, I believe he will, but I hope he makes it to Halloween." Other students said, "We hope he makes it to his birthday after that." Because Judi and her students had discussed the severity of Ryan's illness many times and the possibility that he might die, his death wasn't a great shock to them and they could talk about it with ease. They made comments like "He didn't even make it to Halloween. He loved Halloween!" "I'll miss him." "I sure am sad."

The principal and assistant principal sent a letter to the parents of all the kids in the elementary school. Once they explained that Ryan died after a courageous fight with cancer and that it was a sad day at school for the youngsters, they stated: "We believe that the best thing we can do is to be sure they have honest information—at a level they can understand and deal with—and that there are caring adults they can talk with about their feelings."

Connie, Judi, and the school principals, as well as many other caring adults, worked together throughout Ryan's illness to support him, his family, and his friends until his death. They were honest and open about their thoughts and feelings, giving kids appropriate information so that they could understand what was happening every step of the way during the course of Ryan's illness. They allowed their children to lead by listening to their questions and answering truthfully. Through their behavior, these adults were exemplary role models, which was all the encouragement Ryan's siblings and friends needed to express their thoughts and feelings, even the unmentionable ones.

COMMEMORATION OF RYAN'S LIFE

After Ryan's private funeral, there was a memorial service for him at his school. The service centered around the hundreds of kids who attended. Ryan's classmates sang the song they had created for him with the help of their music teacher. They also sang his favorite song, "Puff the Magic Dragon." His buddy Jules said that the service was great, although very sad. He cried.

Amanda, who had not attended Ryan's funeral, wanted to be present at his memorial service and spoke about her brother at this time. In her grief, she also composed a poem to her brother and shared it with her family. Like most teenagers, Amanda decided how to commemorate her brother's life and death in the ways most meaningful to her. They involved her friends, the memorial service, and her poem.

Following Ryan's memorial service, his teacher, Judi, and the school's guidance counselor, Mary, helped his classmates and former classmates grieve and commemorate his life and death. During recess and for an hour after school each day, Judi made sure that she touched base with many of his friends from second and third grade because they didn't have an opportunity to talk in class about him as her fourth grade students did. She told the kids not to hold their feelings back and to ask any question that bothered them. If students needed to leave the classroom because they were sad about Ryan, they knew that they could go and talk with Mary at any time.

Beth and Scott also visited Ryan's fourth grade class a few times, brought his classmates some of Ryan's favorite candies, and read some of his special stories to them. On Ryan's birthday, about a month following his death, a friend of the McCormick family donated some tulips to the school in memory of him. Beth helped some youngsters from his fourth grade class who wanted to plant them. After they had created the garden, she asked if the kids had any questions about Ryan. They wanted in-depth details— What actually happened when he died? How did he look? What did cremation mean? Because Beth opened her heart to these kids and made them feel safe, they weren't afraid to ask her many questions that adults wouldn't ask. The small garden has remained under the care of Beth's sister, who also placed a stone in it inscribed with Ryan's name, birth, and death day, which helps all the kids of the school remember Ryan each time they pass it.

Following the death of a child, many parents find it difficult to separate from the institutions that were a part of their son's life because this represents a final closure. His classmates and friends from school, Boy Scouts, or karate class can help keep his memory vibrant for his parents. However, friends might need to grieve and go on with life without informally commemorating their friend for an indefinite length of time. Bereaved parents should be mindful of the comfort level of these youngsters and not overwhelm a child's friends with their grief.

In this case, Beth and Scott had made deep friendships and connections with Ryan's teacher, Judi, and many of his school friends since their son's diagnosis. Judi and her class welcomed their visits right after Ryan's death. Ryan's school buddy Jules enjoyed the stories they read and the candies they passed out. He also liked to share with Beth and Scott his feelings about Ryan and the fun they had together.

Unlike Jules, David never expressed his grief openly or talked very much about Ryan. He wanted to visit the McCormick family quite often after Ryan's death, however, and developed a ritual of playing with Scott in memory of his best friend. One evening, after David and Scott built an extensive structure with Legos and other toys across the living room floor, David said that it was a stairway to heaven and their connection to Ryan. Scott helped Ryan's best friend commemorate their relationship and celebrate their friendship in a way that was most significant to David, and this was through play.

Beth made a photo album for David as a keepsake of his friendship with Ryan from the time they were infants until Ryan's death. David particularly liked the pictures in which he and Ryan were dressed in karate costumes. There were also pictures of vacation trips and rodeos that they attended together.

Eight-year-old Lisa made a miniature Ben and Jerry's beanie out of clay and gave it to the family in memory of Ryan. She also wrote a condolence letter to the family saying that she was sad about Ryan, who was one of the nicest people she ever knew. Although they were classmates only in kindergarten, she would always remember what he said when the class let the butterflies go.

Everyone who knew Ryan also knew what he had told his kindergarten classmates about the butterflies they had hatched from cocoons. On that sad day, when the class had to let the butterflies fly from their cage, Ryan said, "This is how our teacher feels about us." His remark spread throughout the community, becoming a legacy to Lisa and many other people. It was painful for his kindergarten teacher to let her students go on to first grade because she would miss them, just as it was painful for them to let the butterflies free to fly as they were meant to do. At the tender and insightful age of five, Ryan understood the meaning of loss and the need to go on in the face of the sadness it engenders.

Beth said that the school has been and continues to be the center of the McCormick family's community. Everyone, from the principal to the guidance counselor to Ryan's devoted teacher and friends, has given the family tremendous and amazing support. In turn, Judi said that Ryan and the McCormick family have been a gift to the school, offering the students and adults of this community an opportunity to stand by their friend throughout his illness and to remember him and his zest for life after his death. Beth and Judi can express their reciprocal love and support because they have worked together to build this kind of relationship for themselves and their kids in the face of loss. They, along with Scott and the other adults of Ryan's community, have been models for all youngsters who mourned for Ryan and learned to understand the impact of his illness and death on their lives.

EPILOGUE

Three years after Ryan's death, Beth, Scott, Amanda, and Jodie still missed him, of course, but things had become a bit easier for the family in this regard. Beth acknowledged that the pain of loss was no longer as acute as it was initially. Amanda had turned twenty, had run through a series of jobs, and had continued to throw herself into her friendships, which gave her strength and endurance to face life. Although Jodie talked more about Ryan than Amanda did, both thought of him as their guardian angel, and he had become a "household word." Many family and single photos with Ryan highlighted the walls of their home. These were a constant reminder to his sisters of the eight years they had shared with him. "Through Ryan's illness and death, the girls have become closer to each other. They only have each other now," Beth observed, "and our future is uncertain."

Eight months after Ryan's death, Scott was diagnosed with a malignant brain tumor. Beth has never asked, "Why me? Why my family, my son, my husband?" She talked candidly about her family's situation and was thankful that they were blessed with each other. "I tell my girls that we were the very best family that Ryan could have possibly had. He was given to us for a complete and full, although brief, life because we were the very best people for him." They were also the very best family for Scott. In the face of this heartache that came on the heels of her son's death, Beth was able to bring humor into the family's life: "My girls and I kid that we're hard on men and they are dropping out of our lives."

As of this writing, Scott remains in remission and the McCormick family and their community work together toward his healing and recovery.

AIDS and Suicide Disclosure:

Mourning Stigmatic Deaths

KEEPING a secret is a difficult task and oftentimes leaves a trail of lies. When we encounter a stigmatic death, however, it seems just as burdensome to tell the truth. The word *stigma*, derived from the Greek language, means mark or tattoo. *Stigmatic deaths are those resulting from an illness or lifestyle that the general population labels as prohibitive. In our society, we attach stigmas to deaths surrounding AIDS, suicide, alcohol or drug use, violence, and criminal behavior.*

Why is it troublesome for us to explain stigmatic deaths, and why are they harder for kids to understand? In addition to understanding the physical cause of a death—for example, pneumonia as a complication of AIDS or a brain injury resulting from an auto accident in which the driver was speeding under the influence of alcohol—there's a judgmental response that is in part cultural. We look on those who steal, contract sexually transmitted diseases, share contaminated needles, drink excessively, use illegal drugs, and kill themselves or someone else as "bad" people. "He should never have had so much to drink!" "Homosexuality is not normal." Certain lifestyles and deaths that results from them carry stigmas to us, although people from other cultures might hold different mores. The Japanese, for example, praise and revere a kamikaze act of suicide.

Disclosing stigmatic deaths involves telling loved ones and the public at large what happened. Due to the judgmental overlay, a person might choose to omit information, share only partial truths, or lie about the actual nature of the death. None of these choices benefits kids as well as the truth does. When adults assist youngsters with understanding a stigmatic death, we have two important responsibilities:

1. Disclose the information without compromising the facts or lending judgment. When correct information is not available at the time of disclosure, address the stigmatic aspect by asking youngsters, "What difference would it make if she had been drinking?" or "if he had been robbing the drug store when he had a heart attack?"

2. Help kids uncover a nonjudgmental response to the death. Expect that they will probably voice their judgments to an extreme in response to the disclosure.

Our twofold task is difficult because we teach children that to steal, kill, drink excessively, and speed are harmful and unsafe to society as a whole; however, if kids blame a person for any death and can't move beyond this point, they will not mourn freely.

For example, nine-year-old Eddie shot basketball hoops with his neighbor "Mr. Roy" every afternoon when Mr. Roy arrived home from his management job at the creamery. Eddie loved Mr. Roy, who also brought him ice cream every week and had barbeques in his backyard on most Sundays during the summer. Mr. Roy enjoyed his beers on the weekends. Eddie's parents also had a few at their barbeques too, but they didn't drink like Mr. Roy. Every weekend Mr. Roy got drunk, which rendered him hopeless at shooting hoops. Even so, Eddie never really thought about what it meant to drink too much.

One Friday night, following a poker game with friends, Roy crashed head-on into another car on his way home. Although he was rushed to the hospital in critical condition, he also killed a three-month-old baby sitting in the backseat of the other car.

"Miss Elise," Roy's wife, told Eddie and his parents about the accident on Saturday morning, but she didn't say that Roy had been drinking. Eddie's parents discovered this from the newspaper and told Eddie why Mr. Roy probably crashed into the other car. In the course of a day, Eddie's emotions swayed from deep sadness to anger. "I hate Mr. Roy. He's just a stupid drunk. That's all he ever was. I'm ashamed to know him. I don't want any of my friends at school to connect him with me."

Eddie's dad said: "I understand how you feel, Eddie, but try to look at this in another way. Mr. Roy will spend the rest of his life dealing with the fact that his behavior killed an infant and left a young couple childless. I can't imagine how I would feel if something happened to you, but I also know that Mr. Roy needs our support so that he can get well, face the consequences of his actions, and quit drinking. He needs his friends right now more than anything else. I think he'll recover physically, but he's living his own private hell."

Although his parents went to the hospital and did what they could to help Mr. Roy's family, Eddie refused to visit him or talk with Miss Elise and their son. When Mr. Roy came home, Eddie didn't have any contact with him. Three months went by. Eddie had closed himself off and refused to talk about his feelings. One day, as he returned from school, Mr. Roy was standing on crutches under the basketball hoop in his driveway. He said, "I miss you, Eddie." Eddie ran into his home and cried. His mom empathized, "Mr. Roy is trying so hard to get better, and he is facing so many big problems. The only way we can help him is to stick by him and be his friend."

After talking with his mother, Eddie found Mr. Roy still standing under the basketball net. Without saying anything, he hugged his friend. Mr. Roy told Eddie that he didn't know what to say or how to apologize for all the hurt he caused everyone. He was deeply sorry, but to say that he was sorry wasn't enough. He was in a program to help him quit drinking, and he wanted to shoulder the consequences of his act. On that day, Eddie and Mr. Roy started shooting hoops again.

Judgmental reasons that kids attribute to a stigmatic loss can keep them stuck in the mourning process and interfere with their ability to develop effective coping skills. Because Eddie's parents were consistently nonjudgmental in their words and actions, he learned to move beyond his anger and shame over a friend he had thought could do no wrong. With time and encouragement from parents and other caring adults, youngsters can discover open and positive paths to channel stigmatic thoughts and feelings. Our aim is to disclose honestly without condoning the act or condemning the victim or perpetrator.

The following two stories, involving adults whose deaths were due to AIDS and suicide, respectively, illustrate model ways of disclosing stigmatic deaths.

THERE'S AN ELEPHANT IN THE ROOM: THE CARLOS ROMANO STORY

My oldest daughter, Melissa, was a junior in high school when Signor Romano, the school's Spanish teacher, told the faculty and student body in morning assembly one day in May that he had AIDS and was too sick to continue teaching daily classes. Because he would remain on campus and continue his involvement with the Latino Club, he invited kids to feel free to talk and meet with him. Signor Romano also shared that his partner had recently died of AIDS.

Melissa had never taken Spanish and knew Signor Romano only as a substitute teacher. Three things overwhelmed her at this time: "Signor came out to us, he told us he had AIDS, and he told us he was resigning. I didn't think he had lost weight or looked sickly. I didn't recognize any huge changes, but then I didn't really know him."

The headmaster of the private school Melissa attended sent a letter to parents, notifying them of what Signor related to the student body. This enlightened administrator (1) respected Signor Romano, regardless of his lifestyle or illness, (2) understood the nature of AIDS and knew the facts about how this disease could be transmitted, and (3) did not isolate parents from information that more than likely traumatized their youngsters. Along with the school's faculty, parents had the opportunity to help their kids tackle difficult and painful feelings.

Because many people in our culture feel that someone shouldn't come out and say that he has AIDS, which might stigmatize him automatically, I asked Melissa how the students and faculty reacted to this teacher after his disclosure. "People embraced him. All the kids who took Spanish with him were really upset. They knew him, had gone to Spain with him, and had a lot of contact with him. I don't think anyone, students or teachers, was turned off by his having AIDS. Our school is liberal and has a gay-straight student alliance. Everyone loved Signor Romano. I never heard students bad-mouthing him or being curious about his sexuality. He told us only that he was dying of AIDS and had lost a partner. He had never come out or said that he was gay."

During Melissa's senior year, Signor Romano died. As the high school principal told the student body, she cried. The school administrators opened the health center and encouraged kids to talk with counselors and faculty. If they didn't attend first-period classes, teachers would understand. If they did, the principal told them that their teachers would support them. As Melissa said, "The administration and faculty gave us a lot of space."

Melissa's first period was contemporary history with Mr. Roland, one of her favorite teachers. As part of the course, he had divided the class into small groups, each having to research and discuss various lifestyles of marginal people in America—that is, those who lived out of society's mainstream. Melissa and four other students composed the group studying gay and lesbian lifestyles. Coincidentally, Mr. Roland had invited a student teacher, who was gay and had come out of the closet, to meet with these five students during history class on the day of Signor Romano's death.

When she showed up for class, Melissa was in shock. Daniel, a friend of hers, hadn't been to morning assembly and didn't know what had happened. Another student came into the classroom, sat in a corner, and sobbed. She had had Signor Romano as a teacher. Mr. Roland didn't say anything. If Signor Romano had died with leukemia, Mr. Roland probably would have been comfortable and willing to talk about his friend. But because AIDS carries a stigma, many people can't even say the word. They call it *that disease*.

Finally, Melissa interrupted the heavy silence that permeated the classroom. "Can we please talk about the elephant in the room?" "The Elephant in the Room" is the title of a poem that an adolescent wrote in his grief. Daniel had no idea what Melissa meant. Another student explained: "When people don't want to talk about something right in front of their faces, it stands out as large as an elephant. Everybody wants to avoid the issue and everybody else knows it." With this icebreaker, the group began to talk about the unmentionable stigma.

Mr. Roland first told Daniel that Signor Romano had died of AIDS early that morning. As he went on to talk about his endearing friendship with Signor, Mr. Roland cried. Melissa had never seen a teacher cry. His vulnerability helped the group open up. Melissa said, "If we, who are the gay and lesbian study group, can't talk about an issue this big, something's wrong with us."

As kids felt more comfortable, they explored their feelings about AIDS. Their guest teacher was able to answer many questions. According to Melissa, "He gave us so much good information, like how long you can live with AIDS. But he didn't cry. I thought that he was so strong. He had been through this a million times. Everybody in his community was dying. As he spoke, I broke down and really cried. I didn't have a connection with Signor the way this man did. I felt guilty about crying. Our guest had more of a right to be upset than I did. At the same time, I kept trying to distance AIDS from me. The truth was that it was just as much in my face as it was in our gay guest's."

Melissa cried, not because she mourned for Signor Romano nor because she judged people with AIDS as immoral, but because she was coming to grips with the feeling that life was no longer safe for her and her peers. "In the bubble of my high school, bad things didn't happen. But something bad had shaken our community. Since seventh grade, I had been learning about AIDS and ways to have safe sex, but Signor was the first person I knew who had AIDS and died of AIDS. This scary omen called AIDS was going to get you no matter what you did, where you were, or how educated you were. I thought that I was educated and that my school was a safe place."

A life-threatening disease had invaded Melissa's safe world and budding generation. "Maybe I have taken risks also and had information. But this wonderful teacher, who educated all of us and was part of my school community, had somehow gotten caught in a trap, which overwhelmed me. If a person like Signor Romano could get caught, I could too. Even though he was gay and I'm not doesn't mean that AIDS isn't a part of my world *now*."

After class, Mr. Roland and Melissa hugged each other. She felt better, was able to talk with friends who knew Signor Romano, and made herself available to those who were grieving the loss of their beloved teacher. Many kids conversed about the dynamics of AIDS—how you get it, what you can do about it, and who is at risk. Being a peer counselor, Melissa had information about how students could get tested and how they could practice safe sex.

In a letter to all parents, the high school principal remarked that Signor Romano shared his personal experience after he retired in order to help youngsters and adults have a better understanding of AIDS. "He put a face on the disease." The dignity and compassion that Signor Romano, the school's headmaster and principal, and the faculty had in disclosing his disease and death mitigated student and parental judgment. These caring adults also helped kids uncover compassion and dignity within themselves.

Students created a shrine to Signor Romano. They displayed his artwork from a class he had taken, along with the many things that he contributed to the school's Latino Club. Shortly after his death, high school faculty and students held a memorial service to honor an outstanding member of their community. A more formal celebration of his life was held later in the year for the entire school and parental community. Melissa didn't attend either service. She didn't need to mourn for a teacher whom she hardly knew. Learning more about the world in which she lived and coming to terms with her own mortality were her issues of loss and mourning.

Following Signor Romano's death, Melissa felt "extremely isolated" at home. She tried to talk with me, an old babysitter, and many other adults about the impact of AIDS on her life. Our message was one of comfort, we thought. We said: "AIDS is a disease that you can *prevent,* you can control." Melissa fought with us: "All of you tell me that it won't get to me. But I have friends who are having unprotected sex. I have a teacher who just died. It will be part of my life no matter how much info I have or who I hang out with."

At the time, I felt that Melissa wasn't able to differentiate between her own safety and the safety of others. Over and over again I pointed out that she could make herself safe despite the fact that AIDS is an epidemic in our society. I wanted to make sure that she would learn from Signor Romano's experience and not go out into the world and say, "What's the use! Here comes the wave, and I'm going to catch it."

Two years following Signor's death, Melissa astutely pointed out to me that she wasn't concerned about herself contracting AIDS or dying from it. "This isn't the real issue for me. But there is something in the back of my head that does affect my behavior and actions. This minute, abstract, intangible, educable disease will remain a part of my world and generation forever." With this statement, I realized that my daughter had grown into a person who was willing to tackle and cope with many onerous issues and fears surrounding life and death.

It's My Fault: The Julie Mann Story

Early one Friday morning, I received a phone call from Sheila, the principal of an elementary-middle school. On the night before, Sheila had learned that Julie Mann, the school's drama teacher, had died by suicide. There was one complication that Sheila didn't know how to handle. Julie's husband had told her that his wife had died suddenly and unexpectedly at home, which is often the case within the first twenty-four hours following a stigmatic death. A family might see blame and shame in this act.

Because the school community was compact and close, a teacher's sister who lived next door to the Manns learned from an ambulance crew that Julie had hanged herself. Sheila's dilemma was, "Which story should we share with the students?" In order to help all of the kids of the school understand what happened, Sheila and her teachers needed to honor Julie's husband's information as well as address the rumors that flew in the face of it: "We learned some very sad news this morning. Our wonderful drama teacher, Julie, died unexpectedly and suddenly at home. Some of you have heard rumors that Julie died of suicide. What difference would it make to you if she did die of suicide?" In this way, we have (1) respected a relative's statement without betraying the confidentiality he wants to maintain and (2) brought an unmentionable to the surface so that kids can openly talk about their thoughts and feelings.

Sheila asked if I would meet with Julie's drama students on Saturday. When I arrived at the school on Saturday morning, anxious parents greeted me. By this time, everyone had heard that Julie had committed suicide. Some parents told me that their kids knew that Julie had hanged herself, and others said that their youngsters didn't know this. They also asked if I could help them address the questions they anticipated that their kids would have. I agreed to talk with all of the parents following my sessions with Julie's students. She had two groups of drama students, ages five through eight and nine through twelve, who were going to perform their plays in a week. I met with each group separately.

As I sat in a circle with the youngest group of kids, I asked, "What happened to Julie? How do you think she died? It's okay to share what you think with me and each other."

Within a few minutes, the younger kids responded to my questions. One said that her mom told her that Julie had "taken her life." Another shared that her mother said the word *sui . . . suiciding*. None worried that he or she was the blame. Their main concerns revolved around the play itself: Would there be a play? Who would help them with their lines and dances? If she was going to kill herself, why didn't Julie wait until after the play? These questions are classic for latency-age children—what will be the same and what will be different? Their needs are egocentric.

I assured them that the after-school program director was going to bring in another drama teacher to help them practice that day. They accepted this answer and seemed satisfied that they could stage the play on schedule. Next, I asked how they felt about Julie committing suicide and if they had any worries about this. Most created theories around her taking some pills. They imagined her asleep in bed with a glass of water by her bedside. One child wanted to know who would take care of Julie's eleven-year-old son, Douglas. I told the group that Douglas's dad would and that both must feel very sad. The youngsters said that they were sad also. I asked them to help me know Julie and their faces brightened. "She was so nice." "Julie had a beautiful voice and sang funny songs all the time." "She made the green room [where the kids gathered before a play] special." "I'll miss her a lot."

Different dilemmas surrounding Julie's death confounded her older drama students. As we sat in a circle, I sensed their anxiety when I asked if they knew why I was meeting with them. They nodded yes and I said, "Can you help me understand what happened to Julie?" Not one youngster mentioned the word *suicide* as we talked around the circle. They wondered if she really died at home or if she was hit by a car. Possibly she had breast cancer and died from that, because she was diagnosed with cancer five years ago. After a very long twenty-five minutes, one girl said, "My mother told me that Julie was a manic-depressive and committed suicide." Immediately, a few other kids jumped on this statement with classic replies: "Maybe I fooled around too much." "I didn't know my lines yet, or the dance routine." "I missed too many rehearsals."

As preadolescents, they struggled to understand cause and effect, particularly over this stigmatic death, and felt guilty. They needed to be told that they were not responsible for Julie's death. No one, not even Julie, was. There was nothing that they could have done to save her. Wanting to blame themselves or anyone else is dangerous because blame distances children from the possibility that one of their loved ones is vulnerable to such an act. It also interferes with their ability to experience the pain of grief.

I reassured them that they would feel better if they expressed whatever feelings they held inside. In addition to guilt, they shared a range of emotions, including anger at the situation, sadness, and confusion. They wondered how they would deal with staging the play: Should they go on? Would Julie want them to? Should they speak about her to the audience? All of a sudden, one spirited boy rose and said, "Next Saturday, we are going to put on the very best play we have ever done and we'll dedicate it to Julie." "Amen!" Everybody cheered at the half prayer, half rally.

Before we concluded, I wanted these preadolescents to remember their life with Julie, just as the younger kids had done with me. They not only talked about how she looked and how sweet her voice was but also about what she had given them—eagerness, confidence in front of an audience, self-esteem, and the ability to achieve their best.

I concluded my consultation with a session for anxious parents by suggesting that they accept their youngsters' feelings no matter what they expressed. If their kids judged Julie as a "bad" person, parents needed to help them understand her death in a more compassionate light. "Your friend, Julie, didn't see suicide as a choice. She had a hurt in her head that was so bad, and she didn't know any other way to relieve her pain. We can't assume that she wished to abandon you and her son. We will never know for sure what she was thinking about and feeling, but I'm sure she loved you and her family. I also believe that teaching you and creating plays with you made her very happy."

In addition, these parents needed to anticipate that their children, particularly the younger ones, might worry about their parents dying and leaving them alone. Kids might show their insecurities by asking to sleep with the light on or in Mom and Dad's bedroom. Parents should provide consistent reassurance and security whenever necessary and expect that any insecure behavior would diminish over a few weeks. For youngsters who are grieving a prior loss, these symptoms might be exacerbated and last longer.

What should parents say about Julie's death to even younger kids, from three to five years of age, who might be the siblings of these drama students? I advised them *not to disclose* the way in which Julie died unless very young children specifically ask. As preschoolers, they are unable to understand causality; therefore, we can anticipate that these youngsters won't have questions. If they ask, "Did Julie die?" I would say yes and then wait to see if they voiced any concerns. I doubt that the majority of three- to five-year-olds would ask anything further. Many would simply say that their grammy, hamster, or some fictional character died too.

The discerning principal of Julie's school realized that the drama students could benefit from outside support in order to cope with their shock and confusion surrounding Julie's death. Because parents and other caring adults initially might be inundated with their own bewilderment and conflicts, professionals can be the first to help children understand a stigmatic death. However, parents know their kids best, so they must adapt, as the parents of Julie's drama students did, nonjudgmental and compassionate language while they observe their kids' ability to cope.

If It's Unmentionable, It's Unmanageable

Adults can cite many reasons for not disclosing the cause of a stigmatic death. A big one is the responsibility they feel to protect a child from the stress of hearing traumatic news. Some adults think that a child is better off not knowing because this knowledge can destroy their friendships and cause others to reject him. Sophie was eight, Janet was seven, and Alicia was four when their parents committed suicide within ten months of each other. Their paternal grandmother chose not to reveal the true cause of either death to the girls, fearing that her granddaughters would be devastated and never recover from their grief.

Although parents or guardians need to decide what's the best information to give their kids, there's a downside to lying about the cause of a death or leaving it as an unmentionable. Youngsters might sense that they haven't been told the truth, or they might eventually hear it from another source. In either case, they might bitterly resent the adult who kept the secret from them as well as feel isolated with the unmentionable truth and unable to express many painful feelings. If we disclose the truth, foster nonjudgmental outlooks, and express our grief, we will create an environment in which kids can speak freely about their unmentionables and overcome any condemning attitudes.

Children can also be our most profound teachers. Many find

that writing is the best means of addressing stigmas and letting us know how they feel. Nine-year-old Yuri wrote and published *Dear Uncle Dave*, a book that she dedicated to her uncle "who didn't live long enough." Yuri was six when her twenty-three-year-old uncle committed suicide. She began by writing letters to him and then, as she grew older, she wrote the book to make sure that she would never forget him and his love for her.

The poem "The Elephant in the Room," by Terri Kettering, teaches us about the desolation youngsters experience with their unmentionable thoughts and feelings.

> *There's an elephant in the room.*
> *It's large and squatting, so it is hard to get around it.*
> *Yet we squeeze by it with, "How are you" and "I'm*
>   *fine. . . ."*
> *We talk about everything—*
> *Except the elephant in the room.*
>
> *There's an elephant in the room.*
> *It is constantly on our minds.*
> *For you see, it is a very big elephant.*
> *It has hurt us all. . . .*
>
> *Oh please, let's talk about the elephant in the room.*
> *For if we talk about death,*
> *Perhaps we can talk about life? . . .*
> *For if I cannot, then you are leaving me*
> *Alone . . .*
> *In a room . . .*
> *With an elephant . . .*

CHILDREN AS
LIVING-ROOM WITNESSES:
Catastrophic Losses

CATASTROPHES affect kids not only directly but also vicariously in their living rooms and on their playgrounds. Television, newspaper, and radio coverage of the bombing of the federal building in Oklahoma City on 19 April 1995 terrorized youngsters. Vivid images of victims and survivors saturated the media and left an indelible mark on people everywhere. On the first day following this devastating act, President and Mrs. Clinton responded to reassure kids throughout the United States: "Almost all the adults in this country are good people who love their children. . . . Talk to grown-ups who are around you about how you feel inside."

The Oklahoma City bombing was a disaster that killed 168 people, 19 of them children, and injured more than 600. Thirty youngsters lost both parents; 170 lost one. The U.S. Department of Health and Human Services distinguishes disasters from catastrophic disasters by definition. *Disasters are traumatic major life events that most people do not normally experience. Catastrophic disasters are those that affect tens of thousands of people and disrupt entire communities.* Generally, we don't differentiate between a disaster and a catastrophe when we talk about these events. In this chapter, I use the words synonymously, specifically because electronic, satellite, and TV communication systems bring major life traumas into the lives of millions of kids around the globe.

The bombing of the federal building in Oklahoma City was a *human-perpetrated* disaster, as opposed to a *natural* one, that left youngsters in the city and surrounding areas anxious, angry, and confused. They had great difficulty separating from their parents, they regressed developmentally, and they feared that a bombing could happen again. Many suffered with *posttraumatic stress syndrome*—numbness, reexperience, and avoidance of the situation (see also chapter 12). Symptoms and behavioral patterns of post-traumatic stress are part of the mourning process that surviving kids endure.

President and Mrs. Clinton, Governor and Mrs. Keating of Oklahoma, parents, teachers, health-care providers, and other professionals from all walks of life worked together to support and nurture youngsters in Oklahoma City as they slowly coped and rebuilt their lives. The task of rebuilding and healing is ongoing and will continue for many years as surviving children grow older and regrieve this horrific loss.

In the Western world, kids face few human-perpetrated disasters; however, all youngsters witness traumatic life events every day through the media, particularly through television. How do kids react to catastrophes that they experience through the media? How can parents, teachers, health-care providers, clergy, and government officials provide a nurturing environment in which children can make sense of these events without undo stress and anxiety? How can we judge which broadcasts are not wise or healthy for our kids to view? How do larger-than-life events—for example, the death of Diana, Princess of Wales—have a catastrophic effect on kids?

A PRESCHOOL STORY: I PRAY AND WORRY ABOUT YOU

Initially following the Oklahoma City bombing, I asked a group of adolescents how they felt about what they had seen and heard. "It didn't happen in my neighborhood, so it doesn't affect me" was their main response. "Things like this happen all over the news every day and in some really bad schools. I know all about it." My oldest daughter, Melissa, had planned to go into Boston with friends on the afternoon of the bombing, but the city of Boston closed down its subway system for the day to avoid copycat bombings. Although this larger event touched her life in a small way, the *reality* of the bombing hit her, so she was anxious. For the most part, however, the Oklahoma City disaster was too far away to distress Massachusetts adolescents, and they were immune to the media images of victims trapped in the wrecked federal building and rescue workers cradling limp infants and children in their arms.

Eve, the director of a preschool located approximately two thousand miles from Oklahoma City, had a different experience with her students. Her three-, four-, and five-year-old kids were eager to talk about the bombing the very next day. Because these kids were so young, Eve and her partner did the healthy and wise thing of letting the children ask questions and express their concerns, without offering any of the information that flooded the news.

The first question Eve's preschoolers asked was, "Is somebody going to come and bomb our school?" Eve's answer was simple and direct: "No! Our school is very, very safe. Our town is very safe, and we have good police officers watching over us. Your parents also know how to protect you."

Another key question was, "Why are there bad people who want to hurt kids?" Eve's answer paralleled President and Mrs. Clinton's: "Most adults are good people who don't want to harm kids. But there are all kinds of people in the world. Sometimes when people were hurt as children, they may grow up to hurt other children, because they don't understand that it's wrong to hurt kids." This salient response offered a plausible explanation about why bad things can happen to good people, but there is no definitive answer. Of course, Eve didn't say that the perpetrator of the bombing was a wicked person who needed to be punished. Deaths from catastrophes are just as much a reality of life as deaths from stigmatic and more benign causes. Only the scope of destruction and loss is much greater.

In addition to these questions, Eve also witnessed how the disaster affected her students on the school playground. The kids played bombing games and made fake bombs. They chased each other around, saying, "You can't bomb me." "I'm going to be the bomber. You run." These games continued for the first few days following the incident. After play period, Eve sat with her students to help them talk about their feelings. Randy, a bright and precocious five-year-old, was particularly invested in the details of the bombing and tried to make sense of it in a preschooler's way. "I saw how the bomb put the building down. . . . McVeigh didn't know there was a day-care center in there, and he bombed it down by mistake, I think." Following Randy's lead, his classmates offered their observations about the pictures they had seen and the stories they had heard on TV.

On the Sunday after the bombing, Eve's pastor addressed the disaster as a part of his sermon. He suggested that parents and kids write letters to the people of Oklahoma City if they wanted to support and boost the psychological morale of survivors. Eve asked her students if they wanted to draw pictures for children in Oklahoma City. She and her partner then wrote letters, which the kids dictated, beneath their drawings of hearts, flowers, rainbows, and children lying under rocks and rubble. Randy wrote, "I watch you on TV, and I'm sorry about your kids." Other kids wrote, "I pray and worry about you." As her pastor suggested, Eve mailed these drawings and letters to the Episcopal Archdiocese of Oklahoma City to be distributed to youngsters in this city.

Thanks to Eve and her partner, the preschoolers channeled their sorrow and anxieties in positive and active ways. Because Randy and a four-year-old boy at the school seemed absorbed by details and wanted to talk daily about the bombing, Eve contacted their parents to make sure that they weren't unduly interjecting their fears onto their preschool kids.

Parental Responsibilities and Roles

Randy knew the names of all suspects, what kind of van they had, and where they lived. He also kept track of how many people were dead in the wreckage and how many were still missing. Each day he gave Eve a blow-by-blow account. When she spoke with Randy's mom, Eve asked how he was doing at home. "We don't talk about this with Randy unless he brings it up. And it's not something that we specifically turn on the news to watch." Eve believed that Randy asked questions because he was bright and inquisitive, and his parents' approach was to respond openly and truthfully to his insightful questions.

She decided to speak with every child's parents and encouraged them to give simple, honest, and age-appropriate information, because the front page of every newspaper showed gory sights daily for many weeks. This is an appropriate response because we don't want to ignore what happened in a community just like ours.

So what are our responsibilities and roles in helping kids filter overwhelming news coverage of human-perpetrated and violent disasters? We know that Randy's need for details is not the norm for preschool youngsters, and we don't want to say, "Isn't life random? We could be the next Oklahoma City. You just don't know what's going to happen these days if you go outside." Because their sense of themselves are rooted in their parents and siblings, children feel hopeless if their families fall apart. As Eve did, we want to make sure that our kids feel protected from life's uncertainties.

Often, they are most vulnerable to scary thoughts at bedtime. Give them an opportunity to talk as you get them into bed and listen to their concerns, whether these are real or imagined. Don't negate or disregard their feelings. To express their fears usually makes young kids feel better and prevents their having fitful dreams or nightmares. Reading a comforting and happy story after your conversation also helps them sleep peacefully.

When children are anxious about a disaster hitting close to home, you also might want to make a "securities list" with them. This list can include what you, your schools, your police department, and your greater community do to ensure their safety and yours. For example, emergency numbers like 911 provide immediate assistance if kids feel threatened and aren't with their parents or another caring adult; home cellars provide good shelters from storms and tornadoes; youth officers in city or town schools watch over and protect kids from harm; after-school youth centers offer them a safe haven until parents finish work for the day. There are many simple activities in which you and your kids can engage to enhance their feelings of security. Playing, writing, and drawing pictures with them help them actively channel their sad or angry feelings.

We also want to monitor media broadcasting of catastrophic events. Although we can't stop the media from spotlighting offending and bloody sights, it's not a healthy prescription to allow young kids free rein to view violent scenes or disasters day in and day out on TV and in newspapers. If a particularly violent story dominates the daily news, you might choose to watch the late news report after you've tucked your kids in for the night, instead of watching the gory details with them from the breakfast or dinner table. In this way, youngsters are less exposed to vivid and brutal images.

Take the time to watch TV with your kids and be mindful of the use and overuse of aggression and violence. You also might observe the nature of TV cartoons and other kids' programs. Many cartoons, like those depicting Power Rangers and Ninja Turtles, can be violent in content, with the rangers or turtles blowing up buildings and killing people at will, even though they have beneficent outcomes. Oftentimes, aggressive play figures make kids feel powerful and invincible; however, let youngsters know that violence is not the path to problem solving or real power and strength.

Along with us, children feel unhappy when something bad, like the bombing of the federal building in Oklahoma City, happens to innocent people just like them. As we do, they wish that they could have kept this disaster from occurring. They also want everything to get better and return to normal immediately. If we are patient listeners, give kids time, work actively with them, and share our grief without overwhelming them with our anxieties, they will feel reassured and secure in their homes, schools, neighborhoods, and world in which uncertain events are rare but can happen.

Responses from Oklahoma City

Fourth graders of a school two miles from the bombed federal building answered Eve's youngsters' letters. "Timothy Schoolmouse" recorded and observed the fourth graders' reactions to the bomb, and each student sent a letter to the preschoolers. The Schoolmouse said: "Our world changed forever that day. Then all of you, the world, came to us. How can we ever thank so many of you for all the love and caring you sent?" By the time the fourth graders wrote letters of hope to Eve's preschoolers, their tears, tummy aches, and headaches had vanished, but they still didn't like thunderstorms because they sounded too much like the bomb. They no longer wanted to stay home from school and were able to concentrate on their work and thank-you notes. Their butterfly drawings, accompanying every letter, were their signs of healing and hope.

I was scared when the bomb went off and it shook the class.

I just want to give you lots of hugs. When the bomb went off our teacher's keys fell out of her pocket.

I went home to find that my cousin was missing in the bombed building. . . . She was dead. I cried all night.

Thank you for all the comfort and love, prayers, thoughts, and support you have given us.

Roses are red and violets are blue. Thank you for sending to me, and I'll send back to you.

I wish I could meet all of you.

Eve's preschoolers shared the letters from these Oklahoma City fourth graders with their families on graduation day. Most adults cried. Eve's pastor and church members, as well as many who saw them displayed at the local library, also shed a few tears. It was, as Timothy Schoolmouse related, "hard to put into words what we felt . . . the hurt was and is so deep." But these Oklahoma City fourth graders and Eve's preschoolers took a giant step toward healing by sharing their fears, grief, and hope for the future.

TV WARS

Over the past ten years, kids have been intimately exposed to global terrorism—specifically wars—through TV. The Gulf War of 1991 was the first covered extensively and live via satellite, although vivid scenes from World War II and the Korean and Vietnam wars have been broadcast and depicted in movies and TV specials for half a century.

Very young children don't have the cognitive skills to differentiate between fact and fiction, but that doesn't mean that they're insensitive to your interests and fears about war. Most school-aged kids understand that the lives of *real* people are on the line in a war. During media coverage of the Gulf War, they witnessed and understood that Scud missiles and explosive noises killed people and destroyed homes. The war was immediate and very real because, for the first time, we watched as it happened. Adolescents, particularly those who had peers in the armed services, were concerned, upset, and emotional about the war. Those whose older siblings were stationed in the Middle East were understandably frightened.

To expose kids to ongoing daily coverage of a war on TV invites unnecessary confusion, stress, anxiety, and fear into their lives. It isn't judicious to keep the TV on such broadcasts for eight, ten, and twelve hours every day. We also don't want to act *unperturbed* by bloody and violent events on the TV screen. So what can we do to help our kids, as well as ourselves, come to terms with the ravages of war and the media's willingness to broadcast each missile or ground attack?

- Address their questions and concerns without allowing our interests, feelings, or needs to dominate their lives. Record coverage of a war on your video machine if you want to follow the account closely, and then view it when your kids are at school or in bed.

- Show compassion, sadness, and understanding for innocent victims on both sides of a war. When you view an upsetting scene from a war on TV or in the newspaper with kids, you should express your sorrow, horror, and wishes for a peaceful solution soon.

- Keep explanations simple and nonjudgmental if youngsters ask how you feel about war. For example, you might say, "War upsets me. I don't like to think about or see innocent people on both sides getting hurt. It makes me sad, and I wish we could do something to help all the people who are getting hurt. There's *one* thing I believe I can do to help, and it makes me feel better. I can pray for peace and *everyone* in the war. Let's do this together."

- Observe your kids' eating and sleeping behaviors and make sure that a conflict being broadcast on TV isn't disturbing their daily routine. A good moment to talk with children is when you are driving together. And when you tuck them in for the night, give them an extra hug to reassure them that you will keep them safe from harm.

Adolescents have philosophical questions and concerns about war, which I highlight under the task of understanding in chapter 2. We might spend many evenings with them listening and then sharing our thoughts. Although we can't provide answers or solutions, adolescents need to explore these life-and-death issues with us in order to develop their own views and outlook on catastrophic events that upset their comfortable lives at home. Most probably have definite opinions and reasons for or against a decision to go to war. Airing their thoughts and feelings allows them to ease their pain and make responsible decisions for their future.

Children whose older brothers or sisters participated in the Gulf War suffered extreme stress. Those left behind want to cling to their parents more than usual. They also might sense parental fears and have disturbed sleep or nightmares. We can help them deal with their anxiety and grief by writing letters, drawing pictures, and sending photos along with them to a relative overseas. Kids derive comfort from letting a brother know that they care and think about him, pray for his safety, and thank him for helping to keep them and the world secure.

As a way of reaching out to their peers in the Gulf War, many adolescents and young adults chose to write to men and women in combat whom they didn't know. Two young adults whom I know met through their correspondence during the Gulf War and have since married. Because Jill was disturbed by the war and wanted to do her part to comfort and ease the suffering and isolation of military personnel in the Persian Gulf, she got Russell's name from a mutual friend and began writing to him weekly. After the war ended, he and Jill met face to face and their romance blossomed.

Kids, as well as adults, need to mourn the catastrophes of war without being overwhelmed by stress or hardened to violence and destruction.

LARGER-THAN-LIFE EVENTS

At the time of the attempted assassination of President Reagan, the ten-year-old daughter of an acquaintance became very upset because, for the first time, this little girl realized that someone as great and powerful as the president of her country was not invulnerable to harm or death. She worked through her feelings by drawing and writing in her journal.

Although the death of a well-known person is not a catastrophe by definition, it can have traumatic effects on kids. Foremost in my mind are the 1986 explosion of the space shuttle *Challenger*, in which a teacher named Christa McAuliffe was killed, and the 1997 deaths of Princess Diana and Mother Teresa.

Millions of children witnessed the *Challenger* explosion live in their classrooms. Parents and teachers had many opportunities following this larger-than-life loss to make sense of it with their youngsters and grieve. Their questions weren't surprising: "How could the president send a mother and teacher into space?" "What about her children at home?" "Is life safe?" The New York Times Company polled 1,120 families with children ages five through eight. Girls were more upset than boys. About half the parents said that they believed their kids were preoccupied with worries, night-mares, and gory images in their drawings because a teacher had been on the flight. Two hundred twenty-four youngsters from nine through seventeen were also interviewed. They were less affected and watched less TV coverage than the younger children.

When Princess Diana died in an auto accident in Paris in 1997, kids saw and heard much speculation about her life and death via the media. Although they weren't deeply saddened or moved because they didn't know the princess personally, they were shocked and worried because (1) she was a mother of two children left behind by the tragedy, (2) she was so young and did a lot of good for the world, and (3) she was supposedly in a safe car with a safe driver, so how could this happen—and could it happen to my mom?

I encouraged parents to answer their youngsters' questions hon-estly but not to dwell on all the conjecture and gossip about the accident or private life of Princess Di. If their kids wanted to view any of the extensive TV coverage, I suggested that the family watch the commemorative funeral together. It gave parents an opportunity to share their feelings of remorse, to talk about how Princess Diana's children might have felt and would be cared for, to assure their kids that they would do everything possible to pro-tect themselves from an auto accident, and to explain Princess Di's commemorative ritual with coffin, flowers, church service, and procession in her honor.

We don't expect that kids will be overly saddened or grief stricken about the death of a famous person because they don't have an ongoing relationship with such an individual. A twelve-year-old boy said that he wasn't affected or shocked by Mother Teresa's death because he wasn't close to her, but he was sorry that she died because she helped to heal and feed many poor chil-dren in India. Three months following her death, he visited his paternal grandmother, who lives in Calcutta. An adult friend asked him to submit brief writings about his experiences for publi-cation on an Internet website. One of the first places this youngster chose to see was the convent in which Mother Teresa lived and was interred. He wrote what he called a "journalist report" about this visit.

Being with Mother Teresa

Today, I visited the tomb of Mother Teresa. . . . Before going in, I had to remove my shoes. As I walked into the room, I saw on the floor a big white box in which Mother Teresa lies. It is made simply of wood, nothing fancy, with a tombstone on top of it. On the stone there is written, "Love One Another As I Have Loved You" [cf. John 13:34]. There is a beautiful ring of flowers on top of the box, too.

Even though I could not see Mother Teresa, I could feel her. It was as if her presence was standing right in front of me. While I was there, many people came to pay their respects to Mother Teresa. Each of them kissed her tomb. Finally, when I stood and thought about all the things Mother Teresa had done during her lifetime, I was overwhelmed.

Then, after I left the room, I spoke with one of the nuns. I noticed that she had a smile on her face the whole time we spoke. Then I noticed that each of the nuns there had a smile on her face. They all enjoy what they do, just as Mother Teresa did.

When I left the building, I felt a cold sweep over me. It was then that I realized that the building I was just in was filled with warmth, happiness, and love.

May her work live on.

Such an eloquent report, which a caring friend encouraged this young boy to write and share, embodies what I believe all kids come to understand, feel, and embrace in time as they confront a catastrophic event. Christa McAuliffe's, Princess Diana's, and Mother Teresa's works surely live on if we, with attention and guidance, give eager children the opportunity to reach out and join with others in the mourning and healing process.

Anatomy of a Crisis:

The Rudie Dodge Story

RUDIE Dodge was a freckled-faced, red-haired sophomore who could have been anybody's teenage son. One Friday morning, Rudie invited the varsity soccer team, of which he was a member, and his close friends to a particular lunch period in the school cafeteria, enticing them with a promised surprise. He asked them to skip class if they had to. At 12:10 P.M., he walked into the cafeteria in which three hundred other youngsters were gathered. After he bought an iced tea, Rudie sat down at a table with his buddies, which included the soccer team and a neighbor with whom he grew up. Rudie was silent for a few seconds and then stood, pulled a .22-caliber handgun from his knapsack, and shot himself in the head. He fell on top of a soccer friend.

Snow was falling lightly as I drove to Rudie's high school early the next morning. Yesterday's evening news reverberated in my mind. As I reflected on the three hundred students, the teachers, and the cafeteria workers who witnessed Rudie's suicide; the other six hundred kids in the high school; the ninety teachers on the staff; and the community of blue-collar, working-class parents and families, I needed the peaceful and quiet snow, not the Broadway tunes I usually played on the tape deck.

The administration of the school had asked me to come in and manage a crisis that sent a shock wave throughout a community rarely touched by violence. Nobody from the school or the larger community wanted to take on this managerial responsibility for two reasons: Those who knew Rudie felt helpless, and although the more than thirty mental health professionals eager to assist from the community were wonderful with one-on-one or small-group counseling, they hadn't been trained to manage a community crisis.

During the five days that I spent at this high school, I established four steps to guide parents and teachers throughout this crisis:

1. To create a safe and inclusive environment in which their kids could understand what Rudie's death meant to them

2. To confront their kids' unmanageable nightmares about Rudie's suicide

3. To help their youngsters face their anger, guilt, impotence, sadness, and fears

4. To help themselves mourn this tragedy and serve as role models for their children

Although this is the story of how Rudie's peers and community met these painful challenges together, these steps serve as a model for any community in crisis.

INNOCENT WITNESSES TO VIOLENCE

Witnessing the violent death of a loved family member or friend is one of life's most stressful events. Chaos ruled immediately following Rudie's act. Many of the three hundred witnesses fled the cafeteria when they realized that the loud bang they heard was a shot. This knee-jerk reaction to apparent danger is part of our natural fight-or-flight mechanism. With a shooting, the urge to flee is wise. If you hear one shot, the likelihood is that another might follow.

Students and friends in the direct vicinity of Rudie's table didn't leave the cafeteria, however. They remained huddled together, crying, screaming, and holding each other while they watched caring adults—a few teachers, cafeteria workers, and the school nurse—rush to Rudie's side as he lay unconscious on the floor. The students didn't possess the coping skills to assist Rudie or call for help. Instead, they regressed in the terror created by their peer's violent suicide.

Sadly, violence is on the rise in our youth today. Psychologists have found that witnesses to an act in which a gun or other weapon is involved often suffer symptoms of posttraumatic stress disorder—numbness, reexperience, and avoidance. In the hours and days that followed Rudie's death, these innocent witnesses in the cafeteria said that they felt "numb." They relived the event—blood and Rudie's blue face—in their nightmares and waking thoughts. Some, being reticent to talk, wanted to avoid the horror they had seen. To alleviate posttraumatic stress in kids, adults constantly need to reassure them that they are physically safe and that an event like this is singular.

Bewilderment, disbelief, and fear were the norm in the other six hundred students when they learned that Rudie had shot himself. What was the best way for them to receive this upsetting news, especially when many heard the shot from their classrooms?

CONTROLLING CHAOS AND PROVIDING SAFETY

Immediately after teachers and workers in the cafeteria rushed to Rudie's side, they called 911 to obtain emergency medical assistance and notified the principal. Within a couple of minutes after he received the news, the principal, Dr. Carl Stivens, intuitively made a brilliant decision: He used the PA system to inform everyone in the school about this incident. Ordinarily, leaders should never deliver bad news over a PA system. When I train crisis teams, I often ask members, "Would you like to hear that your sister died over a loudspeaker?" Of course they wouldn't, but the one time that the PA system should be used to control chaos and relay dire news is when kids' *safety* is involved.

Chaos occurs naturally when a large group of people feel threatened, emotionally or physically. They experience a sense of abandonment and helplessness. Children need to know that adults who care for them are available to make the intolerable and unsafe situation okay. Initially, Carl's primary responsibility as leader in this crisis was to protect all students from harm, inside and outside the school building.

When a crisis involving a violent death occurs, school leaders work to control or prevent chaos. Although controlling chaos is wise and necessary, their decisions about how to do this often inhibit the mourning process. For example:

1. They might acknowledge the incident intellectually but minimize the emotional reaction to it.

2. They might speak as little as possible about what happened; that is, they might avoid helping kids understand what happened and isolate them with their feelings, prompting rumors and more chaos.

3. They might keep everything running as if nothing happened.

A school should not take on the MO (modus operandi) of a mental health agency in a crisis, but it needs to provide a safe place for understanding and expression of feelings. When this doesn't happen, youngsters might intensify the chaos and perhaps jeopardize their own safety by leaving school. When adolescents have each other and the support of adults, the significance of their loss will be validated.

Carl knew that caring adults were already assisting Rudie, whose hopeful rescue by an emergency squad was imminent, so his role as principal lay with the rest of the nine hundred adolescents in the high school, three hundred of whom were witnesses either frozen in terror or fleeing the scene in a vain attempt to find a sense of safety on the icy roads outside. Within a few minutes after the event, Carl went directly to the PA and gave the members of the entire school all the information that he had: "There has been a shooting in the cafeteria, and one of our students has been critically injured. Within minutes, you'll hear the sirens of the ambulance." Everyone heard them as the principal spoke. "And the moment that this student has been taken to the hospital, I'll find out what happened and call everybody down to an assembly in the auditorium to tell you exactly what I've learned." He requested that the six hundred students in classrooms remain there until he notified them to go to the auditorium. He asked the three hundred kids who had witnessed the act not to leave school and directed them to the auditorium immediately.

Notice that the principal didn't give the name or the gender of the person involved, nor did he say that it was a murder or suicide because he didn't know any of this information. He did, however, use the task of *understanding* as a magnet to contain nine hundred youngsters in school. In essence, Carl said to everyone that he would help them understand what took place and why to the best of his ability. As a result, no youngster left the school premises to follow the ambulance or to flee for safety elsewhere.

In the auditorium, Carl told the entire student body and faculty what he had learned about the incident from witnesses in the cafeteria. He gave them Rudie's name and related the details that he knew, describing the size of the gun and the temple area of the head through which Rudie had shot himself. He also said, "I don't imagine that any of us will get much done in class this afternoon. The buses will roll at the usual time, but if you want to stay here, the school will remain open for you until eleven tonight. We will keep the school open from seven until eleven over the weekend as well. I and many of us will be here for you. We'll give you updates on Rudie's condition every half hour in the library throughout the weekend."

Rudie was still alive when Carl addressed the assembly. Through continual reports from the local hospital, the school learned that he had been helicoptered to a large facility in the major city nearby. He remained unconscious and on life-support systems. By early evening, Rudie had been diagnosed as brain dead. Life supports were discontinued late on Friday night after his viable organs were harvested and donated to candidates awaiting transplants. The principal or one of his two assistants announced any and all information in the library as updates progressed.

The meticulous means of communication by which the principal and school administration controlled the initial chaos mediated the terror of all students. By leaving the school open, Carl invited the students to express whatever thoughts and emotions they had. He acknowledged that neither the school administration, the faculty, nor the students could go on with "business as usual" because they had to face their overwhelming loss together. Effective control of chaos is the first step toward nurturing traumatized youngsters and protecting them from additional harm.

CRISIS PLANNING AND INTERVENTION

I arrived at the high school shortly before 8:00 A.M. on Saturday, the morning following Rudie's suicide. Three-fourths of the teaching staff were already present, and many kids and parents had started to flow in as well. After the principal filled me in on how he and the other school administrators initially handled the crisis, we went into the biology lab for our first planning session with the school's crisis team. This team consisted of the school psychologist, the school nurse, the principal, one of the assistant principals, the special education teacher, and about ten other teachers. A cadre of volunteer counselors, psychologists, clergy, and social workers from the community also was eager to participate.

My role as a consultant-trainer was to lead the crisis team and the professional volunteers who composed the planning committee. We needed to make decisions about how the school was going to respond to this crisis over the weekend and during the following school week.

I didn't come as an expert who told everybody what to do. That behavior would have been counterproductive. In a crisis, cooperation is essential to benefit every person of the community. I first asked the members of the planning committee to help me get to know them and the culture of their school and community. I listened, validated their feelings of helplessness and shock, and learned what worried them. From our discussion, we outlined eight issues we needed to address in order to promote positive and healthy intervention and communication:

1. Attitudes toward Rudie's suicide

2. Adolescent grief behavior and effective adult support

3. Adult grief behavior and sharing grief

4. Parental needs and involvement in the crisis

5. Vulnerable kids requiring special attention

6. Media bombardment

7. Nature of classes on Monday and eating in the cafeteria

8. Commemoration of Rudie's death

How did we organize and structure a plan to intervene and communicate with *all* kids, parents, and teachers of this community?

Information/Support Sessions

Our biggest task over the weekend was to offer support meetings for parents and teachers so that they could deal with their issues of mourning Rudie, learn the most effective ways to share them with their youngsters, and understand their kids' mourning behavior. We held two meetings for parents and two for high school faculty. Teachers of the middle and elementary schools required support as well, so we held one meeting for them. I led and moderated all support meetings.

When school began on Monday, I held a final support session for all ninety teachers of the high school faculty, one for the entire student body of the high school, and another solely for Rudie's sophomore class. Through the local newspaper and cable TV network, we advertised the dates and times of our meetings and our intentions to assist and include everyone in this crisis.

Individual and Small-Group Counseling

I also met privately with many of the most vulnerable kids and adults, including Rudie's mother, his next-door neighbors and their son, some members of the soccer team, the cafeteria workers, and Rudie's brother's fifth grade teacher.

Volunteer mental health professionals devised a matrix of services with a structure that could help students, parents, and teachers over the weekend and throughout the following school week. The director of the local prevention network coordinated three levels of counseling services that these volunteers offered, giving anyone the opportunity to meet with a professional. Some counselors set up a space in the library as an informal gathering place for groups of kids or adults. Other professionals "floated" around the building, informally talking with students. They scheduled counseling sessions with more vulnerable youngsters—those who battled with depression or other mental problems, those who had attempted suicide, those who had suffered the recent death of a relative or close friend. The volunteers also identified a group of kids or a parent or teacher who was in distress or wanted to talk. Anyone who wanted one-to-one or small-group counseling could go to the guidance center. In addition, the clergy provided a large and invaluable service by walking around the school and making themselves available to kids, teachers, and parents.

Greater Community Outpourings

The open high school drew an increasing number of students over the weekend. On Saturday, 100 kids showed up. That number grew to about 150 on Sunday. Many parents came to be with their children as well as to attend the support sessions. Members of the Rotary, Kiwanis, and Samaritans, a volunteer group dedicated to suicide prevention, came to assist kids also. Parents, teachers, volunteers, and clergy played basketball and volleyball with youngsters in the gym. Some kids sat quietly with each other and listened to music or played cards. Others sought group or individual counseling. Local restaurants and take-out businesses donated food to the school throughout the weekend. Taxi companies offered free rides to the school. The entire community responded to this crisis. Members of the crisis team and the two assistant principals managed the logistics of our intervention plan and the community outpourings. A place that felt unsafe to kids on Friday afternoon once again became a secure environment for them.

ATTITUDES TOWARD RUDIE'S SUICIDE

In the separate information/support meetings that I conducted for youngsters, their parents, and their teachers, we first talked about their attitudes toward Rudie's suicide. The adolescents and adults employed two common defense mechanisms to deal with his suicide: *denial* and *projection*. Defense mechanisms help us to adapt to a crisis situation; that is, initially we want to protect ourselves against the pain of loss by denying the act or blaming it on someone or something else.

Denial

Some kids and adults used denial to defend against their pernicious feelings about Rudie's intention to kill himself. Many told me that Rudie's act was an accident, a joke, or a threat that he didn't mean. He was just trying to get their attention and he didn't know how else to do it. Rudie was an ordinary kid who maintained a B to C average. He didn't have many complaints about school, nor did he distinguish himself in any way except as a sophomore on the varsity soccer team. On that fateful Friday, Rudie carried a gun to school and skipped all his classes except fourth-period English. Nobody knew about the gun, so they convinced themselves that he didn't really mean to do anything.

Projection

Other adolescents and adults wanted to project the blame for Rudie's act on a specific reason that would not affect them. From the local morning newspaper, they had already learned that Rudie hated his dad and had a terrible relationship with him, so that was the reason. "As long as my children don't hate me, then they're safe and I'm safe" was one rationale some parents used. Rudie's peers sought similar explanations. "He said that he would either have to kill himself or his father," one kid said. "His girlfriend just broke up with him" was another comment.

Distancing Self

When we deny and project, we distance ourselves from such a horrible event in order to protect ourselves. Many who knew Rudie wanted to establish themselves as different from him because, if they weren't, then any one of them could also do what he had done. Thinking this was intolerable, so they tried to place Band-Aids on all their imagined fears: "My child doesn't hate me." "She can talk to us about anything." "All my students can come to me." "I'm not like Rudie. I wouldn't have done this to my friends." These reasons might make us feel safe and normal, but they are unrealistic or forms of magical thinking.

In their efforts to distance themselves, many parents desperately sought information on the warning signs of adolescent suicide to make sure that their kids were "immune" to such a fate. Research has indicated several relevant symptoms: (1) withdrawal from family or friends, (2) inability to attend school, (3) poor grades, (4) large weight gain or loss, (5) insomnia, (6) unresolved grief over a loss, (7) desire or threat to hurt oneself, and (8) self-destructive behavior. Adolescents suffering from prolonged depression and those with impulsive personalities also are at greater risk. Unresolved family conflict, physical or sexual abuse, and drug and alcohol abuse are preexisting risk factors that contribute to stress and teen suicide as well.

I provided the parents of Rudie's peers with a pamphlet containing warning signs, risk factors, and myths concerning adolescent suicide, but I underscored that this information would not help their surviving adolescents nearly as much as understanding suicide in the context of problem solving.

Working Through Denial, Projection, and Problems

Understanding the facts surrounding Rudie's suicide was important, but I emphasized that Rudie's death was *no one's fault*. No one would ever know Rudie's reason for taking his life, but pointing a finger of blame and distancing oneself are mechanisms used to escape one critical fact that the entire community needed to realize: *Suicide is not an antidote for one's problems.* When kids hate their parents, get pregnant, can't handle their sexual identity, or don't have a date for the prom, they have a problem (or several) to face.

Suicide is the ultimate narcissistic act. It suggests total and absolute isolation from others; that is, a kid says, "My problem is so big, worse than anybody else's, and all-consuming. Nothing and no one can help. There's no other way out." But adolescents are unable to fathom the physical consequences of this act. They often are impulsive, angry, and in pain. At the same time, they feel invincible. Their own isolation betrays them. They are unable to reach out for help and feel that the only solution to their problem is suicide.

Parents need to help children deal with stressful life events and develop functional solutions that kids feel they can accomplish daily. We must teach them to share their feelings with us before they become overwhelmed by them. Two effective ways in which we can do this is to let them know daily that (1) we accept and love them no matter what problems they have or what they've done and (2) we expect them to come to us for assistance in managing their lives.

I suggested that, in the weeks ahead, the parental community might respond to this trauma by helping their kids with stressful adolescent issues in a workshop format. Workshops on problem solving throughout the year and for years to come would be an excellent means by which their youngsters could informally commemorate Rudie's life and their friendship with him. Through these workshops, they would learn how to communicate their anxieties of daily living to adults willing to listen and help. In chapter 13, I talk more about problems that adolescents face and why they contemplate or resort to suicide as a solution.

GRIEVING RUDIE'S DEATH

As a crisis of this nature unfolds, the people involved become more open to their powerful grief. After resolving their denial and projection, both kids and adults can move toward the pain of grief, which is critical to working through their loss and its associated trauma.

Although *anger* and *sadness* are the principal feelings of grief, Rudie's peers also experienced *guilt, impotence,* and/or *fear,* depending on the way in which they understood (thought of) their "role" in his suicide. Following a public suicide, these are normal feelings for kids, parents, and teachers to process.

Anger

Some youngsters were readily able to share their anger at Rudie. "How could he have done this to us?" "Why did he have to stage it and make such a scene?" "He was selfish. I would have never done that to him or anyone." Several kids and adults said that he had done this to *their* school and ruined the rest of the school year. They wondered if they could ever look at the cafeteria in the same way. Some sophomores wondered what effect this would have on their class forever. It was as though Rudie had left an indelible black mark on them, their school, and their high school memories.

Guilt

Many counselors and I had to encourage and give some adolescents permission to let their anger surface. These kids felt guilty for being angry at Rudie and they asked, "How can I be angry? He killed himself. He'll never grow up. I can't be angry."

Guilt was particularly profound for Rhoda, Rudie's English teacher, who saw so much in hindsight. On Friday, Rudie had attended only her class, with his knapsack by his side. She wondered why he chose her class. How did she fail him in his moment of need and despair? "I saw things on Friday, but I didn't see them. Linda, one of the girls in my class who is sort of a wallflower, said,

'Mrs. Joy, see what Rudie gave me?' I said, 'No, what did he give you?' At first I thought it was nothing special, but it was Rudie's favorite hockey card and I told Linda that it was real nice of Rudie to give it to her." Rhoda also talked about Rudie as a student. He was a very particular person. When she asked her students to write in their journals, Rudie always wrote in a tiny but neat and precise script. He used ink. On Friday, he wrote in pencil and erased the entry. Rhoda blamed herself because she felt that she should have foreseen Rudie's act.

Impotence

From what Rhoda said, we can also identify her feeling of impotence, resulting from her inability to prevent Rudie from killing himself. The nature of a suicidal death is interactive; that is, both children and adults feel that the person who killed himself did it "to somebody," and this somebody might be them. Rudie's peers, parents, and teachers wondered why they were unable to see his pain and get help for him. His secretive plan and successful attempt to end his life left his peers and community with no recourse to fight the battle or stop him. Although it's normal for kids and adults to have the same feeling of impotence when a loved friend or family member is dying with cancer, the battle is one step removed—it's with the cancer, not with the loved one. With an intentional death, the powerlessness that survivors feel is created by the person who committed the act.

Sadness

Once the initial shock of the crisis was over and Rudie's death began to sink in as a "reality" that no one could avoid, the initial denial and projection adolescents experienced gave way to their sadness over losing him. For some, this sadness catalyzed similar feelings about previous losses. They regrieved their parents' divorce, a move, an adoption, or a death of a parent, sibling, or other friend. Even if kids have adapted well to a prior loss, it's natural for fresh feelings to restimulate past ones. This regrieving usually lasts only for a short period and occurs because youngsters adapt new meanings to old losses as they grow.

Rudie's death also reminded adults of other traumatic losses they had previously suffered. One teacher witnessed her father's death by suicide when she was twelve. On the third day into the crisis, another teacher, named Harry, began to heave with uncontrollable tears that shook his whole body. He told our teachers' support group that he had never been able to face or grieve a traumatic event from his childhood, which involved an attempted murder in his family. Rudie's death enabled Harry for the first time to face his pain over a loss that had occurred twenty years earlier in his life.

When I spoke with the 250 sophomores in Rudie's class, many identified him as a friend since kindergarten. They had enjoyed playing sports with him because he was good at all sports, particularly soccer. Some cried and said that they would miss him during the summer and on his birthday. Others were shaky and said that they couldn't eat or sleep. In general, Rudie's class was sad for him because he gave up three things—his driver's license, the prom, and graduation. These three events are "top priority" in the lives of most adolescents.

Fear

In their pain, some kids feared that those friends who came from broken homes, were abused, or didn't receive much support from their parents might attempt suicide also. Their friends who got high on drugs and alcohol to ameliorate their problems were vulnerable as well. If the seemingly impossible happened to Rudie, then it could happen to other adolescents too. Rudie's act also prompted some to contemplate and question whether they too could ever kill themselves.

The teachers' worst fear was facing their students in class on Monday morning. How could they address and deal with their feelings of grief and those of nine hundred adolescents? This was not a role for which they had received any training, so they felt terribly inadequate.

EXPRESSING AND SHARING GRIEF

Expressing feelings to kids doesn't come naturally to adults, especially to educators who want to contain their emotions in order to appear invulnerable and maintain authority and control, which they see as part of their job. Many educators think that they must be able to handle any and all situations in their classrooms without being affected by them. However, neither parents nor teachers require special training to accomplish the following techniques that foster healthy grief and relationships.

Checking In

During my support sessions with teachers, I checked in with the principal by asking him at the beginning of every meeting, "How are you doing, Carl?" The first time I asked, he reassured his faculty by saying, "I just realized that I'm breathing again because I now know that we can get through this. We'll be okay and our kids will be too." I then asked all teachers to look to their right and left and check in with each other to make sure that the entire faculty felt like a team, including those who were less vocal.

I also asked all parents and youngsters to check in with each other and establish this as a routine in their homes and school throughout the crisis and the rest of the year. "Tell your friend on your right how much you hurt inside. Tell your neighbor on your left that you're concerned about her and want to take care of her. Now pledge that you'll give each other room to express your grief however you need to do it. There's no right way to do it. The only wrong is to decide that there is a wrong way."

Everyone became comfortable with *checking in* during our support meetings. This behavior also extended into the hallways, auditorium, and classrooms where kids and adults gathered or passed each other. Checking in is critical to the process of including all mourning youngsters in our care.

Addressing Competitive Grief

When I met with the entire student body before Monday morning classes, twelve youngsters sat on the floor in front of the auditorium instead of in seats. They chanted a song by John Lennon just loud enough to be a distraction while the principal introduced me.

With a public or private loss, it's not uncommon for humans to experience *competitive grief;* that is, they might say, "My pain is worse than yours," "Rudie meant more to me than he did to you," or "We had a special relationship." Some kids and adults in Rudie's community formed little circles of grief comprising those who were closest to him and those who were suffering the most. Members of these circles wanted to show the entire community that their loss was greatest. These twelve kids needed to tell the entire student body that their pain was important, possibly more important than anyone else's. Their behavior, however, was destructive because it separated them and severed their relationship with the rest of the student body.

We can avoid competitive grief if we are nonjudgmental toward each other's way of grieving and right to grieve. I sat on the edge of the stage and listened to the lyrics these twelve youngsters were singing while nine hundred students waited silently for me to begin our meeting. After a couple of minutes, I asked one of the girls to come to the stage. I told her that the song was beautiful and asked her if she would write the lyrics down for me. When she returned to the group, the chanting stopped.

Although these adolescents separated themselves from others, I didn't separate them or ignore their efforts to show that Rudie was special to them. By acknowledging them in front of their classmates in a nonjudgmental way, I included them in the entire group. During this meeting and all support meetings held over the weekend, I cautioned kids and adults about forming competitive circles of grief that would isolate them from the rest of the community.

Modeling

At the teachers' request, the crisis team made a videotape of me expressing my grief and modeling my behavior for them. One teacher, who was anxious and terrified about facing her students, watched this video over and over again. On Sunday evening, she walked into the local grocery store and found herself surrounded by nine kids. When they asked her how she was doing, she used some of my language to express herself: "I feel like I have a pipe going through my chest. And if we keep talking about Rudie, I'm going to start crying." These kids told her that they felt the same way, and they modeled their behavior after hers. Because of this encounter, this teacher said that she could have spent all night with these nine adolescents. They also taught her that she could be authentic with her students in class on Monday without falling apart.

Accepting Adolescent Grief Behavior

In general, adolescent grief reactions are hyperbolic. In a traumatic crisis, they are more so. The powerful ties that bind them to each other also serve them during a crisis. Oftentimes, adolescents tend to express their pain through moody and aggressive behavior directed at their parents. Many also will cling to home and engage in less risky behavior because they feel vulnerable, but they might not want to talk with their parents; whereas others might want to take wild chances to run from the pain.

The exaggerated behavior of adolescents challenges us to accept them. We want to acknowledge their pain and show them that home is a safe place for them to grieve without criticism. If they criticize one of their friend's reactions, we want to curb their criticism by telling them that they shouldn't judge. We want to let them know that we are present for them at any time, but we don't want to *intrude* upon their grief or their desire to grieve with their peers. Our acceptance of them without being pushy or overbearing during a severe crisis can counter their threats or desires to anesthetize their pain with alcohol or drugs.

Vulnerable Adolescents

In our planning and intervention, each member of the crisis team composed a list of more vulnerable kids throughout the high school; for example, those who had attempted suicide previously, those who had a history of depression or other psychiatric illness for which they were receiving treatment, and those who had suffered recent losses of close relatives or friends. The school psychologist and volunteer mental health professionals counseled these youngsters individually to assess their needs and, if necessary, provide them with ongoing or more intensive therapy or consult with their parents.

When I met with the 250 sophomores in Rudie's class, I asked how many of them felt that they had no one to turn to for help. About thirty hands went up. I reframed suicide for them as an issue of problem solving and told them that no kid need feel alone, because there were many counselors like myself available at school. At the end of our session, a student named Doug walked toward me. His face was pale and his hands were shaking. He told me, "You said you were here to help. I'm either going to kill myself or my father today."

I took Doug to the guidance office and found out that he already had an appointment in the afternoon with a psychiatrist whom he had been seeing for several months. The psychiatrist and I talked with Doug for about an hour. I told Doug that I wanted to check in with him at lunchtime, and he agreed to meet me. When Doug did not keep our lunch appointment, I asked Carl, the principal, to investigate the situation because, unlike Doug's psychiatrist, I felt that the youngster required immediate hospitalization and psychiatric help. An hour later, Carl informed me that he had asked another psychiatrist to see Doug. This psychiatrist brought the youngster to the psych unit at the local hospital for evaluation. That evening, with his mother's permission, Doug entered an adolescent psychiatric facility for further diagnosis and treatment. Today Doug is a young adult working in his community.

Because the first psychiatrist didn't consider it an emergency, did he take Doug's threat seriously? There is no way to know.

With the pathology that this psychiatrist treats regularly and with the crisis to which nine hundred kids were reacting at the school, his response might have been salient. I relate this incident not to judge Doug's psychiatrist or anyone else but to illustrate an important point. This situation suggests the inexact nature of treating psychiatric illness, in particular adolescent depression. Mental health professionals not only must evaluate and reevaluate a young client's mental status, but they also must assess their intuition, and that of a youngster's parents and educators, concerning his well-being.

Media Bombardment

It's difficult for us to see and hear our name, neighborhood, school, or community publicly associated with a violent event. With a traumatic loss, the media's MO seems to be "if it bleeds, it leads." The media often exploit the hype, the hyperbole, and the dramatic without regard or sensitivity to survivors left behind. Major TV and newspaper reporters were on the scene Friday afternoon within an hour and a half of the shooting. They successfully found their way inside the school building. Their cameras captured screaming and terrified kids.

On Saturday and every day following Rudie's suicide, the crisis team made it clear to all students and teachers that they were not to speak to the media. This warning inhibited what could have been a media frenzy for days and days. Of course, the crisis team and administration had no control over what kids could do off school property.

The team also decided to grant only the local community newspaper access to the principal and myself for a limited interview every afternoon. We used the local cable network to announce the times of all support sessions and relay how the school was dealing with the crisis. Twice during the week following the crisis, we allowed the local TV network to interview the principal, the head of the volunteer mental health professionals, and myself. Five days after the crisis, we offered a major TV network the opportunity to do a recap on how the school had handled the crisis.

Journalism that solely plays up blood and gore misses an opportunity to offer a helpful message, not only to devastated survivors but also to millions of kids and adults who hear or read about a tragedy. We can't rid ourselves of the media, but we can talk with them about how our community has chosen to respond to a tragic loss. If we stress the positive things we're learning in the aftermath, we invite reporters to publicize the steps we have taken to bring our community together in a caring and beneficial way.

CLASSES ON MONDAY

After our support meetings and some individual counseling, a handful of teachers were still too frightened to show their feelings in class. They feared that their students might become hysterical and sob uncontrollably or that they would fall silent, leaving these teachers not knowing how to handle either situation. A few tried to conduct class because teaching felt "normal and safe." However, most of the ninety faculty were able to meet the challenge of "being present" for their kids and sharing whatever grief they felt. Throughout their lives, youngsters will remember these teachers, I believe, not for the content of their math or English lessons but for their humanity.

Three of Rudie's teachers expressed their grief with their students in the following ways:

Harry

Harry, who had blocked his grief over a traumatic loss he had experienced when he was a child, told his homeroom class that he had never faced the "grieving scene" before. "I'm the guy who skips funerals and gets people mad at me. I don't know how to do this well because I'm hurting, but I'm here to do this with you. I want to be here with you and for you. It's painful but it feels good not to run away." Harry's students talked about their nightmares and anger: "Rudie's blue face on the cafeteria floor was horrible." "Rudie was a jerk for doing this. Why do we have to mourn him?"

Rhoda

Rhoda, whose English class Rudie attended before he shot himself, had kids who wanted to deal with Rudie's desk. One youngster said, "I'm not afraid to sit in this chair," so he sat in Rudie's place. For the next three to four weeks, Rhoda's students rearranged the furniture in the classroom and played musical desks, many of them sitting in Rudie's desk at one time or another. This was a healthy reaction because these kids didn't "bury" their feelings of distress whenever they entered the classroom.

Rosemary

Rosemary, Rudie's biology teacher, thought that her students perceived her as an "all-business" type of teacher. She gave them the opportunity to talk, but her youngsters were relatively quiet and wanted to grieve among themselves. Rudie's death affected her deeply, and Rosemary found that the best way for her to verbalize her emotions was to write a poem, entitled "In Mourning," and share it with Rudie's class.

Rudie, we hardly knew each other.

You sat in sunshine, in the back. We studied life.
You worked with us; you laughed with us; we thought you
*   felt like one of us.*

We never felt your pain or feared your fears or faced your
*   dreaded demons.*
Our daydreams raced to spring. We couldn't see the winter
*   of your soul.*

You didn't know we cared.
You didn't think we'd help you heal your wounds and fight
*   your desolation.*
You didn't know we loved you,
Or, if you knew, that solace was too slight.

Despair became your partner,
And now you'll never love the girl or write the poem or win
the competition.
Your smile is gone.
Your bud is cut.
Your light is dark.
Your fire is out.

We shudder and we weep. We cry for you and grieve our
disconnection.

Rudie, we wish you'd come to class. . . .

FACING THE CAFETERIA

The principal and some teachers had rearranged the tables in the cafeteria on Friday evening after the crisis. It's instinctual to want to make a setting in which trauma occurred *look* different. Some members of the crisis team felt that we needed to provide an alternative place for those kids who were too frightened or upset to go into the cafeteria on Monday for lunch. The cafeteria would be one of the youngsters' biggest fears. If they couldn't walk into that cafeteria, they couldn't manage their feelings about it. All of the teachers needed to acknowledge this fear up front with their students and arm themselves with the idea that they would tackle this difficulty together. It was also important for teachers to realize that many kids would walk into school, as well as into the cafeteria, on Monday *wanting* to feel normal in spite of the traumatic event they had experienced on Friday. In my meeting with the student body, I explained that, by eating in the cafeteria, we could face our fears and nightmares about it openly.

Some youngsters responded to being in the cafeteria following the crisis by wanting to know why the furniture had been changed. Many also wanted the cafeteria to look like it always did. They wanted the school day on Monday to proceed with classes the same as it had on every other day. Several adolescents did have difficulty entering the cafeteria. They either didn't eat lunch there or grabbed a drink and left. All these responses are normal in children who need to overcome fear of the place in which a violent incident occurred. Within two days, the noise and activity level in the cafeteria returned to what it had been prior to the incident. At the end of the school year, the student body told the principal that they wanted the cafeteria arranged as it had been before Rudie's death.

FORMAL COMMEMORATION OF RUDIE'S DEATH

Most of the nine hundred adolescents of the high school chose to attend Rudie's wake on Tuesday afternoon. Their parents, not the school, were responsible for getting them from the school to the funeral home. Two nearby church halls were open so that all kids would have a place to gather and talk during the wake. Parents, teachers, and counselors volunteered to assist at both halls.

The majority of kids in the high school had never attended a wake. For four days, the parents and teachers of Rudie's community had helped the youngsters understand the relevant issues surrounding his suicide. His wake, however, was a time for them to remember him and express their sorrow. Many wanted to know how to talk with Rudie's parents, two sisters, and younger brother. Usually, a silent hug or a simple "I'm sorry" is the only comfort we can offer family and friends.

When they saw Rudie's body laid out in the casket, most youngsters sobbed. Although they had wanted to go to the wake, they didn't want to be there once they arrived. This behavior was not unusual. For this reason, it was important to have the church halls open and adults available to care for these kids during and following the wake.

LIFE AFTER THE CRISIS

On Wednesday, I felt that my work with the school and community had come to an end. The crisis was over, the grieving had just begun, and the mourning process would continue for weeks, months, and years. The school remained open until eleven in the evening for the rest of the week. Mental health volunteers also remained at the school for the rest of the week and into the following one, after which a mental health center in the community offered pro bono counseling to any student, parent, or faculty member who wished it. The school psychologist said that kids flowed steadily into his office for two weeks after Rudie's death.

I encouraged the principal to allow a major TV network to come to the school and do a wrap-up on how the community had handled this crisis. The network ran a "Checkpoint on Suicide" story on the evening and nightly news. The reporter said that "instead of trying to sweep the whole situation under the rug, school officials encouraged students to talk. . . . This open approach has helped the school mend quickly and better understand the epidemic of teenage suicide."

One student told her: "A lot of kids didn't even want to talk about what had happened, but they wanted to be with each other." A soccer buddy said: "We all played soccer with Rudie. We all stuck together to try and make it a bit easier for each other, thinking that, maybe, if we would have done something, it would have helped him. But everybody pretty much has come to terms with it now and realize that nothing could have been done. Our high school isn't exempt from everything. That feeling of 'what happened' is always going to be there, but I think it's a matter of everyone starting to move on and get things going again."

The reporter concluded her interview with the following note: "There's a new attitude at the school. They call it *inclusion*—making sure that every student and faculty member feels connected. . . . The scrappy hockey team has given everyone—students, parents, and faculty—something to stand up and cheer about. They are working on a state championship. They are symbolic of a larger school community on the rebound."

One teacher, now an assistant principal of the school, said that he was most proud of how the school handled the crisis. "It was by far the finest thing I've ever done in education." From the ashes, the phoenix rises. Rudie's death provided his school with the opportunity to cleanse and heal many wounds on a personal and community level.

Several Weeks Later

What emerges during a crisis are subtle changes in the dynamics within a community. Kids and adults don't cluster in their cliquish groups, and they open up to relationships they never before had experienced. They express their vulnerability and see each other anew without blocking the channels of communication. I call this phenomenon the "wet cement" dynamic. A crisis by its nature creates wet cement for two reasons: (1) its composition is changing or reshaping itself and (2) the persistence of these changes depends on time.

For example, when I returned to the school to check in on the students and faculty several weeks postcrisis, some teachers felt that the staff had returned to the status quo. The faculty room was "back to the way it was," and the generosity of spirit they had experienced during the crisis was missing.

Bobby, the adolescent into whose lap Rudie fell, was at the high school the entire weekend with his dad during the crisis. Bobby's parents were divorced, and his father wasn't always available for him. Over the weekend, his dad had his arm around Bobby's shoulder the whole time they were together. This crisis promoted a caring and intimate relationship between this father and son where none had ever existed. Within a few weeks after the crisis subsided, this relationship unfortunately unraveled and Bobby subsequently faced drug-related problems, attempted suicide in his junior year, and graduated by the skin of his teeth.

Although we can look at this "going back" to past behaviors with a degree of sadness, some kids, parents, and teachers told me that they felt a permanent shift in their lives. Mourning a loss has the power to transform us if we let it and work at it daily.

Two Years Later

How did this tragic event seem two years later to Rudie's graduation class? Graduation provided these youngsters with an opportunity to review and remember past events in their lives as high school students. Rudie's suicide figured significantly in their memories. Graduation also signified their final identification as a group, a group who had, without wanting to, endured a traumatic event. No longer would they grieve together.

At the graduation ceremony, the class acknowledged Rudie by donating a gift of five thousand dollars in his name to the school. The seniors had paid dues and conducted fund-raising events so that the interest from the money they collected could go to providing problem-solving curricula. The president of the class challenged the parental community to match the seniors' donation. To conclude the graduation ceremony, Rudie's friend Bobby dedicated the class song, "With a Little Help from My Friends," to Rudie. Bobby rendered the Beatles' song a cappella and received a standing ovation from the audience.

Although the "attention and glamor" of a teen suicide have the potential to spark the phenomenon of "copycat" suicides (see chapter 13), teachers and parents of Rudie's high school community averted copycat behavior in their youngsters by encouraging understanding and grief expression without glorifying or condoning Rudie's act. During the graduation ceremony two years after the crisis, Rudie's class honored his memory but not his act. Some kids in the school might have felt a sense of relief because his classmates, who might have been reminders of grief, had finally graduated. For some seniors, graduation might have been a painful and difficult transition. Their class gift, their class song, and the yearbook they dedicated to Rudie were icons of their collective grief. Now it was necessary for each of them to go it alone.

Multiple Tragedies in Families and Communities:

Bereavement Overload

W HEN kids experience several losses, either at once or in a series over a short period of time, like adults, they initially express a paralyzing disbelief: "This isn't suppose to happen in my family or my community." "You see it on the news and think, 'That's too bad, but it couldn't possibly happen at our school.' "

Bereavement overload originally defined the continual loss of social contacts that elderly people experienced as their friends died, one after another. Those who lived on were left alone and isolated. Many virtually shut down emotionally. *Today, we say that children and adults of all ages are overloaded with grief if they experience too many losses that thwart their capacity to mourn one or more effectively.* Past experiences might leave bereaved kids depleted emotionally and inhibit the mourning process of a current loss.

When multiple tragedies occur—a car accident that kills three youngsters, a tornado that takes several lives and devastates every home in its path, a family death followed by another within a year—adults need to develop a *balanced intervention strategy* that allows kids to manage what seems like unsurmountable heartaches. A balanced intervention supports youngsters in three ways:

1. It provides openness to engender their emotional expression.

2. It provides structure and routine to ensure their safety.

3. It uses grief and problem solving to mitigate their sense of isolation.

We should aim to give kids space to verbalize their thoughts and vent their feelings while we re-create a structure of normalcy that was shattered by their losses. We also want to help them struggle with questions like "Why me? Why my family? Why my friends?"

THE SIMON FAMILY: IS EVERYONE WHO TAKES CARE OF ME GOING TO DIE?

Mark and Luke's maternal grandmother died just before the twins began fourth grade. Their mother asked Regina, the school psychologist, to assist them in their grief. Three months following this death, the twins' mom was diagnosed with cancer and died a little over a year later. Six months after their mom's death, Mark and Luke's paternal grandmother died.

During her work with the twins, Regina consulted with me on two occasions. We strategized about how she could best guide the boys and their father through their overwhelming losses. Regina highlighted the following concerns:

- Luke talked about his sadness and problems freely and openly. Mark was unable to express his grief with Regina or his family, but he displayed what his teacher described as an "attitude problem" in class.

- Their father, Tom, worked a night shift, necessitating that he bring the twins to their aunt's home in a neighboring town each evening and pick them up for school in the morning. To complicate matters further, this aunt's two younger children aggravated Mark and Luke, and both twins complained that they weren't getting enough sleep.

- Mother's Day was on the horizon a few months after their mom's death. What was the most beneficial way to help the twins handle the delicate situation of making gifts for Mom in class?

Over a two-year period after the twins' mother died, this psychologist, the school community, and the boys' father helped Mark and Luke in the following ways.

Recognizing Bereavement Overload

Regina discovered the twins' coping behavior and styles through their journal writings and weekly counseling sessions, separately and together, with her throughout their fifth grade year. Along with their dad, Mark and Luke also benefited from the assistance of a therapist outside of school.

Mark, who would not talk about his feelings with anyone except his dad, hinted at his vulnerability in his journal. Ironically, from his journal, Regina learned that Luke had been vomiting every day, which might have been a reaction to his paternal grandmother's sickness. She was in the hospital and subsequently died while another of the boys' aunts was in a diabetic coma. At this time, the twins were looking to their extended family to help them normalize their lives; however, they faced yet two more illnesses and two more possible losses, a situation too scary to contemplate let alone live through. Tom had been bringing them frequently to visit their grandmother in the hospital. Regina asked him to reconsider this strategy because these visits might be making Luke relive his mom's illness and death, resulting in his vomiting spells. I suggested that the twins draw pictures and make audiotapes for their grandmother, which their dad could bring into the hospital.

The twins' understandable, but unspoken, conclusion had to be: "All the adults I care about in my life are dying, one after another. Everyone who takes care of me is going to die." There was no safe environment in which Mark and Luke could express their grief, which was also true for their father. They were waiting for the next death or the next bad thing to happen. Attitude problems and acting out are normal grief reactions. Anxiety, nervousness, insomnia, and vomiting are just a few of the physical and psychological symptoms of bereavement overload. In addition, how could a child concentrate in class for five hours a day given this situation?

Establishing a Secure Routine

Because inconsistency had been the twins' reality since their mom's illness, they needed a reliable family life to provide security. Dad was the pivotal person in these young boys' lives, but Tom struggled with his limited capacity to balance his need to grieve the death of his wife with his new role as primary caregiver. Luke said, "I don't feel that comfortable talking to a lot of people about Mom, but we go to Dad. We talk and take care of each other."

Their father needed to create a home for himself and his sons. Having them sleep with their aunt should be only a temporary solution. Tom needed to be with his sons in the mornings, in the evenings, and at bedtime, which might require a change in his work schedule. Including the boys in dinner preparation and establishing morning and bedtime routines would create a normal structure to life, a structure that just about every one of the twins' friends and classmates enjoyed, albeit with a mom as well as with a dad.

Tom also needed to address his boys' most critical and obvious concern: "What would happen to us if Dad died?" Of course, the answer should be honest and reassuring: "I'm very healthy and will take good care of myself because I want to live a long life with you. The chances of my dying are slim, but I want you to know that your aunt has agreed and would like to take care of you if anything does happen to me. Are you okay with this?"

When the twins were in sixth grade, I checked in with Regina to find out how the Simon family was faring. Tom and his sons had found a place of their own in which they created routines and rhythms that suited them without Mom. As they developed a new family constellation, all three were able to begin their work of mourning and coping effectively with their losses.

Celebrating Holidays

As Mother's Day approached, Regina warned Mark and Luke's teacher that this holiday would be difficult for them and awkward for other youngsters in her class. There are several solutions to help make holidays easier for the many kids who don't have a parent for one reason or another. Most important is to involve kids in the solution. For Mother's Day, we want to acknowledge the sadness and isolation children feel if they don't have a mom.

I suggested some classroom alternatives in which the twins could engage during the period devoted to making presents and cards for mothers. They could make an "I remember when . . . " card full of good and loving memories about their mom. Or they could make a card for the aunt who cared for them, or for their dad, who became both their mom and dad.

The day itself might prove to be a sad, reflective time for Mark, Luke, and their father. A wonderful thing that surviving parents can say is: "This day is going to be tough for me. I think it might be for you too. How do you guys think we should get through it?" Dad and his kids might opt to go to the movies, bring a plant to the cemetery, look at some photo albums, or just spend a sleepy day around home. All these choices are good ones. The important thing is that the family do it together and not pretend that the day will be great.

If we want to help kids accept the reality of any loss, it's necessary for us to acknowledge that many have a deceased parent or parents who are divorced. In class, teachers should establish that all families are unique. Single, foster, and stepparents head some households, whereas grandmothers head others. A "Family Day" would be more inclusive for those who love each other and live together no matter the circumstances.

Sharing Grief

Luke, who had been eager to talk about his mom's death, finally got Mark, the taciturn twin, to begin talking about their mom with him, Regina, and other adults before their fifth grade school year ended. In sixth grade, neither boy had any problems with his studies. Regina attributed their progress to the strong foundation of love and security both parents fostered since their sons' infancy. Their progress was also due to their dad's renewed capacity to normalize daily life and make it safe enough for the boys to mourn openly and together.

MARLIN COMMUNITY: NOTHING EVER HAPPENS HERE, BUT NOW EVERYONE IS HURTING

When three adolescents were driving to a favorite park site to slide on the ice, one wanted something to eat. As the car turned into a minimart another one slammed into the passenger side where Nick sat, and killed him. Seventeen-year-old Nick was a senior in the school band and had dreamed of becoming a weatherman. Two weeks later, eighteen-year-old Peter, who liked to reminisce about his days as a catcher on the Little League team, went to a bonfire party outside an old town dump. After he left the party, Peter drove 120 miles per hour past a patrolman. Another patrol car joined the first and they chased Peter, whose car flipped and landed on its side, killing him. Peter was a good kid and hadn't been drinking, so why would he run from the police? A third death followed within a week and a half when fifteen-year-old Steve, whose trademark was outlandish hairstyles, was struck and killed by a driver who thought that he had swiped a deer walking alongside the road. After these three fatalities, an adult of the Marlin community said: "Everyone is just so confused. No one knows what to make of this. Nothing ever happens here, but now everyone is hurting."

Parents, teachers, and community leaders faced the following issues as a result of these successive tragedies:

- Three adolescent deaths had scared everyone, interrupting life's daily routine. Kids were afraid to go out and parents were afraid to let them leave home. Who would be next?

- Parents were angry and frustrated because they thought that the school leaders had lent minimal support to grieving kids and faculty. The administration was unwilling to bring in outside assistance.

How did the community confront these issues?

Establishing a Safe Environment

A pastor in the Marlin community asked if I would help his community heal. I addressed the question on everyone's lips: "Will my child be next?" We want reasons to alleviate our fears and pain; however, every child is vulnerable to accidents, and there are no reasonable answers as to why accidents happen. I asked these parents to talk with their kids about their own anxieties and sadness while reestablishing a routine home life. As we explain that accidents happen to the best of people and remind youngsters of some safe rules of the road, we also want to assure them that tragedies like these are rare and will abate.

After Peter died, community leaders passed a law that prohibited adolescents from throwing parties and drinking at the old town dump. Fires, alcohol, dirt bikes, motorcycles, and guns were forbidden, but the old dump remained open to walkers and hikers. Following Steve's death, community leaders decided to look into the possibility of installing sidewalks along the road that he had been walking when he was hit. Town workers cleared overgrown bushes from the side of this road to improve driver visibility. From these tragedies, Marlin's town council took many opportunities to make their community a safer place for their kids, which also addressed and reduced anxiety and fears.

The media provided extensive coverage of town leadership and my meeting with concerned adults of the community. After I spoke, one TV station aired a summary of the issues I discussed as its "Top News Story." The news reporter outlined the four tasks of mourning that youngsters experience and stressed my advice: "The best you can do is not hide the pain, and remember, grief shared is grief diminished." This was responsible broadcasting because viewers were able to learn the best ways to assist bereaved kids, not the best ways to blame or sensationalize tragic events.

Allowing Time to Heal

Parents blamed the school for not supporting their grieving kids, which isn't unusual when tragic events send an entire community reeling. We want to project our anger. We want someone else to be responsible for controlling accidents; however, no person or organization can. Neither can they ease our pain or our youngsters'. My invitation to speak to the Marlin community was in response to this anger. Projecting anger only divides and isolates. I encouraged parents to put their differences aside, to work as a united community, and to listen and allow their children to lead. I believe that my presence mitigated parental discomfort and facilitated *their* need for support.

I also pointed out that their kids had banded together and mourned for their friends. When they left the church following Nick's funeral, his friends passed around a photo album of his life. Flowers and mementos marked the spot where Steve was killed. Eight of his friends were pallbearers, and many wrote farewell notes on a poster board at the front of the church following his funeral. "I'll see you when it's my turn," one said. Kids placed yellow roses on Steven's coffin at the cemetery.

Time itself was the eventual hero in this community. There were no further incidents as adults and children commemorated their losses and picked up the pieces of their daily lives.

RIDGEDALE HIGH: I IMMEDIATELY NEEDED MY FRIENDS

Jay, a seventeen-year-old senior, and two sixteen-year-old juniors, Ben and Stuart, died when the car in which they were riding crashed into a large oak tree. Although there were two survivors in the backseat who were wearing seat belts, no one knew exactly what had happened, except that the driver was going very fast and lost control of the car. Twelve hundred students and over a hundred faculty members at Ridgedale High School suffered bereavement overload in the wake of this fatal accident.

The high school was located in a large metropolitan area, and coverage of the tragedy received wide media broadcast. Six weeks following the accident, I was invited to cohost a weekly TV program that featured adolescents discussing issues relevant to their world. Throughout our conversation, six Ridgedale adolescents, who had agreed to do this program with me, shared their valuable insights.

SCOTT: *Kids from our school went to the oak tree, brought flowers, and burned candles. Everyone was crying and holding each other. The tree turned into a hangout where kids could share some funny stories and lighten up the mood. After I visited the tree, I felt better.*

KELLY: *I immediately needed my friends. Your immediate fear was about yourself and your friends. When I found out about the accident, I picked up the phone and called every single one of my friends to make sure they were okay.*

LISA: *I was hysterical after a friend called. I ran around the house crying. I think it would have been easier had I had friends there. Although my parents understood, they were looking at it from a different point of view.*

MARIA: *What's the different perspective that parents have?*

LISA: *Everybody is sad, but parents look at it and say, "It could have been my kid." We look at it and say, "It could have been me, but at the same time, it was a friend, not just another kid."*

MARIA: *Is it good to know details of what happened, or would you rather know less?*

LARRY: *I kept watching the same news segment over and over again. It never reached a point where I couldn't watch it.*

CLAY: *I needed a videotape and I wasn't willing to give up until I found out what happened.*

MARIA: *As adults, we need to ask kids what they need, even if we don't have the answers and want to know less than they do, which is usually the case.*

RHODA: *But when an adult says, "I know how you feel. I'm in so much pain too. Let's work this out together," I say no! I need to grieve the way I need to grieve. I don't want Mom telling me how to do it. I appreciate her being there. Someone is there to love me, but she doesn't have to treat me like a two-year-old and be all nice and sweet to me.*

MARIA: *You've made a good distinction.* I'm talking about understanding and you're talking about grieving. *Adults can help kids understand. I don't think we can help you grieve. You want each other.*

SCOTT: *What did I learn from this? Don't speed, and definitely wear your seat belt. Right after the accident, kids drove at a snail's pace, but some went back to their old ways of driving after a week or so.*

RHODA: *Our school opened for us over the weekend. Teachers came in and the crisis team helped us. The school had food and it was a safe place to go.*

MARIA: *How did you handle going to the wakes?*

SCOTT: *I just went to Jay's and was shocked to see how well his parents were taking it. I was happy for them. They had a photo album of Jay as he was growing up. His casket was closed.*

LISA: *I found an open casket, like at Ben and Stuart's funeral, a lot better. I felt by seeing them, I got one last look and could say good-bye. I had a hard time at Jay's because it was a closed casket.*

CLAY: *I decided not to go to any of the wakes. I thought it would be too hard. The deaths didn't hit me until a couple of weeks after the accident. I don't regret not going. I don't think I could have handled them.*

KELLY: *There was competition about who went. How many wakes and funerals did you go to? There's definitely a competitive edge about who did what and who did more.*

MARIA: *Do you feel as if you've become closer as a school and family?*

ALL: *Oh, yes, definitely!*

LARRY: *I think some of the closeness will die off just like the [decline in] speeding. Some people have learned a lesson about driving fast, but others haven't. Some of us will remain close, but others will go back to the way things were.*

RHODA: *Everything happens for a reason, I told one teacher. She said, "I don't think there's an explanation." But I need to find one. How do we know that their lives weren't already determined—like they were fated to have cancer and be horribly ill for ten years? That pain is worse than sudden death. Maybe that's why they died in the accident, but there's really no answer.*

Learning from Children

Throughout our conversation, these insightful teenagers were comfortable and open with my nonjudgmental questions. The lessons that they have taught us about adolescent needs and adult ability to stand by them after they were overcome by the sudden death of three friends are:

- Adults can help adolescents understand what happened by providing as many details as kids require, but adolescents have different issues from their parents and want to grieve with each other without adult interference.

- Speeding and recklessness in the wake of this type of tragedy are foremost in the minds of adolescents and are reflected in their behavior, but many return to their normal driving speeds and risk-taking habits within one to three weeks.

- The scene of a tragedy symbolizes a shrine and legacy to deceased friends and promotes memory embraces that many adolescents will cherish throughout their lives.

- The formal commemoration of a wake provides closure for some adolescents but not for others; however, to participate or not to participate should not be used to promote competition.

- The openness of a school community provides inclusion; responds to youngsters' needs to grieve together in a safe environment; fosters peer and adult closeness as a by-product of emotional outpouring; and gives structure to the chaos adolescents experience following bereavement overload.

The Ridgedale youngsters benefited from parental and school understanding, and the producer of this weekly TV program gave the greater teenage community an opportunity to learn about life and death from their peers.

BRENTON COMMUNITY: GLAMOR OF SUICIDE AND COPYCAT BEHAVIOR IN PREADOLESCENTS

One Thursday evening at a Brenton Middle School dance, a preadolescent girl attempted suicide. During the following week, seven older preadolescent girls from the same school also attempted suicide. Thankfully, no deaths resulted, but parents, teachers, and community leaders were outraged by what one resident called "copycat" behavior in this small and sleepy middle-class community. Rumors ran rampant and adult feelings—fear and panic being the greatest—collided. Many parents called the health coordinator of the Brenton school system with questions: "Are these kids crazy?" "Is this contagious?"

A national TV network heard about the attempts and wanted to interview me on its morning news program. The producer asked what was different about this community. There was nothing different. This kind of tragedy defies all statistics and odds and could have happened in any community across the United States.

The school administration and crisis team, as well as the police department, responded quickly to each suicide attempt. If a youngster attempted suicide in school, the health coordinator or psychologist called her parents and made a psychiatric referral immediately. Following each attempt, the school's psychologist and health coordinator visited all classes at the middle school and spoke to students about the nature of each incident. They, as well as all teachers and administrators, maintained an open-door policy, remaining accessible to all kids at any time.

Shortly after these incidents, the superintendent of schools organized a meeting for parents and other concerned adults in order to calm their fears and panic and to correct erroneous information or thinking. He wanted all members of Brenton community to understand how the school staff was handling this overloaded situation and returning the school to a safe environment for all kids. Members of the clergy, mental health organizations, and police department also outlined their resources available to kids and families. As a bereavement specialist, I was invited to give a keynote address. We highlighted the following intervention and prevention strategies at this meeting.

- Don't trivialize any child's problems. One young girl explained her reasons for attempting suicide: "I wanted to stop the hurt. I can't hurt like this anymore. I had a fight with my mom, my dad is constantly rapping me, my best friend and I had a fight, and this boy I like doesn't want to pay attention to me. When I told my mom that this boy I like doesn't like me, she said, 'Don't worry about it. You'll have fifteen boyfriends before you're a senior.' "

- Helping kids to not feel overwhelmed by everyday and ever-changing problems is a continuous process. Parents, teachers, and other caring professionals need to shoulder and share the responsibilities that go along with this process. An easy exercise for adolescents involves a blank piece of paper on which you ask them to list all the problems they have today. Stick that list in an envelope, seal it, and file it away. Three weeks later, take it out and give it to your youngsters. What do you suppose they'll find? This set of problems has been resolved or supplanted by another equally traumatic and overwhelming set.

- Explore the hidden nature of kids' problems—lack of self-esteem, feelings of inadequacy, fear of being isolated by peers—and help them to realize and understand any nonovert thoughts and feelings accompanying a problem.

- Although parents and teachers have to maintain certain rules to which kids must adhere for their well-being, give youngsters the reasons behind these rules and your perspective about them.

- Police officials can work with the school administration, crisis team, and psychologist to check in and keep a close eye on troubled kids; however, they require parental concern and cooperation if they are to work effectively with kids.

- Knowledge of a classmate's desire to commit suicide is not a secret that friends can afford to keep. Parents should instruct their kids to sacrifice a friendship, if need be, in order to obtain help for a depressed friend. Along with sex and AIDS education, suicide prevention also should be part of the preadolescent health curriculum in schools.

- To glamorize attempted suicides or deaths by suicide, like the suicidal death of rock star Kurt Cobain in 1994, can suggest to kids a harmful way of getting attention and notoriety when they are vulnerable or feeling isolated with their problems.

- According to the Samaritans, a volunteer organization dedicated to suicide prevention, the majority of kids who attempt suicide do so in unsupervised time after school.

Remember, when youngsters are overwhelmed by pressing problems relating to peers or home life, too much time alone or unsupervised might exacerbate their feelings of helplessness and isolation. It's a family's and community's responsibility to reach out, listen, and involve themselves in their children's activities in order to mitigate feelings that overpower and harm kids.

HARLOW HIGH SCHOOL: WHEN SOMETHING LIKE THIS HAPPENS, IT CHANGES YOUR LIFE FOREVER

The six hundred students of Harlow High had to confront four peer deaths within a seven-month period. Three boys—Jeremy, Bruce, and Patrick—took their lives by suicide and another, Rusty, died due to a ruptured cerebral aneurysm, although his death was initially rumored to be drug related. I was not involved in the immediate crises that the school and parents faced with their kids after each death. Subsequently, because the principal felt that he and the faculty had not been prepared adequately, he asked me to provide some much needed consultation to this exhausted community.

Harlow High School was located in a blue-collar rural community with a depressed economy and large drug- and alcohol-dependent population. By the time I came to meet with all members of the school community, they had suffered ostensible bereavement overload and didn't want to dredge up intense emotions they were trying to leave behind. After my two-day sessions, however, I believe that parents, teachers, and kids came together and shared their relevant issues. I was particularly struck by candid youngsters who willingly shared their thoughts and feelings.

Problems of Pole-Vaulting

When I asked an auditorium full of six hundred adolescents how they had faced their peers' deaths, they told me with *drugs*, *work*, and *sports*. Drugs, as well as alcohol and sleep, numb the pain of a loss. With drugs, adolescents say, "I don't want to feel this pain. This is enough. I don't like and I don't want these awful feeling inside." Work and sports help us to focus on the moment and forget the past, so they are effective painkillers as well.

Why did the kids of Harlow High look to drugs, work, and sports to run from pain? Understandably, their grief feelings were intense. But if we leave these kids alone and allow them to bury their pain, their fretful feelings might reemerge in fits of depression or anger throughout their lives.

The day before I spoke with the Harlow High student body, I observed four students pole-vaulting after school as the track team practiced for a meet. One pole-vaulter tried and tried, but missed the bar time after time. To my amazement, this didn't discourage him. During our session the next day in front of six hundred students, I told this kid that I had enormous regard for his ability to persist and asked him two things. What were his feelings as he missed the bar each time, and how was he going to overcome this problem of missing the bar? He said that he felt fear, pain, and discouragement, but he knew that he had the support of his teammates and coach. He also had cleared eight feet for the first time yesterday, so he was happy and thrilled. "But what about the times you missed?" I insisted. "I just got up and tried again." This youngster provided his peers with a wonderful lesson in dealing with loss and problem solving. He faced his uncomfortable feelings and losses, he reached out to his coach and peers for help, and he didn't give up.

Advice from Problem-Solving Experts

After I talked with the Harlow High student body, I invited any interested kids to meet with me. I wanted to hear *firsthand* what suicide meant to them and how their peers' deaths affected them. The following excerpts from our dialogue illustrate what was important to these vulnerable and wise youngsters.

RUBY: *It makes it hard on us and the person who is doing it when he doesn't say anything about it [his desire to commit suicide], when he keeps everything inside. I was one of those people who kept everything inside. My childhood was a living hell. It got to me when I came to high school and saw so many kids with their parents. . . . I want you guys to know that you've got to keep your heads up. You can't go screwing up because there's a problem. There are people out there who can and want to help. I tried to commit suicide more than sixteen times and it hurts. The way I help myself now is by opening up.*

CRAIG: *I've been there. I attempted and I hurt a lot of people by doing this. It's not worth it. You have to open up. I went crazy when Jeremy did it, and I had to seek help. It helps to open up and reach out for help.*

ALAN: *Suicide is selfish.*

EDDIE: *When I tried to commit suicide twice, I didn't feel selfish at the time or think about who I was leaving behind or who I was going to hurt. I just thought about getting out of what was bothering me. So I get angry at the situation but not personally at Jeremy, Bruce, or Patrick for committing suicide.*

JENNY: *My father died and my mom gave me away, so there's not much I can do about that. I don't think I'd try suicide again because I see how others react. I realize that this is my mother's loss because she doesn't have me, so I've come a long way.*

MARIA: *People abandoned you, but you solved the problem. You have learned that nothing is worth dying for and that you're a beautiful person.*

ALICE: *I write. I wrote a letter to Jeremy and one to Bruce. As stupid as it sounds, this helps me be brave. I find people I know I can talk to and I write.*

RUBY: *What about memories, guys? Memories are always going to be there. Our friends might be gone, but our memories aren't. I'll always remember that Jeremy was the first guy who taught me how to throw a baseball.*

JUDY: *I know memories are good, but I don't want any memories of Jeremy or Patrick right now because I know that things will never be the way they were.*

MARIA: *From what other kids have shared with me, I know that the same memories that make you cry now will make you feel good someday, but it takes time.*

COLBY: *No matter what, when something like this happens, it changes your life forever.*

MARIA: *Why do you think that some of you can handle and manage feelings better than others?*

BOB: *If you meet high expectations, you're expected to do it again and again. It's pressure. I've been in a lot of sports at a lot of schools. Sometimes team members can hound you—"Why didn't you do this?" I'm not saying that this makes some kids want to commit suicide, but kids blame themselves if they don't measure up to expectations.*

JILL: *I feel like I have to be the one everyone leans on, but I don't have anyone to lean on. Nobody is there for me. [A classmate reaches over, hugs Jill, and tells her that she is here for her.]*

ALICE: *I basically have no parents. I haven't heard from my father in eight years, and my mother is an alcoholic. I don't live with her. As much as I despise them for giving me up, I know that they are my parents and they do love me in their own way. . . . I'm brave because I know myself. I love myself too. I know how to handle situations. I know myself well enough to know that I could help someone through a bad situation.*

RICH: *I was brought up in a loving family and we always have kids over at the house. When sixty people are coming and going, there are always problems. So you learn how to help people out.*

ALL: *We say, Let's go to Rich's house. His mom is my mom.*

MARIA: *Did all of you know each other as well as you know each other now?*

ALL: *No.*

MIA: *I don't know how I'm going to make it through the prom. It seems too much to bear without Jeremy. You think you know yourself and then something like this happens, and you don't know yourself at all.*

MARIA: *What just happened in this room in forty-five minutes?*

ALL: *We all came together and shared. We opened up and all have similar feelings.*

MARIA: *Now, when Mia goes to the prom, she'll know that all of you will be there supporting her one way or another.*

RUBY: *I've been at this school for five years, and I've gotten to know more and more people. What Mia said about knowing yourself and not knowing yourself I compare to a house. It's always going to be under repair, and I'm not sure that anyone is ever going to know themselves exactly. Like a house, you have to put on new shingles and new paint from time to time.*

As they struggled with four deaths, faced their own problems, and reached out for assistance, these adolescents experienced the power of healing. They learned about love and friendship. They learned that caring adults want to help them.

We can learn from them, from the Simon twins, and from the youngsters of the Marlin community, Ridgedale High, and Brenton Middle School if we listen. Not only with bereavement overload but also with all losses and problems that kids confront, our intervention strategy must first and foremost build loving connections and relationships. Kids have taught me that, as with grief, any big or small problem is diminished if shared.

Part 3

NONOVERT LOSSES

Fragmented Families:

Mourning a Divorce

YEARS ago, we looked at divorce as the legal dissolution of a marriage between two people. Now we see general books on the market highlighting divorce as a *process* that unfolds for kids and their parents over many years. Although parents become ex-husbands and ex-wives, they don't become ex-moms and ex-dads.

Divorce represents the "death" of the family that a child has known. Accidents or illnesses are the agents of grief in the death of a loved one, but parents are the agents of grief and stress in the divorce process. Divorce is also the grief that keeps "giving," in that kids often long for or fantasize about their parents' reunion for many, many years, even if their parents quarreled continually when the family lived together. Just as adults vow that their marriage is "forever," so kids trust that their family union is "forever."

As divorce has become more prevalent in our society, researchers have investigated its effects on youngsters. Even five years following the divorce, many experience stress from family instability and continued parental conflict. In 90 percent of divorces, Dad leaves home and the kids live with Mom; however, a child's emotional ties to each parent remain strong. Because the breakup of their marriage usually devastates a husband and wife, parents don't recognize or acknowledge how *their* separation and untoward feelings about each other wound their kids.

A child's adjustment to parental divorce depends on three factors:

1. The phases of the divorce process

2. The child's age and level of development

3. The child's gender

How parents help a child come to terms with their divorce, as well as how they behave toward one another, dictates the youngster's adjustment and ability to accept her family's fragmentation without extensive or lasting mental anguish.

PHASES OF THE DIVORCE PROCESS

The physical separation of two parents ushers in an intense crisis. For some families, the crisis can last a month or two, but for others, it can continue for a year or more. Boundaries between the three phases of the divorce process—*acute crisis, short-term transition,* and *long-term adaptation*—are far from rigid and depend on specific family dynamics rather than on time. How parents resolve their conflict, deal with their emotions, and establish new patterns of living determine the length of each phase and their kids' reactions to the entire process. Due to each youngster's unique personality, developmental stage, and gender, family dynamics and circumstances affect kids in different ways within each phase.

Acute Crisis

The first phase of the divorce process begins as parents separate. Regardless of the nature of parental tension that kids might have experienced for years, they are shocked, frightened, and saddened because one parent has left physically, changing their world dramatically and crushing their belief about family togetherness forever.

During the acute crisis, parental rejection, anger, and guilt generate intense conflict in children. Separating parents who feel rejected or diminished often respond with anger or rage. Kids might witness verbal, and sometimes physical, abuse and vehement arguments. Enraged spouses also might abandon their kids' needs and feelings—what Neil Kalter has termed "diminished parenting" in his book, *Growing Up with Divorce*.

Between explosive exchanges, or perhaps in place of them, parents might debase each other in less volatile but obvious ways. For example, the first time a dad comes to pick up his five- and seven-year-old boys for the weekend, their mom says, "You didn't tell me you were taking the boys skiing. I don't want you to do this. You better watch them closely—and don't leave them to ski down the slope by themselves, *like you always do*." Their dad replies: "I *did* tell you I was taking them skiing. You just don't remember because you were crying so much when I phoned you. They don't want to be cooped up with a mother who feels sorry for herself all the time." Whether through yelling or insidious bickering, kids view the two people whom they love most at each other's throats continually.

While a rejected spouse might feel unworthy of being loved, the one who decided to leave might feel guilty. Both rejection and guilt can produce states of chronic depression, another name for anger turned inward. Divorcing parents often cry, sleep, or eat excessively, while giving little attention to their kids. Other parents evade depression, anger, or guilt by working all the time or establishing an extensive social life, either of which also deprives kids of parental attention.

Financial constraint is another stressor on kids. Dads usually become burdened with maintaining two households instead of one. Many moms, who left college or the workplace when they had children in order to devote themselves full-time to raising a family, must find substantial employment and/or further their education to compete in a challenging job market. Even if women continued to work after they had kids, oftentimes their pay is less than that of men, so they are strapped financially following the separation.

During a *cordial separation*, in which parents manage to appear friendly and caring toward each other in front of their kids, many youngsters can't understand why their parents want a divorce. They can cling to false desires and fantasies about parental reconciliation. Contrary to what we might assume, therefore, a *measured* level of conflict between parents can help kids as they begin to come to terms with the reality and finality of their parents' divorce.

As custody is established and becomes routine, the loss that youngsters endure over the parent who moves out slowly begins to mollify. Today, many parents opt for *joint custody* in which they both spend more or less equal time with their kids and decide together about their religious, educational, and health-sustaining needs. When parents cooperate and manage their conflict in front of their kids, joint custody provides a more comforting transition for children throughout the divorce process.

Short-Term Transition

Continuing conflict and hostility between parents can only enhance kids' stress as the time of separation marches on. Parents who argue and disagree about custody arrangements, financial settlements, and level of child support after the acute crisis subsides and a transitional routine begins to place added anxiety on kids. Financial problems also won't subside as long as the parent at home, usually the mom, must work long and hard to establish a career, reducing her time and energy for child rearing.

If parents don't assume joint custody or responsibility, the parent away from home, usually the father, becomes "Disney Dad" who takes his kids off for fun-filled weekends; however, the fun that Dad brings into their lives every other weekend doesn't make up for their feelings of losing hold of him and the deeper relationship they had when he lived at home and cared for their daily needs. When parents have joint custody, kids constantly move back and forth between two homes, which poses added stress even if the divorce process runs smoothly. Adjusting to custody settlements can be particularly difficult for youngsters if parents:

• Place them in the middle as go-betweens—"Tell your dad that he's late again with your tuition. He's only hurting you, because you won't be able to go to this great school if he doesn't cough it up." Kids can develop a fear of both parents and suffer deep wounds.

- Use them for emotional support—"I'll be too lonely if you spend the night with Jill. I want you to stay home and watch our favorite TV program with me." Kids can lose their sense of independence and confidence, as well as feel guilty for wanting to do their own thing.

- Ask them to be parents—"You'll have to cook dinner every evening and put your brother to bed because my course is from five until eight, three nights a week, and I have to study on the nights when I don't have classes. Just make sure you get your homework done before dinner and you shouldn't have a problem." If kids are forced to give up the freedom of youth, they can resent these heaped-on burdens for the rest of their lives.

During the transitional phase, kids also must begin to face their parents' *sexuality and dating*. For a mom or dad to have a sexual relationship with someone other than each other is unacceptable to most youngsters and creates inner conflicts of loyalties. As parents develop a social life and date, they have less time to spend with their kids, and the enormous loss of the parent who doesn't live at home sinks in further. Kids must "compete" for their parents' time and affection, enhancing their fears about being even less significant in their parents' lives.

The short-term transition in the divorce process can last up to two years following the acute crisis. If adults don't neglect their role and responsibilities as parents, children will be able to cope effectively with their stressful feelings and adapt to the finality of the divorce.

Long-Term Adaptation

Anger, jealousy, emotional dependency, depression, or desire for reconciliation that persists in one or both parents can cause emotional and behavioral disorders in kids.

At the same time, *remarriage,* which happens in many cases during this phase, can magnify some previous stresses and deluge youngsters with a whole new set of issues:

- The competition kids feel about sharing a parent with a new spouse can intensify.

- The relationship kids develop with a new spouse can conflict with their loyalty toward the parent whom the spouse replaces.

- The anger kids harbor against a new spouse who crushes their wish for their parents' reconciliation, disciplines them, and tells them what to do can dominate their ability to adjust.

- The place that kids lose in the new family can cause them to resent their half- and stepsiblings as they compete with these new family members for their parent's attention.

Although these issues seem overwhelming, a warm and loving marriage between a parent and his or her new spouse can boost kids' self-esteem, give them an effective masculine or feminine role model daily, increase their confidence in being accepted by their parent's partner, and help them feel comfortable in relating to a person of the opposite sex who isn't their parent. Children who grow up in single-parent households can lack opportunities in educational and growth-enhancing experiences because of ongoing economic constraints. They also can act immature and lose many of their friends because of their overly close ties to a parent who doesn't foster their autonomy and independence.

Throughout every phase of the process, every parent's top priority should be to minimize the many stresses and trade-offs that can confound their kids.

EFFECTS OF AGE AND GENDER ON CHILDREN'S ABILITY TO COPE WITH DIVORCE

Anger, sadness, anxiety, abandonment, loneliness, and jealousy, as well as being out of control and overburdened with the responsibilities of absent parents, are all feelings that kids might endure in their grief. The age of a child can help parents identify which stresses of a divorce will be paramount.

Preschool children (ages three to five) usually regress behaviorally. An inconsistent daily routine and parental hostilities and emotions can make them tearful, irritable, aggressive, and less interested in play. Their greatest fear is parental abandonment, so they might fuss considerably when they have to be separated from either parent. Preschool youngsters more likely than older children will be inclined to blame themselves for the divorce. Parents need to observe their behavior because very young kids don't have the capacity to verbalize specific feelings of anger, sadness, fear, and rejection.

Latency-age youngsters (ages six to eight) usually are very sad and preoccupied with the parent who has left. They might feel rejected and voice their longing for him to return home. "If he loved me, why did he leave?" They might not be able to concentrate on learning, they might act out in class, or they might become socially passive and withdrawn, losing the friends they had made. Many young school-aged kids want their teachers to know about their family's situation because they believe they can do better in their studies if their teachers understand. Parents need to check in often with their latency-age youngsters and listen to them. If they are having problems in school, parents should make teachers aware of the divorce. Teachers, in turn, should be compassionate and help a child express his feelings through play, art, music, and relevant children's stories.

Preadolescents (ages nine to twelve) are affected most by their internal conflicts and misperceptions about both parents. They might be angry, jealous, out of control, and feel burdened by their parents' absence, lack of attention, or preoccupation with their own psychological and social needs. Preadolescents can be psychologically aggressive—using bullying tactics to provoke their siblings and peers, for example—as a defense to intellectualize their grief and release their inner conflicts without appearing out of control. Words of reassurance from parents often won't suffice to comfort these kids. Parents need to engage in and share activities with them routinely, which provides preadolescents with consistent commitment and love.

Adolescents (ages thirteen to adulthood) are self-absorbed and experience great stress as they attempt to integrate self-autonomy and self-image with their awakening social life and internal biological changes. Although they are in the process of separating from their parents, adolescents rely on parents to listen to their problems and frustrations as they become independent and responsible. How adolescent cope with divorce depends on their parents' sensitivity toward their issues and respect for their autonomy.

How do boys and girls differ as they attempt to cope with their grief? Older latency-age and preadolescent boys often identify with their dad and want to please him. They might talk or behave like Dad just to irritate Mom, and they might act out their distress, neglecting to do chores, for example. By being aggressive toward relatives and friends, these boys make it challenging for their parents, teachers, siblings, and peers to talk effectively with them and have compassion for them.

Latency-age, preadolescent, and adolescent girls often attempt to maintain good relationships with both parents. To free themselves of emotional pain and to earn praise, they convert their anger and sadness into loving and solicitous help. As I highlight in Natalie's story later in the chapter, this benevolent behavior can hold hidden costs in that girls might harbor delayed anger into their adolescence and adulthood or never work through their painful feelings about their parents' divorce.

Both boys and girls can suffer from lack of a masculine and feminine role model. Parents represent male and female models that kids rely on to identify with characteristics of their same sex and learn to interact with their opposite sex. Although both boys and girls are at risk of becoming overly involved with their mom in the absence of an ongoing relationship with their dad, a mother who spends an excessive amount of time working or socializing also will be unavailable, diminishing a feminine role model in their lives.

LISTENING TO AND COMMUNICATING WITH CHILDREN OF FRAGMENTED FAMILIES

To help boys and girls of all ages express their grief and cope with the physical and psychological adjustments of parental divorce and family fragmentation, we have to *put them and their concerns and needs first*. This advice is much easier said than done, especially when divorced parents have erroneous beliefs about their youngsters. Here are some *false assumptions* parents commonly make:

- Kids want to hide their feelings from parents, not think about them, hope they will go away, and act as if nothing has changed. The truth is that kids want to express their feelings and let parents know how much they are hurt.

- Kids will take a step backward and observe their feelings and thoughts. The truth is that the ability to observe and analyze one's emotional and cognitive pain takes enormous maturity. In the midst of a loss, few adults have this coping skill.

- Kids will put their conflicted and painful feelings into words. The truth is that kids are overwhelmed by their feelings, and even older kids can't necessarily separate one feeling, like loneliness, from another, like rejection.

- Kids will consider their parents' distress, despite their own grief, by being good and appealing children. The truth is that kids are often ill mannered, temperamental, rude, and bad.

It's not enough to understand how youngsters grieve and display their painful feelings. As the perpetrators of their children's grief and stress, divorcing parents have to learn the most beneficial, comforting, and nonisolating ways to communicate with their kids. Keep the following points in mind:

- Use simple language to explain what's taking place and what's going to happen with living arrangements, financial status, and school and social needs.

- Allow and encourage kids to vent their feelings, concerns, confusions, conflicts, and wishes, no matter how hard it is to face the pain that you've brought into their lives. Check in with them daily, or more often during the acute crisis, and don't isolate or ignore bereaved kids as you grieve.

- Don't ever put kids in the middle of your conflicts or make them choose between you and your ex-spouse.

- Remember that kids often think that they're the cause of your divorce. Remind them that they aren't, and tell them that your love for them has not changed nor will it ever change.

- Remember that kids continue to hold on to the cherished fantasy of parental reconciliation for years, often into their adult life. Don't give them mixed signals in the event of a cordial divorce.

- Share in many activities with kids, and remember that they deserve to have both parents participate in important events in their lives, such as school plays, teacher meetings, birthdays, graduations, and sick days.

Because many parents are overwhelmed by an unhealthy relationship and can't cope with their own feelings, they never learn how to communicate with their youngsters or understand their children's stresses. For example, as long as Timmy could remember, his parents argued off and on at the dinner table in the evenings. These arguments increased with time. His dad would scream at his mom, while she sat and cried. Every now and then, she tried to stand up for herself, but to no avail. His dad would scream even louder and then ask his three boys to "look at your crazy mother. She has no backbone. When you finish your dinner, all of you are coming to the workshop with me. You don't have to sit here and listen to her."

Sometimes Timmy felt that these arguments were his fault. If he would have brought home better grades or helped his dad even more than he did already, Dad would not have been so angry. At other times, Timmy hated how his dad put him in the middle and tried to turn him against his mom. He also hated that his mom cried so much and didn't stand up for herself or him. His brothers were six and eight years older than he. They were in high school and seemed to ignore the arguments. Not only that, they didn't listen to his mom or dad. When Dad told them to help him in the workshop, they said they had too much homework. He excused them, but he made Tim help him constantly. Tim gave up most every weekend with his friends to help his dad work on the car, fix the washing machine, or paint the house.

Finally Timmy's parents separated when he was ten. He spent every other weekend with his dad, but his parents' behavior toward him didn't change, except that his father wasn't around so much. Every time his dad saw his mom, they argued. Timmy was never able to talk with either parent about *his* feelings—and they never once asked him how he felt. When Tim was nineteen, his dad died suddenly with a heart attack. His mom never verbalized her feelings of rejection and low self-esteem. She depended on her sons to sustain her every need, and they did until she died in her seventies. It wasn't until Tim was in his thirties that he confronted his painful feelings about his parents' inability to help him because of their desperate needs. He had suppressed great anger and resentment. From his mom, Tim learned how to suppress feelings very well.

After many therapy sessions, Tim channeled his anger into developing self-respect and an honest self-image, and he shared his grief with his brothers. Not so remarkably, they had experienced many of the same feelings—isolation and lack of love and attention. With Tim's encouragement, his brothers sought counseling, and the three men have learned to make time to listen to each other and to their own kids.

Tim and his brothers had to go it alone and didn't confront their grief until they were parents themselves. In order to give youngsters relief and hope, all divorced parents should take the time to listen to, understand, and empathize with their kids. Children will then know that they can survive a divorce without losing the love, care, and devotion of both parents. Putting your kids first, keeping your conflicts in their proper place, being sensitive to your youngsters' stresses, and communicating with them every step of the way are the keys to healthy relationships and recovery throughout the divorce process.

GRACE'S STORY: A KIND AND LOVING DIVORCE?

When Grace was eight, both her parents explained that they weren't getting along, that they no longer loved each other, and that they were getting a divorce. Grace's dad was going to live in a condominium not far from their home. Together Grace's parents, Claire and Greg, also told her that they would always love her and that their divorce was not her fault.

Grace's parents rarely fought or exhibited any conflict in front of Grace before or after the separation. They agreed to keep their emotional and financial disagreements out of Grace's earshot. Greg said, "We didn't cry or carry on, nor did we ever trash each other in front of her."

Before the separation, Greg worked outside the home and Claire was a full-time mom, but he shared coparenting responsibilities and activities with Claire and was very involved in Grace's daily life. Immediately following their physical separation, Claire and Greg continued to coparent Grace. She went shopping with her dad to pick out her bedroom furniture and personal care articles for the condo because Grace and her parents decided that she was going to live equally with each, alternating one week with her mom and one with her dad. Grace seemed comfortable with this arrangement and had little trouble adjusting to it.

Shortly following the separation, Greg decided that he would drive Grace to school daily, even when it wasn't the week she lived with him, as a way of reassuring his daughter that he had not abandoned her. Initially, when Greg had Grace for the week, he didn't know how to fix her hair. On these mornings, he would drive by her mom's home before school so that Claire could do

Grace's hair. Once he learned the technique, however, Greg was able to help Grace with the hairdo that she liked. When Claire decided to go back to school to complete her bachelor's degree, driving an hour each way to college and back, Greg compensated by becoming more involved in Grace's ballet and tutoring schedule after school.

Two years following the separation, I asked Greg what his ten-year-old daughter would give as a reason for her parents' separation. "She would say that she's happy her parents get along now and aren't upset with each other anymore." The most difficult challenge for this preadolescent was family vacations and trips. It was different taking a trip with only her mom or her dad. Grace hadn't voiced any wish for her parents' reconciliation, which is unusual for a child. Although her parents rarely argued in front of her before or after the separation, possibly Grace felt their tension and unhappiness together and was relieved that she no longer had to suffer these effects.

For two years, Grace has appeared to have experienced minimal stress in adjusting to her parents' separation. During this time, she complained of occasional stomachaches. Her pediatrician found her to be lactose-intolerant and altered her diet around the foods that precipitated her discomfort. Since then, her abdominal pains have ceased, and Grace has had no other physical maladies. Neither has she had any psychological symptoms or behavioral problems in school. Her grades are excellent and she has many friends. She also has strong and consistent feminine and masculine role models in her parents.

Will this cordial divorce pose any difficult stresses for Grace in the future? Her parents see one possible bump in the road ahead—their dating, which neither has embarked on yet but probably will eventually. However, if they continue to put Grace's needs first, listen to her, be honest and authentic as they explain what will be different and what will remain the same in her life and theirs, Grace will have the necessary coping skills along with the love, care, and attention of both parents to help her weather and work through any distress she might feel over her parents' divorce as she grows up.

NATALIE'S STORY: I HAVE NEVER WISHED
FOR MY PARENTS' REUNION

Elaine and Ron separated when their daughter, Natalie, was two and a half. Natalie had only one vague but fond memory of her parents being together on a vacation in Bermuda. If her parents had told her that they were separating, she certainly didn't remember at that age. Until she went away to college, Natalie lived primarily with her mom but spent every Tuesday and every other weekend with her dad.

The last time I met with Natalie, she was nineteen and majoring in premed and biochemistry. She received a partial scholarship, and both her parents contributed financially to her education. As Natalie reflected on her living arrangement with Ron, she said, "It was good. I didn't feel alienated from my dad. We didn't have to catch up every time we saw each other because we did this frequently enough. In the summer, I would spend a week or two with him. At Christmas, I'd go skiing with him. My time with him was flexible."

Natalie first realized that her parents were divorced when she was about five. "I wanted to figure out why they weren't together, like other kids' parents, so I asked Mom. She told me that she still loved my dad but that she wasn't *in love* with him. At the time, I believed her, but later on I didn't feel that Mom really loved Dad." Elaine's answer was too complex for this young child to understand. But when Natalie was eight, she had the ability to observe her parents' behavior, and she then was able to grasp a realistic understanding about why they divorced.

"My parents are both chiropractors and had a practice together, until Mom basically threw Dad out of the house when she found out he was having an affair with their secretary, Maureen. Mom is a no-nonsense, dominating person. She's meticulous and plans for the future. My dad is just the opposite. He's quiet, nonaggressive, youthful, and fun loving. He's active, likes sports, and lives for the day. Dad never talked about how he felt, so Mom kept pushing him. He would say, 'I don't want to hear it. I don't want to deal with it.' I could definitely see a lack of communication between them, and I never wanted them to get back together. Ultimately, I think my parents would have divorced anyway because they are so different. I feel that Dad did it poorly and gave up on their relationship too soon. He agrees with me."

Natalie has lived seventeen of her nineteen years in a fragmented family. During this time, "I've never felt that I had anything to do with their divorce. As soon as I was conscious about who was around, Maureen was there. Maureen was always there. I never even felt that she was responsible for the divorce, not then anyway. Now I think that my parents and Maureen—all three—are responsible and had a part in it." For a youngster *not* to feel responsible or wish for her parents' reconciliation is most unusual. Possibly, because Natalie has never known her family together, she can't wish or feel responsible for something she has never experienced.

Natalie pinpointed the greatest stress of the divorce on her during her childhood and early adolescence—her stepmother. "Maureen was a manipulative person who set her sights on my father and got him. My dad moved into her house, and Maureen was very nice to me at first. Her five children were much older than me, and I never had any problem with them. When I was about eight or nine, I started to understand many things about my parents' divorce and why it happened. That's also when Maureen began being mean to me. I don't know why. Like, I would sit on Dad's lap if there was no place else to sit in the living room sometimes, because Maureen had five kids. She would tell me to get up and say that it was improper for me to sit on Dad's lap. She didn't go for affection either."

Natalie couldn't share with Ron her feelings about Maureen. Once, when he drove her back to her mom's, she was in tears. Ron asked if she felt that Maureen loved her. "I didn't say no. I remember driving home a lot of nights thinking, 'Just say it. I hate her. I want her out of my life.' I never could say this until Dad and Maureen split up. I think I just wanted to avoid conflict with them because I wasn't with her that much. I was afraid, but I don't know why. I knew Dad would never let her take him away from me. I don't know what I thought except that she would make my life more of a hell if I told him and then he told her."

As a young child, Natalie showed enormous resilience to cope with a father who never stood up to his second wife on his daughter's behalf. Instead of revealing her anger, she said what she knew would please her dad to make him happy and assure his acceptance of her. She wanted to find a way to make life with her dad, Maureen, and Maureen's older kids work smoothly, which was quite a mature but not atypical undertaking for a school-aged girl. Natalie wanted the love, care, and attention of both parents. Although both always went to her soccer games, graduations, and birthdays, and Ron never deserted her or made her feel left out or unwanted, Elaine was "my primary caregiver."

When Natalie was sixteen, Ron and Maureen divorced. At that time, Natalie laid her angry feelings out on the table, determined not to hold anything back. "I told Dad that I called Maureen 'the witch' and that she was mean. Maybe she was jealous of our relationship, but he should have taken up for me. He should have been more protective of me. When I told my dad all this, he cried. It was a formality that I would go to his house and do this and that. I'd kiss him good night, but I was never that close to him. He knows that now. Since his divorce from Maureen, we've become best friends. He has learned a lot about relating to me and understanding my needs. I talk with him daily now, even though I'm away at college. I talk with Mom about every other day. I think she might be jealous of my relationship with Dad, but she denies it."

What was Natalie's relationship with her mom? "I've always felt close to Mom and could tell her everything. I've never felt like a mom to her, just a friend. She has had three serious relationships but never put me second, made me feel responsible for her life, or ever left me behind. I never felt threatened by any of these men. I never felt a huge attachment to them, but they were a part of my life as much as they were of Mom's. I was okay with her relationships, and all her boyfriends were nice to me, but I didn't always like the way they treated her. I was more concerned for Mom than anything else."

This concern shows Natalie's hypermaturity and adultified behavior. It's normal for an eight- or ten-year-old to be *self*-centered, but Natalie worried about her mother's well-being. She adjusted to someone moving into her home and sharing her mom with him because she wanted her mom's happiness. I asked Natalie if she felt that she had to *protect* both her mom and her dad. "Yeah. I'm not sure why. They've both had problems with relationships. I think that Mom has been dealt a raw hand with her marriage and her work."

Natalie's insight into her parents' behavior, the divorce, the choices they made, and what it cost her to adapt to these things has evolved as she has grown. "I would have liked to have had a stronger relationship with my dad, but I had a stronger one with my mom. I never felt emotionally starved for his affection, and I always had someone to talk to. I think I've also benefited from the divorce because it's made me strong and helped me to cope with problems. The greatest cost of the divorce to me—I was determined to make everyone my friend. I just want everyone to like me. I guess that's a little bit of a problem—that I want everyone to be my friend and if they aren't, it really bothers me. I go overboard to make people like me, and I try to be a people pleaser. But I'm learning to give this up. I don't have to be in every sport or every organization to make people like me. Now, I do what pleases me, and when I do something to please someone else, I feel good about it. I've learned. And when someone does something I don't like, I stand up to them no matter what."

Kids of all ages want everyone to like them, but this is especially true for girls who live through a divorce. Natalie has had to adapt to how her parents engaged in other relationships, how they had problems with intimacy, how her stepmother treated her, and how her dad married for the third time and took on another new family. She witnessed her mother's relationships fall apart and her career decline. But because Natalie felt loved by both parents and could share her deepest feelings with her mom, she was finally able to express her anger to her father, develop a meaningful relationship with him, and not be as solicitous to both parents as she previously was. She has acquired a good self-image and learned that she and others can love her for who she is. Her schoolwork and sense of self-esteem were not affected, nor did her trust for either parent plummet.

Growing into a young adult, Natalie carries all the painful but positive lessons she has garnered from her parents' divorce as she creates her own philosophy about life, develops her career, and builds future relationships.

LIVING WITH DIVORCE

Like death, divorce is not something for which people plan; yet today, more and more adults and kids live with divorce. No matter how cordial two ex-spouses try to be, divorce is a grave loss for them and their youngsters. Although Grace seems to have undergone minimal stress and grief, she is still young and has not had to adapt to the many changes that Natalie has. Natalie has not had to confront the problems and trying relationships with stepsiblings that other kids have had to contend (see chapter 15).

Each family, and each divorce, is as unique as each person is, but what creates honest and loving relationships is universal. When parents understand why divorce is a process, what affects their children at different stages of development, and why kids respond in a certain way to the stresses of fragmented families, they will find caring words and communication modes to address their youngsters' needs while they cope with their own problems and loss.

15

I Think Sam Is Starting to Like Me a Lot:
Blended Families

TODAY, when divorced adults with children remarry, they must blend two already established families together. In contrast to a first marriage, blended families comprise a "packaged union." By default, the children must accommodate their parent's wish for them to live with a new spouse and his or her children. Lurking in the backdrop of this less than idyllic family picture are two ex-spouses, who will share the parenting duties with their ex and the new spouse.

Situational losses also can create blended families, or stepfamilies. If a parent dies and the other eventually remarries, stepsiblings need to come together as a new family constellation. Among immigrant and naturalized citizens, some grandparents head families composed of their children, grandchildren, and nieces and nephews. If both parents die or desert their children for whatever reasons, grandparents, godparents, aunts and uncles, or foster parents might bear the responsibility of the youngsters left behind.

Curly haired and vivacious Hannah was two when her father died and five when her mom remarried. Her stepfather chided her about everything, from her grades in school to her ability to do chores around the house. In his eyes, she was never good enough and could do nothing well. He dismissed his own children in the same way, although they didn't live in the household. Hannah's mom always stood up for Hannah. Now in her twenties, Hannah has taken time to reflect on her family life and absence of a father figure. She appreciates her mother's consistent love and attention, which got her through difficult preadolescent and adolescent years, but she realizes that she has a hard time having intimate relationships with men because she didn't experience intimacy with a father or within a family unit.

When blending a family, couples need to place their kids first and keep in mind what's best for the children. Because youngsters of all ages continually fantasize about their divorced parents' reunion, not only immediately following a divorce but for many years to come (see chapter 14), they don't envision the thought of either parent remarrying, nor do they necessarily want a divorced parent to date.

Once you and your children have adjusted to life after a divorce, or to one in which your partner has died, keep in mind the following tips as you contemplate dating and eventual remarriage:

- Discuss your reasons for wanting to date with your kids and let them know that their feelings about it are important.

- Establish with your new partner, if a relationship becomes serious and you decide to remarry, that your children's welfare—financially, psychologically, and spiritually—is foremost. Consider prenuptial agreements in order to protect your assets for your children in the future.

- Make sure that your spouse to be is a healthy role model and one with whom your children can develop a meaningful relationship because she will become an integral part of their daily life. Remember that your new spouse will not replace your children's other biological parent.

- Begin to develop an ongoing relationship with your new partner's children as your relationship together grows.

- Discuss parenting styles with your new partner, your roles in disciplining each other's youngsters, and your financial responsibilities to the new family.

- Establish with your partner and children some guidelines and rules of household responsibilities before remarriage to make blending easier as the new family begins living together.

- Help your children to develop relationships with stepsiblings. Realize that they have to share you with these siblings as well as lose their former place in the family, a situation in which anger, rejection, and competition can reign. A stepsibling also might stir up latent sexual feelings in a youngster, which can generate confusion and guilt in kids and uneasiness in you.

- Include your children in your wedding plans and marriage ceremony.

You're in love and see grand things for your new family as you and your partner join in matrimony. Despite both your efforts to create a smooth road ahead, your youngsters initially might view a stepparent and stepsiblings as an "intrusion" into the safe and comfortable life that you have built with them. The two stories in this chapter reflect the discomfort and grief that children work through as they adjust to their place within a blended family.

The Dixon-Keen Family

Annie, who has her master's degree in nursing and directs a large research project at a major medical school, was separated and divorced for six years before she met her second husband, Sam. Prior to Sam, she had another serious relationship and introduced her two boys, Jeremy and Aaron, to this man shortly after they met. He became closely involved with the boys in their everyday life. When things didn't work out for this man and Annie, her children suffered another loss.

For this reason, Annie decided that she didn't want them to

become attached to Sam or develop an ongoing relationship with him until she and Sam had dated for two years and then decided to marry. The boys liked him. Twelve-year-old Jeremy already knew Sam through one of his friends before Sam and Annie met. Jeremy said, "Oh, you're going out with Uncle Sam. You better not blow this, Mom, because he's a nice guy." When Annie and Sam were clear that they wanted a permanent commitment, she discussed this decision with both kids. Jeremy told her, "You deserve to be happy. I want you to be happy. You're too good for Dad. He doesn't deserve you."

Aaron, who was nine and had never felt ready for Annie to date, was concerned about sharing her with Sam. Annie assured him that she still loved and cared for him as much as ever, and she always put Aaron's needs before hers and Sam's. On the evening that they returned from their honeymoon, they and the boys had their first meal together. Aaron said, "This is our first dinner together as a family."

Annie would not have considered marrying Sam unless he was a person whom she would want her boys to live with. "He had to be a good model for them, although we were both clear that we didn't need or want another parent for our kids. In spite of his flaws and drawbacks, my kids' father is active and involved with them. Sam's ex-wife adores their children.

"In a second marriage, two people need to establish that the kids come first. Sam and I both know this about each other. In fact, it's something that I value. I wouldn't want him to put me in front of his kids. I don't expect him to want to put me first. We talked about who our kids were. We didn't structure how he would get to know my boys. We just decided that we would get to know each other's children as things happened naturally in our lives."

Sam was a sports trainer and taught health in a private high school. Every year, he trained a football team to compete in a fund-raising game. The first thing that he did alone with the boys was to take them to this game. Jeremy went with Sam one year, and Aaron and a friend of his went the next.

Sam's three children were older and wouldn't be living with him, Annie, and the boys. His eldest daughter was on her own. His son and youngest daughter, who had lived with Sam when she was in high school, were both away at college and stayed with their mother during holidays and summer vacation.

Unfortunately, Sam's ex-wife had talked negatively about him to her children. After being divorced for twelve years, she and Sam still had a contentious relationship when they discussed the children's needs and well-being. Although none of his kids lived with Annie and Sam, Annie didn't know what role she should play in their lives. She didn't want their mother's anger toward Sam to alienate his youngsters from her. Annie was careful to respect them and their mother as she took time to develop a relationship with Sam's three older children.

When Alyssa, Sam's youngest daughter, was accepted into many fine colleges, Annie shared her opinion about which school she thought would best suit Alyssa, but then Annie stepped back. "Sam and I welcome each other's input, but it wasn't *my* decision. Along with Alyssa, her mother and Sam needed to come up with what was best."

As the relationship between two future spouses evolves, they need to define comfortable boundaries that they will not cross as they blend their families together. A couple needs to think carefully and realistically about expectations and ground rules. No matter how great the people coming together are, each family member must make major adjustments. The fact that children retain both their parents in the picture helps a new couple set roles and responsibilities for the stepparent.

After being married for three months, however, Annie admitted that she and Sam struggled with his role in their new household. "Before we married, we talked about our different parenting styles and Sam's responsibility toward my kids because he would be living with them on a day-to-day basis. I felt that there was enough of a match so that we wouldn't have a big problem. But the honeymoon period was over about a week after we were married. Jeremy had mouthed off to me in an obnoxious way. I have more tolerance than Sam, who jumped all over Jeremy. My son and I both just sat there with our mouths hanging open, and then Jeremy walked off."

At this point, Jeremy and Annie became allies. Both realized that Sam had crossed a boundary with which neither mother nor son felt safe or comfortable. It's healthy that Annie immediately discussed this encounter with her new husband. "I looked at Sam and said, 'I'm really unhappy about the way you talked to Jeremy, about how you responded. My kids aren't used to getting yelled at like that.'

"Sam said, 'Well, he shouldn't be talking to you like that.' He was absolutely right. We both agreed on this, but I had to reiterate that I don't discipline as he does, and he needed to respect how I parent my kids. Before we married, I don't think we talked enough about what the day-to-day stuff was going to be like. We didn't put it on the table consciously and verbally, so that's what we're trying to work out now."

Rules by which a stepparent governs his stepchildren are, as Annie said, "murky and gray." Parent, stepparent, and children need to sit together and detail specific responsibilities for everyone in order to maintain a well-functioning household. If Aaron comes home from school with a friend and they drag out half the things in the refrigerator to make a big sandwich, they also must clean up their mess. If the kitchen is left in shambles, Sam must and should discipline them without screaming or yelling. If Jeremy leaves his dirty clothes in the corner of the bathroom after his shower, Sam has the right and should inform Jeremy that dirty clothes belong in the hamper. Families need household rules in order to avoid chaos and disorder. Every family member should be clear about these rules and know that Annie and Sam will both take responsibility to see that they are honored.

Sam also had to resolve issues with Aaron being Annie's "baby." The family suffered through an ugly divorce. Aaron slept with Annie a lot during this time and since. Her bed became a "family bed." When Annie and Sam decided to marry, they gradually weaned Aaron from their bedroom. First he slept in a sleeping bag on their bedroom floor. Then he got used to sleeping in his own room right across the hall. Finally Annie and Sam built him a new bedroom downstairs so that they would gain their privacy upstairs.

After they were married, Sam began locking their bedroom door so that Aaron wouldn't disturb them. Annie never locked the door and said that she always had to be available to Aaron. He needed the security of knowing that he could come to his mom during the night if he was having any problem. The solution wasn't to unlock the door, which is now the case, but to create one in which Aaron could feel safe in his own space.

"Aaron now has the coolest room in the house. We got him new posters, and Sam bought him a new desk and armoire, gifts to help keep Aaron happy in his room. He still sleeps with his tennis racket because his room is next to the garage and that's scary for him. A couple of nights after I've tucked him in, I've fallen asleep in his bed and Sam has come to retrieve me. Sam's fine about this and doesn't say, 'Don't you think Aaron is too old for you to be doing this?' "

As they rearranged the house to accommodate their blended family, Annie and Sam wanted to make sure that Sam's kids also felt welcomed in the home, so they gave his two daughters Aaron's old room. The girls told Annie what colors they wanted their room painted, and they picked out new bedspreads to make the room their own. Annie and Sam placed a comfortable pullout couch in the TV room for Sam's son, Greg.

Annie and Sam also needed to figure out Sam's financial role within the new family. Before they married, they discussed finances at length and drew up a prenuptial agreement. Because Sam owned a home as well, it was clear to them that they would each keep their own assets and support their own children separately. Annie received child support from the boys' father, so there was no reason for Sam to contribute anything financially to her kids, other than what he chose to give them. To keep their joint household running, Sam and Annie decided that he would give a bit less than she because he had to maintain another home.

It was also important for the newlyweds to include all their youngsters in their marriage and wedding plans. They postponed getting married until Alyssa, Sam's youngest, who was living with him, went off to college in the fall. Annie and Sam didn't want to disrupt Alyssa and Sam's last summer together by blending an entire family just when Alyssa had to make a major transition in her life. During their wedding ceremony, Annie and Sam welcomed all the children into the family by presenting each with a rose. They honored the children's contribution to the relationship.

Although this was one of the happiest moments in Annie's life, she reflected on the loss she faced with her decision to remarry. "A remarriage is a nail in the coffin for every family member. Up until the day Sam and I got married, my kids and their father had hopes that we would reconcile. My ex verbalized this with our kids, which reinforced their fantasy that we would get together again. For me, the loss of my family with my first husband is and always will be a tragedy. Remarriage is a last letting go—not that I ever wanted to reunite with my ex. I told my kids, 'I know this is really sad, and it makes me sad that your father and I couldn't make it work out. But we couldn't. It's important for us all to be happy. When I'm happy, you're happy and having fun.' "

When children are involved, divorce is a grief that keeps giving. I can't stress this fact enough. You will have a relationship with the other parent of your kids until they reach adulthood. Even then, you might have to deal with their other parent when your children come to you for help. For this reason, your divorce and relationship with your ex-spouse has a meaningful impact on your second marriage and blended family. Annie feels that family counselors, as well as divorced "citizens," don't think about this. "We just think, 'Get me out of this nightmare marriage, and then I'll be done with him.' "

You begin a different relationship with an ex-spouse by changing streets, but the road is still ahead and now includes your new spouse as well. Annie and Sam step back, support one another, and allow each other to deal with ex-spouses as each sees fit. "Sam is able to contain himself around some of my ex-husband's extraordinary behavior. He would deal with him in a different way, but he lets me do my thing, which is good for our relationship."

In terms of Sam being a stepparent, Annie feels that he is still groping in the dark as he tries to relate to her boys. After three months of marriage, she hasn't felt a moment in which Sam clicks naturally with the boys or cares deeply for them. "This hasn't really happened yet. I think Sam is trying to decide how much he wants to be involved and attached. It has to happen to a certain extent, but if it doesn't happen to the level that I want, that would be okay because my kids have their dad and other caring people around them. Although I've told Sam that I wish that he and my kids were closer, that I wish he would spend more time with them and get to know them better, he's such a guy about it and says, 'Well, I've asked them to help me fix the window or put the garbage in the back of the truck.' I then tell him that I'm talking about relationships, not tasks, but to Sam, you form a relationship by doing stuff together."

One day, Aaron commented to Annie: "You know, Sam doesn't talk a lot about his feelings, does he?" Annie said, "Well, he does sometimes, but it's with me." Aaron replied, "Jeremy doesn't talk much about his feelings either," to which Annie gave a salient explanation that reflects how youngsters change through successive developmental stages. "Jeremy has feelings too but as guys get older, sometimes they don't think it's okay to talk about feelings." Aaron responded: "Well, I always want to talk about my feelings," and Annie told him that he could always talk with her.

Jeremy and Aaron call Sam "Mr. Warm and Fuzzy" as a joke. They've complained that he's too tough and lays down too many rules. On the one hand, Annie has encouraged them to talk with Sam about this, and she also shares their feelings with him. On the other, when Sam complains about the boys not listening to him, she says, "Bring it up with them. Please don't place me in the middle."

At this time in their lives, Annie has suggested that the family seek counseling. She and the boys have benefited from counseling through her divorce, and Sam also has had therapy for many years. They are seeing a family therapist whom the boys know and feel comfortable with. No matter how smooth things are going, I advise all new families to seek counseling as their lives begin together. With this preventive, rather than interventive, therapy, everyone can spill out differences while someone trained to provide a constructive framework of communication helps the family solve immediate and future problems as they adjust, change, and grow together on a daily basis.

New families also must realize that humans don't develop common ground or work through differences over one wonderful celebration or dinner, but each daily event, small or large, helps relationships deepen. Annie and Sam gathered all the children for their first Thanksgiving together. "I have a tradition that everyone says what they are thankful for. I began at the table and said that I was thankful for my new family and for having this opportunity to be together. I loved them all and felt really blessed. The kids then each said something about our new family, and Sam spoke last and was grateful to have us all with him. It was a Norman Rockwell painting!"

Aaron yearned for a complete family unit because he was so young when Annie divorced and never had the chance to feel a part of one, as Jeremy had. A week or so after Thanksgiving, Aaron told Annie, "I think Sam is starting to like me a whole lot. We watched a whole movie together."

To reinforce the relationship her kids would like to have with Sam, Annie shares her mother-son conversations with her husband. "I tell Sam that it doesn't take much. My kids don't need much. Jeremy wants Sam to go out in the woods and shoot trees [it's called paintball], which Sam would love. One day soon, I hope he will do this with Jeremy, not as a coach or as a parent but as a spouse who cares about my boys because I care about them."

Annie doesn't place any expectations on her family for the future. "We are evolving, and there are no signposts that we have to reach." This positive outlook enhances a family's ability to grow closer according to each member's timetable, without confining anyone to an artificial framework. Annie's wisdom stems from the most essential fact that all parents should remember each day: "It's easy when you're in love to forget about the kids. After you've been through a miserable time, you think, 'Finally it's my turn. I have some happiness.' But I think that families really need to pay attention to kids and kids' feelings. Kids don't ask for remarriage, so it's important to appreciate and have compassion for what they go through. My kids come first."

THE NEW FLANNIGAN FAMILY

Two seemingly ordinary parents in their midthirties committed suicide within ten months of each other, leaving their three young girls orphaned. Their paternal grandmother fabricated untrue stories about the cause of both deaths. In his will, their dad requested that his brother's wife, Helen Flannigan, raise his girls if something happened to him. Helen and her husband, Joe, had two boys of their own. Being a strong, pragmatic, and tolerant forty-something woman, Helen bore the brunt of bringing the new Flannigan family together.

Craig was Helen and Joe's oldest son. When his cousins came to live with the Flannigans, he was fourteen, handsome, athletic, and popular in school. Following his father's model, Craig displayed a macho and sarcastic wit. He didn't share his feelings readily and hung out with his peers, staying out of the house as much as possible.

Alan, who was displaced as the youngest in the family, was smart and creative. He was a worrier, mature beyond his twelve years and close to his mom. His cousins moving in with the family wreaked havoc on his life, changing Alan overnight. He fought against one conflicting feeling after another.

Sophie, quiet, pretty, and shy, was eight when she went to live with the Flannigans. Being displaced as the oldest in the family, she wasn't accommodating or sympathetic to boys who dominated her in age, stature, and know-how. She became moody and argumentative with her sisters and cousins.

Janet, who was seven, manifested the greatest difficulty in adjusting to her new family. Before her dad had left on his last business trip, she had clung to him and agonized about being afraid to let him go. She constantly had guarded her dad after her mom died, not ever wanting to leave him. Janet wouldn't even spend a weekend with her grandparents or friends. Within weeks of moving in with the Flannigans, Janet began a ritualistic behavior of pacing and washing her hands repeatedly. She insisted that Helen read to her every evening and leave the bedroom light on throughout the night. This obsessive-compulsive behavior stemmed from issues of insecurity and abandonment, neither being unusual for a girl of Janet's age who had lost both parents within a year.

Four-year-old Alicia remained the baby of the family, receiving lots of attention from everyone who knew her. She needed a mother, so she adjusted quickly to Helen's loving care.

The new family came together in the modest home that Helen and Joe had bought many years before to suit themselves and their two boys. This couple slept on a pullout sofa in their finished cellar so that the girls could be more comfortable together in a spacious bedroom of their own.

An Acute Crisis: Alan's Conflict and Dilemma

After the girls' mother committed suicide, Helen read an article in the newspaper about the Good Grief Program. She contemplated whether to seek advice then because she didn't know what to expect from her nieces or how to help them through their grief. "I had boys and didn't know anything about girls. I needed tips. I was afraid to be in the same room with them. They didn't live very near us, and I wasn't that close to them. How was I going to help them and my brother-in-law?" Her brother-in-law's anger flared when she told him that she wanted to talk with a bereavement counselor, so in the end Helen didn't contact me.

Immediately after her nieces moved into the Flannigan household, however, Alan came apart at the seams, his cheerful personality changing dramatically. One evening he became so distraught that he was unable to sleep or attend school the next morning. He cried all day long. Helen finally prevailed upon him to talk about his obvious misery. Alan implied that he couldn't stop thinking about a situation from many years ago. When he was eight, he had played "princess" with another girl cousin, who was six at the time, and had kissed her. He said that nothing else had occurred, yet he felt that he had taken advantage of her.

An innocent kiss haunted a twelve-year-old boy because it had awakened his sexuality and aggravated his fears about becoming attracted to three cousins, whom he also hated for displacing his position in the family and taking his mother's attention from him.

IIe told Helen, "I want to talk with someone who can help me feel better." The guilt and anger that flooded Alan's waking and sleeping moments and his cry for help finally brought Helen to my office.

Due to his mom's persistence in encouraging her son to communicate, Alan's conflicted and unmentionable feelings bubbled to the surface. The first thing that he said unequivocally was "They took my family away." Alan was a thoughtful child who felt very badly for his cousins, despite the moments when he wanted to kill them. If he wanted to feel better, he needed to express his thoughts and feelings in our sessions no matter how horrible they seemed. After six weeks of counseling, he learned to articulate (1) his guilt about hating the girls' intrusion, (2) his ambivalence about wanting them to leave, (3) his fear of being sexually attracted to them, and (4) his jealousy over the time his mom spent with them. Slowly Alan understood that these feelings were *normal*. He also realized that he had found a safe place to verbalize them, so they no longer dominated his life at home and in school.

Helen needed to devote some undivided attention to Alan each day. She and Alan decided to make dates apart from the rest of the family. Once a week, they either went to a movie or shopped at his favorite mall. She made a point of attending his hockey practices whenever she could. I advised her to talk with Alan's teachers, who proved understanding about the work he had to make up.

Alan overcame his guilt about his sexual thoughts without difficulty, but he tended to hold his anger in, not only because he empathized with his cousins but also because he feared that he would explode or lose control of himself. As the girls grew more a part of the family and Alan got to know them, he became more comfortable with his anger and understood it. He saw that his mother loved him as much as ever and that his cousins weren't a threat to his wellbeing. When he skirmished with them, Alan's anger proved nothing more unusual than what every sibling exhibits.

Joe and Craig didn't want or feel that they needed counseling. Unfortunately, Joe thought that Alan's feelings were nonsense, and he didn't give his son or his wife much emotional support or everyday assistance.

A Family in Transition: Bereavement Overload

"Deep down inside, none of us, including myself, wanted to take the girls in," Helen admitted. "We were hostile and angry about what had happened and what we had been stuck with. Yet, when my husband, my boys, and I talked about what we should do, we never talked about *not* taking the girls. After the girls got settled in with us, we were wrought with too many problems, but each of us was afraid to say we weren't going to do this. Joe and the boys carried on endlessly and dumped their feelings on me, but they never said no."

Joe retreated to the cellar and put on a "bad guy" act with the girls. He would tell the girls, "If you girls do this one more time, you're out of here. Shape up or ship out." After a while, his abrasive demeanor softened somewhat. Helen remarked: "When I was working evenings, sometimes Joe would give them money—a couple of dollars—to spend on themselves. The girls would tell me, but he wouldn't. And then they'd say to me, 'But we don't like it when you aren't here to help us.' "

Fourteen-year-old Craig stayed away from home as much as possible, finding it too difficult to cope with the girls. Almost every day, Craig showed up before dinner and told Helen, "Your girls aren't going to live much longer if you keep this up." He was referring to their occupation of the couch, on which they lounged. Craig was never very tolerant of the girls, nor did he become a part of his new family. He stood off by himself, never getting into "the meat of things."

After his acute crisis dissipated, Alan would talk with the girls sometimes and help them with their homework. In the end, he accepted and adjusted, better than Craig, to his cousins living with the family.

Sophie, who turned nine shortly after her dad died, was the least communicative of the girls. She never cried or talked about her mom or dad, but she wore toughness and anger on her shirtsleeve. She harassed Janet and Alicia constantly, always trying to tell them what to do.

Seven-year-old Janet displayed the most grief and adjustment problems. She refused to sleep unless Helen lay with her and read to her. One day, when Janet knew that Helen was coming to see me, she pleaded with her aunt, "Oh, promise me you'll never make me go talk to somebody, Helen." Helen asked why. "My mother made me do that once and it was terrible." It was actually Janet's paternal grandmother, not her mother, who had asked the school psychologist to talk with Janet after her mother had died.

Janet's bedtime rituals, which included several trips to the bathroom to wash her hands, needed to be watched but posed no concern unless persistent. Because she had so much to adjust to so quickly, she attempted to manage her anxiety and fear of abandonment with this obsessive ritual. To help her fall asleep, I suggested that Helen lie with Janet every evening as long as her niece needed the extra closeness and reassurance. After a while, Janet's anxiety and fears subsided along with her obsessive-compulsive behavior.

Alicia was a delight to the family and never gave any problems. Being four, she adjusted to Helen, who attended her primary needs with care and affection. Even as Alicia grew and began kindergarten, she was the family favorite.

During the first year after the girls moved in, I suggested that Helen and Joe have dinner alone once a week. Along with their sons, these parents also needed to do a few things together without the girls. Before the girls had moved in, Helen and Joe watched TV with the boys just about every evening. If the girls could spend at least one weekend a month with their grandparents, Helen, Joe, and the boys could plan an enjoyable weekend among themselves. They decided to take a four-day cruise about six months after the girls came to live with them. In the end, however, the trip was bittersweet because their "old family feeling" was so short-lived.

Despite the pain and hardships, Helen continued to listen to every family member's grief day in and day out. Eventually, her determination to keep her new family together "began to sink in to Joe, Craig, and Alan."

Adapting a Blended Family Perspective and Survival Strategy

Helen gave up much of her life to accept her new motherhood and peacemaker role. She sacrificed a job, which had provided her spending money, autonomy, and social life, to care for young girls who were, as she said, "aliens to me. I didn't know anything about taking care of girls." In church, she found strength and often reflected on the hymn "Is It Me, Lord?" She told Joe, "We have a chance to make a difference in others' lives. It really isn't all that much sweat off our backs when you think about it. This is an opportunity for us." After three years, he relented and said, "Yeah, you're right, Mother Teresa," and then Joe would joke with his friends, "I had a great life until Mother Teresa decided that she was going to bring up all those kids."

Sophie, Janet, and Alicia gradually learned to develop a sense of trust in their new family and saw that neither Joe nor Helen would abandon them. Joe's hostile threats were benign. Letters that the girls wrote bear this out. The Catholic school that they attended had all students write a letter of appreciation to their parents. Sophie wrote a little note to "Dear Mom and Dad" on a scrap piece of paper. She had never called Helen or Joe "Mom" or "Dad" before. In fact, from the time they moved in with the family, all three girls called them "Helen" and "Joe." Helen wrote Sophie a "mushy letter back, telling her how much I loved her and that her class was great, her teacher was great, and the school newspaper was great. You're also a great writer, Sophie."

Janet wrote to "Dear Helen and Joe," but told Helen that "you are the best mom I've ever had." She drew a picture of Helen, Joe, and herself together. On Joe's shoulder was a little emblem that said "coach." He was a hockey coach, and many people called him "Coach." Alicia, who was in first grade, wrote a long, mushy letter only to Helen.

Craig, who was a senior, prepared to leave for college the following year and was looking forward to being on his own. He never embraced a close relationship with his cousins. To be away from home finally would release him from a family unit he never wanted nor came to accept. Alan, who was a sophomore, had learned to enjoy and appreciate having the girls as a part of his family, despite their squabbles, their wanting to have friends sleep over on the weekends, and their silly girl talk.

What Does the Future Hold for These Sisters?

After people have met Sophie, Janet, and Alicia and learned of their parents' suicides, they have commented to Helen, "Wow, you'd never think that anything is wrong. You'd never guess what they went through. They act like nothing has happened, that everybody's life is like theirs."

Although their grandmother told them that their mom died from a brain hemorrhage and their father from an auto accident, Sophie and Janet probably know of their parents' suicides because their teachers, neighbors, and friends know. The fact that neither girl has talked about the deaths nor asked obvious questions suggests that they have buried this information and learned to survive it through Helen's love and care. Someday, Sophie and Janet, as well as Alicia, will need to sort out their feelings, particularly about why their parents "orphaned" them and why their grandmother lied to them.

As the transitional person who rescued them and became their safety net, Helen will continue to be a pivotal support for all three girls. So far, she has chosen not to encourage them to share their unmentionable feelings about parents who have been the direct agents of the girls' enormous distress and sadness. Helen felt that they didn't need to face the pain of suicide or the lies about what happened on top of adjusting to a new family. When the time is right, Helen will be the one caring adult to whom each girl can go to express her feelings because they trust Helen and know that she won't let their world fall apart.

Hopefully each girl, in her unique way, will eventually look on their mom as a person who suffered with untreated depression. They will have to forgive their dad, who was too consumed by loss to know how to help his girls or himself. In the meantime, the Flannigans have given three sisters a sense of family and security. Very few families could have taken on this task and come out on top.

BLENDING TIME, ENERGY, AND CARE

The losses that youngsters suffer in the blending of families depend on the temperament and age of each child. Any change, even one beneficial in many aspects, encroaches on the security that you have built with them. Sharing a parent and adjusting to new family members are dynamic forces that can undermine a child's comfort zone as well as his ability to learn, play, and communicate.

If parents place the welfare of children before their own, as Annie and Helen have done, youngsters will survive any threat to their self-esteem and unique value within the family. Letting them know that they come first assures kids of your unconditional love and openness as they struggle to build relationships with new family members and accept different household rules and discipline. This message also ensures their financial, psychological, and spiritual well-being, even when the family has to compromise its lifestyle and living situation for the good of all members.

Continuous effort, time, and family counseling help to channel effective communication and listening skills as a couple endeavors to foster an authentic family constellation and close bonds with their children and stepchildren.

16

Mourning the Brother
I Once Had:
Chronic Losses

My disabled brother, Frank, is fifty-two and lives with my eighty-two-year-old mother. As I relate in chapter 1, my brother's life, as well as my family's, was altered forever following his first seizure at the age of twelve. His seizure disorder, as I call it now, wreaked havoc on his physical, mental, and emotional development. No one, not even Frank or his neurologists, was prepared for the painful deterioration that he would suffer. I felt that my family was even more isolated from those who had experienced a death or an infant born with a specific anomaly because we didn't have a name for Frank's illness nor did we know anyone like him.

Being a child, I didn't reflect on *my* anger, sadness, and fear about Frankie, as we called him then, and his disorder. How could my parents know about my feelings if I didn't acknowledge or voice them? When I was a young adolescent, my worst nightmare was his scary and unpredictable seizures. My mother seemed nervous all the time, especially if my brother was having a "shaky" day or eating out at a restaurant. Every evening when the family watched TV together, I secretly battled with my nerves. One eye would always be on Frankie, watching his tremors, waiting for one to escalate into a seizure, which did occur from time to time.

Sometimes, I couldn't stand my anxiety and would leave the room, never revealing my fears.

Now, with a mixture of intense feelings, I look back on my childhood relationship with my brother. As a bereavement specialist and parent, I understand how each member of my family tried to cope with a bewildering series of events that redefined Frank's future—and ours. Forty years ago, without understanding or psychological support from professionals, my parents did their best to care for their disabled son and two daughters by creating a "new normal," one day at a time. They were remarkable for their courage, faith, and love.

Not long ago, my daughter Melissa reminded me that I don't have nearly as rich a relationship with Frank as she has. Although I'm devoted to my brother and care for him when my mother is sick or away, Melissa chided me because I sometimes lose patience and rarely engage in conversation or laughter with him. I miss the fun that my daughter shares with her uncle Frank. Like Paula, my younger sister, Melissa knows Frank only as disabled, but I knew him as a robust boy who had everything going in life. When he had his first seizure on that fateful hiking trip with the Boy Scouts, I lost my big brother and became his caregiver and advocate. I'm proud that I found a marvelous volunteer position for him as a transport attendant at a local nursing home. He has worked there for nearly nine years and is great at his job. On his sixth anniversary, the staff and residents of the home celebrated and honored Frank as "volunteer of the year," giving him a Red Sox baseball cap. As I congratulated him and sounded in perfect control over the telephone, tears streamed down my face.

Unraveling the tight weave of feelings about my brother and the meaning of my life as his sister is arduous work and a continuous process. With teenage daughters ready to leave the nest, I feel isolated from my contemporaries as I face middle age and embrace the complicated question of how my sister and I together will care for Frank after my mother dies. Understanding my own childhood loss has helped me address this question openly and honestly.

Sometimes it's painful to watch my brother stammer or spill catsup as he tries to eat a Whopper. When I get a lump in my throat and a hollow feeling in my heart, I now know the nature of this pain. It's called *grief*. Bereaved youngsters with siblings or parents who have cognitive and/or physical disabilities have been my best teachers and greatest inspiration. Many kids in this situation don't realize the tremendous loss they endure throughout their childhood until they suffer a crisis, which ushers their feelings to the forefront, or until they face the loss in adulthood, as I have done. Some children live without ever confronting this nonovert but insidious loss.

Changes in the mental, physical, and developmental status of the disabled person influence his and his family's ability to mourn and remourn this chronic loss. No matter the specific family circumstance, these changes are ongoing and four issues usually come into play for normal children:

1. They sustain stresses from responsibilities of family life that their parent's or sibling's disability demands.

2. They encounter new adjustments as their parent's or sibling's health changes or declines.

3. They hide their anger, sadness, and other feelings from themselves and their parents so as not to upset the family. Instead, they appear to manage their lives well by "adultifying" their behavior.

4. They perceive themselves as different from their peers.

Parents don't necessarily understand that their healthy kids have suffered a loss. If these youngsters don't acknowledge and express their pain at some point in their development, they will remain forgotten mourners. It's our job to recognize that their seemingly well-adjusted routine of living with a disabled family member only masks their hidden or unacknowledged grief.

RICK'S STORY: MOM'S A LOT MORE UNDERSTANDING OF LUKE

Right after Luke's birth, Barbara's obstetrician's eyes filled with tears as he told her that her newborn had Down's syndrome. Barbara became involved in an early intervention program for kids with similar disabilities and joined a family support group in a neighboring town. "I can't stress how helpful it was to have a group of people with whom I could be totally honest. We could support each other's children as well as ourselves. The grieving is the hardest for the first few years. It comes at your child's different developmental stages also. You never know when something can trigger your tears. Only recently I've been able to attend the Special Olympics Games without crying."

Two and a half years after Luke was born, Barbara gave birth to a second child. "I was thrilled that Rick wasn't born with any disability. I tried to do my best with both children. In retrospect, with all the programs that Luke was involved in, I became wound up with his progress. I had milestones and goals for him all the time and focused a great deal of attention on Luke. I believe I should have had a better balance. I regret that Rick didn't get as much attention as he deserved from me, especially during the early years of his life."

Rick actually made his mom aware of her inattention to his needs. When he was four, she would drive both boys ten miles twice a day so that Luke could participate in a summer program for challenged kids. Along the way, they would sing, attempting to make the trip fun. One day during this drive, Rick said to Barbara, "Mom, I'm not going with you anymore."

Although Barbara heard her younger son's distress, Luke's special needs dominated if he were going to grow into the best person possible. She chose to focus on her younger son's bright and outstanding qualities, instead of on his distress, because these qualities buoyed family life and helped Luke. She was proud that Rick, even as a preschooler, was so perceptive of his disabled older brother. "Rick was tuned in to Luke. He understood that Luke was struggling to learn things that Rick took for granted. There was quite a difference in the boys' physical skills. It was wonderful to see Rick helping Luke. He actually taught Luke how to swing by himself. I tried and tried, but it was little Rick who taught Luke how to pump himself on the swing."

As Rick grew older, he learned to fend for himself and do things independently from Luke. Barbara compared her sons' relationship in high school: "Luke has developed his own friends and feels so good about himself. Rick doesn't belong to the health club [where Luke swims with other disabled children], nor does he do as much with Luke as he used to when they were little. As Rick got older, I think he perceived Luke as a nonperson. As a teenager, Rick has been protective of himself. That has hurt me, but it's probably what he has needed to survive, to get through adolescence, to live with a disabled brother, and to live in a single-parent household."

Rick was five when his parents divorced, leaving Barbara with the primary care of both boys. I talked with seventeen-year-old Rick right before his high school graduation. Just as I had done at his age, Rick seemed to shrug off his "second place" feelings. "I don't think Mom treats Luke so much differently from me, but she definitely gives him a lot more attention. She's a lot more understanding of him sometimes, but it's not like I'm around the house that much now anyway—only for dinner. Life would be different if he was normal. You spend a lot of time watching, driving, and being with my brother, even if you don't have to do anything for him. It takes up your time."

In a roundabout way, Rick said that Luke came first and received special treatment. He then relegated his own feelings as unimportant, unless they concerned Luke's well-being, and saw his life as different from his peers because of Luke. "If things get to Luke—but they usually don't—I can be around him because I'm so used to him. He doesn't get me down. I used to fight with other kids over him. That's the only thing I ever fought about—when kids teased my brother. It's the only thing that made me angry. My friends like Luke now that he's older. They treat him more like a person because they are older and understand he's retarded. It makes me feel good that my friends accept him."

Although Rick was very willing to talk with me about Luke, he was reticent to discuss any untoward feelings unless I prodded. For example, I asked him if he ever felt any jealousy or sibling rivalry or if his mom had expectations or wishes about his behavior toward Luke. Rick replied: "Luke and I used to fight a lot, especially when he was bigger than me, but it was playful fight. We don't do this anymore since we're older. A couple of years ago, I used to get really mad and mouth off at him. Mom would say, 'Nobody treats your brother like that.' I would say, 'Well, nobody else has a brother like that.' "

I sensed from Rick that he always tried to suppress his anger and sadness about Luke being "special." When he didn't, his mother, without realizing it, might have made him feel guilty. As a result, seventeen-year-old Rick developed a one-way relationship with Luke. He hid his true feelings and did what he could to make Luke safe, happy, and comfortable, but he wasn't able to make Luke more a part of his own life. "We're never together except on the weekends. I'm home by seven in the evening, have dinner, and then do my homework, so I don't see Luke very much. On weekends, I'll pop into his room and sit with him sometimes. He's lethargic and doesn't want to do very much except watch TV. If I ask him if he wants to play football, he'll say no. I try talking with him, but most of the time I don't get anywhere."

Rick didn't know how to relate to Luke in the same way that I didn't know how to relate to my brother, Frankie. Neither Rick nor I learned how to express our loss over our brothers' disabilities. To the best of his ability, Rick tried to act mature so that he wouldn't upset Luke, his mom, or everyday life. When he reached adolescence, he did the normal thing of hanging out with his peers, with whom he could identify and share similar interests. With Barbara's help, Luke did the same with his own friends.

I asked Rick, whose conflicted feelings about caring for Luke were apparent, what the future held for him and his brother. Rick already had thought about this and discussed it with Barbara.

"I've told Mom that Luke is definitely not living with me. I've squared that away. I hope that my brother lives somewhere that he wants to live. I don't care where it is as long as he is happy there. I don't picture him living with me, but if he wanted to, I wouldn't mind if he became more independent. I think it would be pretty cool if he had an apartment off my home—he would be there but on his own. I just want him to be happy."

Rick's father was unable to cope with the stresses and responsibilities of Luke's disabilities. After he and Barbara divorced, he began drinking and was not able to parent Rick or Luke effectively. Barbara labored in "overdrive" to compensate for his absence and to raise Luke to be the best possible given his disabilities. He received the bulk of her attention, which is understandable. Rick, who appeared to need less care, got less. As a single mother, Barbara didn't have the energy or time to parent her sons equally. She had one hope for them as they entered young adulthood: "Lately, Rick is more attentive to Luke and is giving him the respect that Luke deserves. I hope that they will have a great relationship one day. I do know that Rick cares very much for Luke deep down. If anyone says anything against Luke, Rick is right there defending him."

TRACY'S STORY: I DIDN'T ADMIT THAT I COULDN'T HANDLE IT BY MYSELF

Twelve-year-old Tracy was in sixth grade when her mom came home from the doctor and told her that her breast tumor was cancerous. "I was alone with Mom and sat next to her. I asked her why she seemed okay about it. She said, 'Things like this happen, and I'm going to deal with it. And so are you. We are going to get through this.' I didn't feel as positive about it as my mother did. I believed 90 percent of what she said, but I also thought that the disease was stronger than she was. But I knew that once Mom said she was going to do something, she did it, so I thought she was real and honest with me. I just didn't know how to feel because I had never had anyone that close to me have something life-threatening."

Tracy didn't have past experience from which she could draw. As her mom, Lucy, went through chemotherapy and bone marrow transplantation, the secure life that Tracy knew and loved completely vanished. "Our house changed. We had to take care of it. Mom was a major part of running it. Her power had to be divided between my older sister, me, and my dad. I didn't get too much work because I was the youngest. Dad worked pretty hard and had a lot to do. My sister, Andrea, didn't like her responsibility. She was like the mom and felt that she shouldn't have to deal with that. I figured it out from her behavior. She would get mad if my dad would ask her something, like to take me somewhere."

Tracy couldn't talk with Andrea, who was five years older than she and seemed angry about everything and with everyone. Neither did Tracy want to burden her mom or dad with her feelings. She acted mature and did what she was asked without complaining. Although Lucy would check in with her daughter, wanting to know how Tracy was holding up, Tracy lied to her mother: "I would say, 'I'm okay.' I felt guilty to share my feelings. I didn't want to say anything to Mom. She already had too much to deal with, and I didn't want her to worry. I didn't want to let her know that I was angry at her for getting cancer, even though it wasn't her fault. But I would think, 'Why is she doing this to me? Why is she putting me through this?' " In Tracy's eyes, her mother had *abandoned her* to survive or die from a life-threatening illness, in essence, leaving her alone to keep her world from falling apart.

As time went on, Tracy regressed and withdrew into herself. "I went through a lot of emotional changes when Mom was sick. I would cry and get angry but not talk about it. I grew up a lot during those months. I was very scared. My aunt from Colorado came to take care of us when Mom was in the hospital the first time. She was a good listener. She told me to be positive and how to think. She told me what a good outlook was and that I should have it, but it was hard to have this deep down inside. I also had a couple of friends I could talk to about Mom. They weren't really that helpful because they didn't know much about what to expect either."

Both Tracy's mother and her aunt maintained positive outlooks about Lucy's prognosis. They showed their concern for Tracy's well-being, but they dismissed her "negative" feelings. As Tracy said, "Everything was positive. There were no other thoughts." Tracy interpreted this as "I'm not allowed to have or express *my true* thoughts."

Seeing her mother in the hospital was the most fearful experience Tracy endured. "Every single time Mom went into the hospital for a complication, I would worry. When she had the bone marrow transplant, she was in the hospital for nineteen days. That was the hardest part for me because Mom was the weakest then. She had practically no blood cells. I saw her a lot, probably two to three times a week. I didn't want to let her know I was upset and had to do everything I could not to cry in front of her. I cried when I left the hospital and was alone."

Lucy recovered from the transplant and showed no signs of cancer after a year. She regained her strength, the strength and vigor that Tracy had always seen in her mom and that made life secure for her. Although the family seemed to bounce back on an even keel, with Lucy organizing and maintaining the household, when Tracy began junior high, she became severely depressed, which prompted Lucy to seek my assistance. Tracy said, "I had feelings that I had never had before and didn't know what to do with them. I was very sad, and I'm sure some of it had to do with keeping a lot of my feelings from my mom. In junior high, kids were changing. It was a big change for me, and I don't like change. All the changes I had known were bad, especially when my mom got sick. I hated going into junior high. I didn't know any of the teachers or many of the kids. My two best friends kind of dropped me, and I didn't know why."

Lucy, whose determination helped her survive and recover from a life-threatening illness, understood that her daughter had a delayed grief reaction to the stresses and adjustments this illness precipitated. In addition, Tracy was going through puberty and experiencing many changes within herself and with her school life. Through the eyes of a budding adolescent who had just been through an insecure time with her mother's cancer, Tracy again faced a new situation in which she knew no one and lost her best friends. Her scary thoughts revolved around suicide.

I referred Tracy to a child psychiatrist with whom I worked. This psychiatrist prescribed an antidepressant for Tracy, and I continued to see her for a year. During this time, Tracy was gradually able to express her intensely painful feelings because she felt safe. Two years following therapy, she recalled, "I had you to talk to, to tell my feelings. That's how I got through this. I think that, to a certain degree, I needed to stop and look at what I had. I took everything for granted. I didn't realize how important my family was, how important we are to each other. What happened to Mom made us a lot stronger, not just my mom but the rest of the family. That was good for us. I learned a lot about myself, like I have to be positive, which was a problem for me before. I was always worrying a lot. My sister is away at college now, but we talk a lot. She listens and understands me. I can talk with her about my life now."

If in the future Tracy felt that she had no one with whom she could talk, what would she do? "If I needed help, I would come to you. The problem I had to admit to myself was that I couldn't handle the situation alone . . . and that's okay. I shouldn't have and don't need to handle it by myself."

Tracy has learned an insightful lesson that she can carry with her as she confronts other problems or crises. For example, even though Lucy seemed to have "beaten" the cancer, Tracy acknowledged and voiced one reason why she was still concerned about her mom's health. "I worry about her cancer returning because she's always on the go, always doing something. They say it usually won't return after five years, but that's no guarantee. I don't feel I need to talk about this worry now because it doesn't really bother me. Mom also knows what is going on with herself. If she thought that her cancer could come back again, she would tell me. So I don't feel as if I'm protecting her or hurting myself by not talking about it. If it bothers me, I would talk with her and my sister."

Another worry that Tracy no longer kept to herself was her concern about having the particular gene that caused her mother's breast cancer. "If your mother has breast cancer, you have a one-in-five chance of getting cancer, so that's a big chance. I have to be very careful. I don't drink caffeine because that causes lumps in the breasts. I have to be extremely careful of the sun because skin cancer is also in my family. If I have a problem with my period, I have to have it checked out right away because that could cause something as well. I might have a cyst on my ovary. I don't think it's related to breast cancer. It just causes me pain, which makes me nervous. Mom knows how much pain I'm in. She made an appointment with the doctor for me."

Tracy's abdominal pain subsided, and she discovered that she didn't have an ovarian cyst. She has grown into a thoughtful and deliberate adolescent, although it has been difficult for her to articulate her worries with her family and reach out for help from them. Lucy, a fighter, voiced only that she would recover from her life-threatening illness. Although she checked in with her daughter, she didn't give Tracy an opening to express her negative feelings—abandonment, fear, anger, and sadness—until she understood that her daughter's depression stemmed from delayed grief and fear of adolescent changes. The last time I spoke with Tracy, she was a sophomore who had adjusted well to school and made many new friends.

In working with me, she learned that her painful feelings got out of control—manifested in depression, anxiety, and poor adjustment in an unknown school environment—because she hid them. I encouraged both Tracy and Lucy to talk with each other often about Tracy's fears and worries, no matter how big or small, in order to bolster Tracy's self-image, self-confidence, and ability to admit that she doesn't need to go it alone at any age.

LILY'S STORY: I HAVE PANIC ATTACKS WORRYING ABOUT DAD

Lily was five when her father, Adam, went into the hospital and came back home with a walking cane. He had multiple sclerosis (MS), a progressive disease of the nervous system that affects brain and generalized body functions over a long period of time. Remissions, flare ups, and numerous symptoms characterize MS.

Nineteen-year-old Lily recalled that she, her dad, mom, and older sister talked together about his diagnosis. "My parents explained what it meant, but it was so long ago. I think they said that Dad had scars on his spine that went up into his brain. He didn't really need his cane when he first came home. His MS started bothering me when my friends would come over, because they were scared of him. He had a big Irish thorn cane. I was never afraid of the cane, but when I was in junior high, he used to embarrass me. He would stare at my friends. He would say embarrassing and inappropriate things too. He couldn't help it and didn't realize it. I knew that."

Lily never felt that her dad was in charge of her. "He was my father figure up until third grade. After that, he was never really a father to me. My mom was in charge." Neither was Adam a father to Lily's sister, Grace, nor was he a husband to her mother, Rose. "When my dad first got sick, my parents mostly fought. He couldn't work, so Mom would leave him to do two simple things, like call the plumber or take the chicken out of the freezer, but he couldn't get anything done. I hated to come home from school and hear my parents screaming at each other. Mom got much better after a while because they did marriage counseling."

Lily looked to Rose as the hub who kept family life going. Rose's anger, which she verbalized well, allowed no room for feelings of sadness in the home. Grace retreated into her own world and was unable to articulate her feelings. Lily appeared normal, happy, and protective of her dad. She was called "Little Miss Sunshine" because she always smiled.

"When my dad would get very sick, his temperature would go very low, and I would hate to leave the house. I'd go to [high] school, but I would never stay over at a friend's house. I would call home as soon as I got out of school. If he was okay, I would hang out with my friends until four. Then I would go home and do whatever he needed. I relieved his home-health aides. When he went through a bad phase, I had to feed him. Once, when we couldn't get his temperature up, we had to get an ambulance to take him to the hospital. He could have died, but he didn't. That's when I started having panic attacks. I couldn't breathe. I would get so anxious and shaky. I couldn't eat. I wouldn't go anywhere. I think it was a fear of my father dying and me not being there."

By being with her father, Lily felt safer. If she took time for herself and was not always there for him, she also felt guilty. Adam eventually went into a nursing home, this ordeal being the most heart-wrenching for Lily, who was seventeen at the time. "It happened suddenly. One day, we just couldn't care for him anymore. It wasn't safe for him at home, and it wasn't safe for the nurses taking care of him. He needed a protected place where he couldn't get hurt if something happened, like if he fell. His going into the nursing home was really hard. We didn't talk about it with him. Dad couldn't be in on the decision because he wasn't functioning well enough. It was almost like somebody died. I was just sad."

Within weeks of her father's move, Lily's mom created a new life for herself. "My mom, who had *no* life for years, started dating her boss intensely. He is much older. I was angry but told her it was all right. She deserved it, but it was such a shock, and I didn't expect such a serious relationship so fast. Mom didn't neglect me, but she didn't understand. She tried to understand me, but she didn't." Lily could intellectualize that her father needed to be in a safer place and her mom deserved a relationship, but the cost to herself was dear. Her dad, who had emotionally abandoned Lily to his illness years ago, was severed physically from her daily life while her mom left her bereft as well. Grace was away at college, leaving Lily with no one with whom she could share the brunt of the family's drastic and sudden changes.

I had counseled this family off and on for many years during periods of exacerbated stress around Adam's illness. At this time, I began to meet weekly with Lily. She was an overly anxious and panic-stricken seventeen-year-old girl responding to a profound loss. Rose could not understand why Lily could not accept her mom's new friend. She also didn't see how difficult it was for Lily to accept her father's move. "When Dad first went to the home, it was really hard for me to visit him, but I would phase out in classes thinking about him so much. I would go to see him once a week. He is physically there, but he isn't there in his mind. I grew less anxious about him than when he was at home because he was in a safer spot, but I feel I'll always be coping with something new with my dad."

Rose asked her daughter to "grow up" and accept her dating behavior. Lily correctly identified her mom as the agent of her new loss. "Dad couldn't help it but Mom could." Lily felt abandoned by the one person, her mother, whom she had thought would never change. Adjusting to college was next to impossible for Lily, who completed her freshman year on probation. The following summer, she was an angry and sullen eighteen-year-old who clung to home and did everything possible to punish her mom for dating and creating a new life with another man. When September came, Lily felt that she had no home and no other choice but to pack the car and leave for her sophomore year. In the middle of packing, she suffered a panic attack in which she literally could not move from a kitchen chair, necessitating that she withdraw from college.

Rose, who had developed a new life for two years and was adamant to move forward in her relationship with her friend, was shaken by Lily's severe attack. Finally, Rose was ready to listen to her daughter. No matter how unfair it appears to an adult parent in Rose's situation, she must put her children's feelings and grief *first*. Rose had consciously assumed that Lily and Grace would adjust to her new life in time. Of course, this was not the case.

Rose's way of handling her grief over her husband's disability was to hold back her sadness but verbalize her anger openly. After Lily's dramatic panic attack, Rose and Lily worked regularly with me. Rose was gradually able to empathize with Lily's feelings and learn to express years of repressed grief along with Lily. Together, they found a new vocabulary to discuss their feelings and points of view. Tears eventually flowed with ease as mother and daughter talked about their sadness, disappointments, and fears about the future. Rose came to realize that Lily, and Grace also, needed her to slow down, spend more time with them, and form a family constellation on their own, which they did for many months, before bringing a new person into their lives.

Presently, the three of them are cleaning out their home of twenty years and packing their belongings. The house is for sale, and they will move with Rose's friend across town into a lovely home that they all felt was right for them, one complete with a pool for Lily. Lily also found a job as a receptionist for a stock brokerage firm, was promoted to sales assistant, and is taking one course at a time at a local community college. Being sensitive and conscientious, Lily still worries about her dad and his relationship with her mom. She also worries about her mother's new life and future with a man twenty years her senior. Will Rose's friend and possible future husband die soon and leave the girls alone once again? Will the family cycle repeat itself?

I explained to Lily that Rose made a conscious decision to engage in a relationship with a man who cared deeply about her, Lily, and Grace. The cycle might very well come around again; however, Lily has developed more mature skills to recognize her feelings and articulate them, which bodes well for her future ability to deal with any life change. And, as she said, "I have my father's sense of humor and optimism and my mother's strength. My friends get anxious about everyday things that seem stupid to me. Overall, I don't think I would have been as strong and sensitive about a lot of things if my father didn't have MS."

ADVICE FROM PARENTS AND KIDS

Children who have grown up with a mentally or physically disabled parent or sibling have matured beyond their years. Like myself, they see the upsides and the downsides of what they have gained and lost.

From what she has learned, Tracy had the following advice for her peers, especially for boys: "Boys tend to keep their feelings in, like I did. It's much better if you talk about them with somebody. Just talking helps a lot." Lily advised parents "to move slowly and talk more with their kids." Rick's mom, Barbara, recommended that parents like herself "consider their other children and their disabled child as part of a whole. Don't simply focus on the disabled child. Make room for the other kids. Couples should consider themselves and their relationships as husbands and wives and as mothers and fathers."

Many children in the same boat with Rick, Tracy, and Lily are forgotten mourners because their parents are unable to give them permission to feel and then express their range of feelings. My advice: Get the ongoing support that you need so that you can (1) *make room* for *all* your kids, (2) *listen* to them, (3) *put* their needs *first,* and then (4) *work* steadfastly and conscientiously over the long haul to bring your family's needs *together.*

17

IF IT'S UNMENTIONABLE, IT'S UNMANAGEABLE: Everyday Losses

IN *The Wind in the Willows,* when a flock of swallows prepares to migrate south for the winter, they make plans and arrange things. They talk about their voyage so that all the birds in the flock will know what route they're flying, where they'll stop, and how they will forage en route in order to arrive safely at their winter home. The first swallow tells Mr. Rat that talking about the move is "half the fun." "Fun?" said the Rat, "Now that's just what I don't understand. If you've got to leave this pleasant place, and your friends who will miss you, and your snug little homes that you've just settled into, why, when the hour strikes I've no doubt you'll go bravely, and face all the trouble and discomfort and change and newness, and make believe that you're not very unhappy. But to want to talk about it, or even think about it, till you really need—" The second swallow interrupts Mr. Rat to make his point about leaving a secure summer nest.

Every September, like migrant birds, thousands of children face the awesome task of making a giant move. Some step onto the big yellow bus for the first day of kindergarten, whereas others transition to middle or high school. These eventful changes, while loaded with adventure and delight at first glance, define growth in a child's life. For most kids, they also hold emotional losses that make Mr. Rat wonder *why anyone would ever want to think or talk about such changes*.

During the normal course of development, youngsters experience several other life events encompassing losses that they need to *grieve*. These include:

- Becoming a sibling when parents bring home a baby sister or brother

- Moving to a different part of the country

- Not making the team

- Not getting into the college of choice

- Breaking up with a boy- or girlfriend

- Adjusting to future realities and vocational choices ("I'm never going to be a ballerina; I'm not tall enough.")

Frequently, like Mr. Rat, adults don't see the value of acknowledging or talking about these losses and fears of the unknown, in addition to the possible fun they will hold. How often have you heard a caring but misguided parent say to her son or daughter:

- "You'll love the baby. Someday, you'll have so much fun together!"

- "Of course you'll love our new house. You'll see!"

- "You were better than the other kids. The coach just showed favoritism. Besides, the Eagles aren't such a great team anyway!"

- "Look on the bright side. You'll be closer to home!"

- "What's the fuss about? You'll go through this many times before you're grown up. It's just part of life!"

- "Your sister is short too, but that never bothered her!"

In an effort to mitigate or deny any hint of pain with these comments, parents distance themselves from their kids as they rationalize, distort, distract, or confuse the issues, leading youngsters to think that feelings of sadness, anger, longing, fear, and jealously are outlawed.

I believe that everyday developmental losses, if acknowledged, immunize children against running from normal, painful responses to future losses, both great and small. How do parents and other caring adults face inevitable childhood losses with their kids? Keep these three strategies in mind:

1. Nourish and increase the trust between you and your child by speaking truthfully about the specific life event. Don't sugarcoat it or deny the facts at issue.

2. Empathize with your child by listening to his concerns without judgment.

3. Emphasize your child's growth by calling attention to particular skills he has learned, which will equip him to face the new and daunting situation. Identify similar past experiences in which he ultimately felt powerful.

The following story illustrates the effectiveness of these strategies.

MOLLY'S STORY: I JUST WON'T GO

Jeremy and Maggie would have been absolutely thrilled with the news of his promotion, except that it required uprooting their fifteen-year-old daughter, Molly, from Lincoln High in Boston in the middle of her sophomore year. Together, both parents had carefully considered Jeremy's career move. Ultimately, it meant a better lifestyle, with more family time together, greater opportunities for Jeremy to move up in the company, and a chance for Maggie to live near her aging parents in Indianapolis.

Molly wouldn't even entertain the idea of a potential move while she was in high school. "I just won't go. I'll live with Shelley and her family until I graduate." After saying this, she refused to talk further about the move.

When she was twelve, Molly had experienced a difficult transition to middle school. Having been born with a cleft palate that required several surgical repairs, Molly was self-conscious of a slight scar on her upper lip, particularly when she reached puberty, despite the fact that no one could really notice the scar. Being shy, she had a hard time making friends at the middle school and was slow to warm up to changing classes and teachers. Finally, Molly blossomed into a solid B-plus student who liked school and had many friends, especially in her church youth group. Her tennis acumen had distinguished her in the spring of her freshmen year after she earned a place as third singles on the varsity tennis team. With this successful season, she looked forward to spring tennis and competition in her sophomore year.

On the evening that Jeremy accepted the promotion, he and Maggie approached Molly after dinner. They tolerated and accepted her angry outburst: "I'm just not going. You can't make me." Nothing more was said that evening.

Two days later, Maggie asked Molly to go out to breakfast with her. Reluctantly, Molly agreed. Over breakfast, Maggie said that she understood Molly's feelings. She, too, had ambivalent emotions about leaving their home, neighborhood, friends, and church. She recognized that it was even harder for her daughter, who was so happy, successful, and involved with school. But, for many reasons with which Molly might not agree, she and Jeremy saw the move as benefiting the family, which was the most important consideration in their decision-making process.

Molly's initial reply, "But it's not fair to me," provoked a heartfelt conversation between this mother and daughter.

MAGGIE: *I know you think it's not fair, and I hear how angry you are. I know how much you value your friends on the team and at school and church.*

MOLLY: *I'll never make new friends in Indiana. I don't know anybody. Dorks probably live there.*

MAGGIE: *We're going to fly out next weekend to visit Nana and Gramps and to find a house. We want you to come. We want you to look at schools, neighborhoods, tennis clubs, and homes that interest you. Would you like to bring a friend along?*

MOLLY: *I'll go if I can bring Trish . . . but that doesn't mean I like the idea any better.*

MAGGIE: *I understand, and I'm not going to force you to be happy about this. It isn't easy for me either. One thing, though, I want you to think about. Remember when you went to overnight camp the first time? Your tummy cramped during the whole ride to the Adirondacks. You were so scared to break into any of the camp groups on the lawn. Dad and I wouldn't leave until you felt settled. We were all pretty nervous, remember? But, as it turned out, Explorations became the best experience of your life. You faced your fears and found that you could make wonderful new friends—and you discovered tennis that summer!*

MOLLY: *But that was just camp. This is my life! I'm missing it already. I feel so accepted, so sure of myself. I know everybody. A new school . . . everyone already has friends. It will be so hard.*

MAGGIE: *Facing anything new is hard. Leaving behind the familiar is sad. I'll miss our home and all our friends too. What could help make the move easier for you?*

MOLLY: *E-mail, lots of trips back home, and invitations for all my friends to visit me. Maybe for the summer I could stay with Trish and then return in time for school.*

MAGGIE: *Sounds like a good plan!*

MOLLY: *But don't think I'm happy about this. Life is tough.*

MAGGIE: *I agree. But I want you to know that I'm proud of the way you are growing up.*

After about sixteen months, which is the normal adjustment period for an adult making a move, Molly loved her school, church, and friends in Indianapolis. Her parents' empathetic response to her, their patience, and their allowing her as many choices as possible helped Molly adapt to this major life change without undo problems. Her prior ability to confront and overcome her fears about middle school and overnight camp assured this adolescent that she had the necessary psychological skills to adjust again to a new situation involving a significant loss. She didn't have to like the loss, nor did her parents deny her grief.

ANGELS WITH HEADLIGHTS

We can reframe growing up as a series of gains and losses. The trajectory is far from linear and spans a series of regressions and spurts in youngsters of all ages. Of course, all losses, no matter their severity, are painful, but collectively they promise kids a mastery of emotional upheaval that will serve them over a lifetime if we help them face and manage any loss every step of the way.

How kids work through the mourning process and grow from it is up to us. We must be guardian angels who illuminate the shadows and paths of loss so that youngsters can understand, grieve, commemorate, and go on in the midst of emotional devastation and confusion. Although some might label this a "death book," these pages reveal the story of life. When we look on ourselves as parents and nurturing adults, our work to help children accept death and other losses is about promoting life and loving relationships every day.

Appendix:

Resources for Children, Families, and Communities

You can choose from the following selections of books and videos to help youngsters as they cope with a death or other loss. The first section, with its subsequent subsections, lists books for kids. These also will give you different insights into how children view loss and help you uncover meaningful language as you talk with your own kids. The second section encompasses readings for adults, and video materials are offered in the last section.

Books for Children on Death and Other Losses

General Literature

Armstrong, William. *Sounder*. New York: Harper & Row, 1969. This is a beautiful story, for children from eight to thirteen, about a young African-American boy and his dog who dies.

Buscaglia, Leo. *The Fall of Freddie the Leaf*. Thorofare, N.J.: Charles B. Slack, 1982. This book for all ages is a wonderful metaphor of life and death depicted by the changing seasons.

Cohen, Miriam. *Jim's Dog Muffin*. New York: Dell, 1984. When Muffin dies, Jim's first grade class helps him feel better; a book for kids from four to eight.

Gravelle, Karen. *Teenagers Face to Face with Bereavement*. Englewood Cliffs, N.J.: Julian Messner, 1989. This book deals with adolescent issues of grief.

Grollman, Earl. *Straight Talk about Death for Teenagers: How to Cope with Losing Someone You Love*. Boston: Beacon Press, 1993. A poetic and thought-provoking book for teens who have experienced the death of a friend or relative.

Mellonie, Bryan, and Robert Ingpen. *Lifetimes: The Beautiful Way to Explain Death to Children*. New York: Bantam Books, 1983. This book offers meaningful ways for youngsters ages three to nine to understand death.

Rogers, Fred. *When a Pet Dies*. New York: Putnam, 1988. This book of photographs and words helps kids from four to seven express what they feel and can do when a pet dies.

Viorst, Judith. *The Tenth Good Thing About Barney*. New York: Atheneum, 1971. A family comes together to grieve and commemorate the death of a pet cat, a story that will capture young children from four to eight.

Parental Death and Illness

Krementz, Jill. *How It Feels When a Parent Dies*. New York: Alfred Knopf, 1981. Eighteen vignettes written by children from seven to seventeen who share their feelings about their parent's death.

Lanton, Sandy. *Daddy's Chair*. Rockville, Md.: Kar-Ben Copies, Inc., 1991. A touching story for children and adults about the death of Michael's dad and how Michael deals with it in the Jewish tradition of Shiva.

LeShan, Eda. *When a Parent Is Very Sick*. Boston: Little, Brown, 1986. A self-help guide that highlights feelings and situations in which a parent is temporarily, chronically, or terminally ill. Youngsters from ten to fourteen can understand how illness affects entire families.

————. *Learning to Say Good-Bye: When a Parent Dies*. New York: Macmillan, 1975. This book helps bereaved children, ages eight and older, deal with their feelings when a beloved parent dies.

Madenski, Melissa. *Some of the Pieces*. Boston: Little, Brown, 1991. A family shares happy memories about a dad one year after his death and cremation. Kids from ages five to nine can identify with this story.

Sibling Death and Illness

Cohen, Janice. *Molly's Rosebush*. Morton Grove, Ill.: Albert Whitman and Co., 1994. This book deals sensitively about how children five years and older can understand miscarriage and loss of a premature fetus or infant.

Guest, Judith. *Ordinary People*. New York: Ballantine Books, 1976. A classic for all ages relates the story of Conrad, whose older brother died in a sailing accident in which he survived to struggle with guilt and turbulent feelings about his family.

Lowry, Lois. *A Summer to Die*. New York: Bantam Books, 1977. This is thirteen-year-old Meg's story about her family, her sister's death from leukemia, her new friendships, and her special talents. It speaks to youngsters from eleven to fourteen.

Richter, Elizabeth. *Losing Someone You Love: When a Brother or Sister Dies*. New York: Putnam, 1986. Fifteen youngsters, eleven and older, reflect on a sibling's death, giving honest reactions and feelings about their loss.

Grandparent Death and Illness

Hesse, Karen. *Poppy's Chair*. New York: Macmillan, 1993. Kids from ages four to six will enjoy this book about sharing memories with Grandma after Grandpa's death.

Miles, Miska. *Annie and the Old One*. Boston: Joy Street Books, 1971. Annie, a Navaho Indian girl, wants to prevent her grandmother's death by undoing a rug her grandmother is weaving. Her grandmother helps her to understand dying as a natural process of life; a book for kids from eight to eighteen.

Thomas, Karen. *Changing of the Guard*. New York: Harper & Row, 1986. A new girl at school encourages sixteen-year-old Caroline to open up, share her grief, and become friends after Caroline's beloved grandpa dies.

Friend's Death and Illness

Coerr, Eleanor. *Sadako and the Thousand Paper Cranes*. New York: Putnam, 1977. Children express their love and commemorate the short but spirited life of Sadako, a young Japanese girl who died from leukemia. Kids ages six to ten will enjoy this story.

Cohen, Janice. *I Had a Friend Named Peter*. New York: William Morrow, 1987. This book, for children from five to ten, talks about Peter, who dies suddenly after being hit by a car. Parents and teachers help Peter's friends understand death and carry on his memory in their lives.

Knowles, John. *A Separate Peace*. New York: Macmillan, 1959. During World War II, two friends in a boarding school share their trials and tribulations. An accidental death of one friend leaves the other to deal with his grief and guilt feelings about being responsible for the accident.

Paterson, Katherine. *Bridge to Terabithia*. Camelot, N.Y.: Avon, 1977. A story of friendship between a preadolescent boy and girl who have created a wonderful fantasy world. After her death, he must deal with his grief.

Smith, Doris B. *A Taste of Blackberries*. New York: Thomas Y. Crowell, 1973. Two best friends are picking blackberries together when one is stung by a bee and dies from an allergic reaction to the sting. The surviving friend learns to cope with the cause of this death and asks many questions in order to understand, heal, and go on with life. Kids ages eight to twelve will appreciate this story.

Suicide and HIV/AIDS Literature

Bunting, Eve. *Face at the Edge of the World*. New York: Clarion Books, 1985. After Jed's best friend hangs himself, Jed is left with many unanswered questions. This book realistically deals with interracial relationships, peer pressure, and drugs.

Cameron, Eleanor. *Beyond Silence*. Eight months after his older brother committed suicide, Andy continues to suffer from recurring nightmares. He goes on a journey of healing when he visits his ancestors' home in Scotland. This is a poignant story for teenagers.

Dougy Center. *I Wish I Were in a Lonely Meadow: When a Parent Commits Suicide*. Portland, Oreg.: Dougy Center, 1990. A book written by children who share their experiences and feelings about a parent's suicide. Youngsters from nine to fifteen can identify with these stories.

Girard, Linda Walvoord. *Alex the Kid with AIDS*. Morton Grove, Ill.: Albert Whitman and Co., 1991. A fourth grader writes about his new friend, Alex, who has AIDS, and the class learns that Alex is like any other kid. A book for youngsters eight to eleven, it offers a good description of what to do when someone falls and is bleeding.

Kolehmainen, Janet, and Sandra Handwerk. *Teen Suicide: A Book for Friends, Family, and Classmates*. Minneapolis: Lerner Publications, 1986. Frank discussions highlight what we know about suicide—the myths, misconceptions, causes, and warning signs. Hypothetical case studies demonstrate methods of prevention and coping with grief and guilt in teenagers.

Lerner, Ethan. *Understanding AIDS*. Minneapolis: Lerner Publications, 1986. Vignettes address preadolescent and adolescent myths, misconceptions, and fears about AIDS.

Quinlan, Patricia. *Tiger Flowers*. New York: Penguin, 1994. A young girl shares her memories of her uncle who died from AIDS. Kids seven and older can understand what a homosexual relationship means.

Thesman, Jean. *The Last April Dancers*. Boston: Houghton Mifflin, 1987. Sixteen-year-old Cat is frustrated by her mom's inability to recognize her dad's depression. After he commits suicide, Cat struggles with guilt and a strained relationship with her mother. Teenagers will benefit from this reading.

Divorce

Brown, Laurene. *Dinosaurs Divorce: A Guide for Changing Families*. New York: Little, Brown, 1988. This book deals with the sensitive issues that all kids face when their parents separate. It's especially poignant for youngsters from three to seven.

Fassler, D., M. Lash, and S. Ives. *Changing Families*. Burlington, Vt.: Waterfront Books, 1988. This book on coping with divorce, remarriage, and new families is for parents and children, especially those from four to eleven.

Krementz, Jill. *How It Feels When Parents Divorce*. New York: Alfred Knopf, 1988. Youngsters seven to sixteen share their feelings about their parents' divorce.

Stein, Sara Bonnet. *On Divorce: An Open Family Book for Parents and Children Together*. New York: Walker and Co., 1979. This book can motivate discussions with kids ages four to eight because it contains thoughts and feelings of kids on one page and views of parents on how to talk with children about their divorce on the facing page.

BOOKS FOR PARENTS, TEACHERS, AND OTHER CARING ADULTS

Brett, Doris. *Annie Stories*. New York: Workman Publishing, 1986. These are stories you can read to children under ten who have to deal with death and divorce.

Fox, Sandra. *Good Grief: Helping Groups of Children When a Friend Dies*. Boston: New England Association for the Education of Young Children, 1988. This is an excellent resource for any adult working with kids who have experienced the death of a friend. To order the book, call the Good Grief Program at 617-414-4005.

Gordon, Dennis, and Audrey Klass. *They Need to Know: How to Teach Children About Death*. Englewood Cliffs, N.J.: Prentice Hall, 1979. This book stresses the importance of kids learning about death and dying.

Graveline, Denise, and Jamie Quackenbush. *When Your Pet Dies*. New York: Pocket Books, 1985. Pet owners can benefit from understanding the many feelings children experience after the family pet dies.

Grollman, Earl. *Explaining Death to Children*. Boston: Beacon Press, 1967. This book offers wonderful language to explain death to kids.

————, ed. *Bereaved Children and Teens: Support Guide for Parents and Professionals*. Boston: Beacon Press, 1995. This books highlights writings from bereavements experts who answer some of the most provocative questions about childhood mourning.

Kalter, Neil. *Growing Up with Divorce*. New York: Ballantine Books, 1990. This highly informative book has copious details about the stages of divorce, the effects of fragmented families on children's development, the trade-offs involved, and the best ways to communicate with grieving kids throughout this process.

Kübler-Ross, Elisabeth. *On Children and Dying*. New York: Macmillan, 1985. This classic offers families guidance and information as they cope with a dying child.

Merrifield, Margaret. *Come Sit by Me*. Ontario: Women's Press, 1990. This book can aid parents and teachers to help four- to eight-year-olds understand AIDS and what it means.

Tasker, Mary. *How Can I Tell You?* Bethesda, Md.: Association for the Care of Children's Health, 1992. Written with knowledge and heart, this resource offers an abundance of information for parents, teachers, and community leaders to help them disclose and talk about AIDS with children and clear up associated stigmas and untruths.

Wolfelt, Alan. *Helping Children Cope with Grief*. Muncie, Ind.: Accelerated Development Inc., 1983. This psychologist helps parents, caregivers, teachers, and counselors understand bereaved children and talk with them.

Videos for Children and Adults

Aquarius Productions. "What About Me?" Wellesley, Mass.: Aquarius Productions. Call 508-651-2963. Children from various cultures and ages four to fourteen discuss their unique but universal grief experiences.

Centering Corporation. "Standing Tall: Teen Grief." Omaha: Centering Corporation. Write to 1531 N. Saddle Creek Rd., Omaha, NE 68104 or call 402-553-1200. Seven teens share how they heard about the death of a loved one, their feelings, and what helped them to go on with life.

Compassion Book Service. "Children Die Too." Burnsville, N.C.: Compassion Book Service. Call 704-675-9670. Parents and siblings who have experienced the death of a child, brother, or sister, candidly share their reactions and experiences.

————. "It Must Hurt a Lot." When Joshua's dog, Muffin, dies, it's the worst hurt Joshua has ever endured. He expresses his different feelings over time and realizes that his loss has given him strength and insights. A book of the same title is also available through Compassion Book Service.

Ellman, Deborah. "Shattered Dishes." Boston: Fanlight Productions. Write to 47 Halifax St., Boston, MA 02130 or call 800-937-4113. Three young women and men confront the intense emotions surrounding the breakup of their families and discuss how this experience has affected their own development and relationships.

Good Grief Program. "The Death of a Friend: Helping Children Cope with Grief and Loss." Boston: TMT Enterprises. Write to 200 Riverside Dr., Norwell, MA 02061 or call 781-826-0609. The psychologist Susan Linn and her puppets Catalion and Audrey Duck share their questions, worries, and feelings after their friend Allison was hit by a car and died. This video is for three- to twelve-year-old kids.

Hunt, David, and Daal Praderas. "Hope for the Future." Boston: Fanlight Productions. Write to 47 Halifax St., Boston, MA 02130 or call 800-937-4113. This video examines the effects of pediatric AIDS on four children and their families; also available in Spanish.

Kussman, Leslie. "What Do I Tell My Children?" Wellesley, Mass.: Aquarius Productions. Call 508-651-2963. Joanne Woodward narrates this video depicting experts, adults, and children sharing their feelings and thoughts about death.

ENDNOTES

PREFACE

p. xiii No one says this more poetically . . . : *The Complete Works of Swami Vivekananda*, vol. II, 10th ed., Mayavati Memorial Edition (Calcutta: Advaita Ashram, 1989), 226–27.

p. xv In the last verse of *Song of Myself* . . . : Walt Whitman, *Leaves of Grass* (New York: New American Library, 1958), 96.

CHAPTER 1

p. 3 Every fifteen minutes . . . : All statistics on children and adult deaths are from vital statistics reports issued by the National Center for Health Statistics, Department of Health and Human Services. I've obtained these statistics from two sources: (1) Population Reference Bureau, Inc., 1875 Connecticut Avenue, N.W., Washington, D.C. 20009-5728, telephone 202-483-1100 and (2) Stand for Children, 1832 Connecticut Avenue, N.W., Washington, D.C. 20009, telephone 800-233-1200.

p. 4 Rick's older brother, Luke . . . : A brief explanation of Down's syndrome can be found in *Taber's Cyclopedic Medical Dictionary* (Philadelphia: F. A. Davis, 1988), 489–90.

p. 7 In *The Tibetan Book of Living and Dying*,

Sogyal Rinpoche . . . : (San Francisco: HarperCollins, 1992), 7.

p. 7   What is Tommy telling us . . . : Twenty years ago, most clinical psychoanalysts believed that true mourning occurred in kids only after adolescence. See J. B. M. Miller, "Children's Reactions to the Death of a Parent: A Review of the Psychoanalytic Literature," *Journal of the American Psychoanalytic Association* 19 (1971): 697–719; M. Osterweis, F. Solomon, and M. Green, eds., *Bereavement Reactions, Consequences and Care* (Washington, D.C.: National Academy Press, 1984).

p. 7   Earl Grollman, a friend and colleague . . . : Rabbi Grollman's books include *Straight Talk About Death for Teenagers* (Boston: Beacon Press, 1993) and *Bereaved Children and Teens* (Boston: Beacon Press, 1995).

p. 8   In *Motherless Daughters,* Hope Edelman . . . : (Reading, Mass.: Addison-Wesley, 1994), 160.

p. 9   "Going through an active grief process . . . ": The quote, from Evelyn Bassoff, is cited in Edelman, *Motherless Daughters,* 160.

p. 9   Persistent nightmares, sleep or eating disorders . . . : Sandra Sutherland Fox, *Good Grief: Helping Groups of Children When a Friend Dies* (Boston: New England Association for the Education of Young Children, 1988), 17, 41–42.

p. 10   What happens to this child's family as a psychosocial unit . . . : Therese Rando, *Grief, Dying, and Death* (Champaign, Ill.: Research Press, 1984), 374–403; G. P. Koocher and J. E. O'Malley, eds., *The Damocles Syndrome: Psychosocial Consequences of Surviving Childhood Cancer* (New York: McGraw-Hill, 1981).

p. 10   She outlined four tasks that they work through . . . : Fox, *Good Grief,* 20–27.

p. 10   Bill Worden, a colleague of Sandra's . . . : J. William Worden, *Grief Counseling and Grief Therapy: A Handbook for the Mental Health Practitioner* (New York: Springer, 1991), 10.

p. 11 In *Motherless Daughters* . . . : Edelman, *Motherless Daughters*, 185.

CHAPTER 2

p. 13 *Understanding, the first task of mourning* . . . : Sandra Sutherland Fox, *Good Grief: Helping Groups of Children When a Friend Dies* (Boston: New England Association for the Education of Young Children, 1988), 21–23.

p. 14 Perhaps communicating about death . . . : E. Furman, *A Child's Parent Dies: Studies in Childhood Bereavement* (New Haven, Conn.: Yale University Press, 1974), 57.17

p. 17 Their fears and fantasies also help them . . . : Ibid., 45, 260–61. Kids watch others as they are getting information. If there are gaps in a story, they're inclined to fill in missing pieces.

p. 19 Although infants and toddlers respond to separation . . . : Maria S. Mahler, "On Sadness and Grief in Infancy and Childhood: Loss and Restoration of the Symbiotic Love Object," in *Psychoanalytic Study of the Child,* vol. 16 (New York: International Universities Press, 1961), 332–51.

p. 19 Preschool kids, between three and five years of age . . . : Maria H. Nagy, "The Child's View of Death," *Journal of Genetic Psychology* 73 (1948): 3–27.

p. 21 Youngsters in latency, between the ages of six and eight . . . : Ibid.

p. 21 Yes, our kids want to know . . . : Furman, *A Child's Parent Dies,* 14–17. Children not only need to understand death but they also need to feel safe in a secure environment. John Baker, Mary Ann Sedney, and Ester Gross also have noted that children look to protect themselves, their bodies, and their families in "Psychological Tasks for Bereaved Children," *American Journal of Orthopsychiatry* 62 (January 1992): 106.

p. 23 If Grandpa Henry is placed in a heavy metal casket . . . : Dennis Daulton, a licenced funeral home director and director of Dodge Laboratories, which manufactures funeral equipment and products, stated in an interview that worms cannot invade sealed caskets, 23 July 1997.

p. 24 Unless we can talk about what happened . . . : Furman, *A Child's Parent Dies*, 236–37.

p. 25 Most preadolescents have an adult understanding . . . : Nagy, "The Child's View of Death," 3–27.

p. 28 At puberty, young people . . . : M. Gilead and J. Muhlaik, "Adolescent Suicide: A Response to Developmental Crisis," *Perspectives in Psychiatric Care* 21, no. 70 (1983): 245–57.

p. 28 Although adolescents have an adult understanding . . . : Nagy, "The Child's View of Death," 3–27.

p. 33 What Rabbi Grollman has referred to as "straight talk" . . . : Earl Grollman, *Straight Talk About Death for Teenagers* (Boston: Beacon Press, 1993).

CHAPTER 3

p. 34 *Grieving, the second task of mourning* . . . : Sandra Sutherland Fox, *Good Grief: Helping Groups of Children When a Friend Dies* (Boston: New England Association for the Education of Young Children, 1988), 23–25.

p. 35 By avoiding his kids, he added . . . : John Baker, Mary Ann Sedney, and Ester Gross, "Psychological Tasks for Bereaved Children," *American Journal of Orthopsychiatry* 62 (January 1992), 106.

p. 35 *Unlike adults, children grieve* . . . : E. Furman, *A Child's Parent Dies: Studies in Childhood Bereavement* (New Haven, Conn.: Yale University Press, 1974), 23–24, 56–58. In "Psychological Tasks for Bereaved Children," 106, Baker, Sedney, and Gross have noted that if this painful task is not endured, bereaved kids will cling to the lost person as their primary source of internal emotional support; thus, the grieving process will be incomplete.

p. 36 Although aggression and obstreperousness . . . : Baker, Sedney, and Gross, "Psychological Tasks for Bereaved Children," 107. These authors have noted that younger children rely heavily on daily routines and physical care. The caregiver should provide environmental consistency and routine as much as possible to provide ego support and help kids contain their intense separation anxiety.

p. 39　All children regrieve a significant loss . . . : Furman, *A Child's Parent Dies,* 14–17.

p. 40　How strong the relationship was that a child . . . : Ibid., 25, 64–67.

p. 40　Rabbi Earl Grollman tells a wonderful story . . . : I've heard Rabbi Grollman relate this story during many of his speaking engagements.

p. 40　A powerful relationship does not necessarily . . . : Furman, *A Child's Parent Dies,* 25, 64–67.

p. 42　We might not see overt manifestations of grief . . . : The psychiatrist E. Lindemann first outlined and described anticipatory grief in "Symptomatology and Management of Acute Grief," *American Journal of Psychiatry* 101 (1944): 141–48. See also J. William Worden, *Grief Counseling and Grief Therapy: A Handbook for the Mental Health Practitioner* (New York: Springer, 1991), 108.

p. 43　In our culture, children suffer many *nonovert losses* . . . : Kenneth T. Doka, ed., *Disenfranchized Grief: Coping with Hidden Sorrow* (Lexington, Mass.: Lexington Books, 1989).

p. 44　Kids who protect their grieving parents . . . : E. Furman, "On Trauma: When Is the Death of a Parent Traumatic?" *Psychoanalytic Study of the Child* 41 (1986): 160–61, 192–93.

p. 44　Hiding our grief . . . : Ibid., 106–11.

CHAPTER 4

p. 47　*Commemorating, the third task in the mourning process.* . . . : Sandra Sutherland Fox, *Good Grief: Helping Groups of Children When a Friend Dies* (Boston: New England Association for the Education of Young Children, 1988), 25–26.

p. 47　We commemorate the dead in *formal* and *informal* ways . . . : Ibid., 25.

p. 49 First, you would have to explain how we care for . . . : In her book, *What to Do When a Loved One Dies* (Irvine, Calif.: Dickens Press, 1994), 15–58, Eva Shaw offers adults brief information and guidelines about autopsies, organ donations, cremation, embalming, wakes, funerals, burials, memorial services, and various religious services.

p. 51 My explanation is, "A *wake* doesn't mean . . .": *Merriam Webster's Collegiate Dictionary*, 10th ed., defines the word *wake* as "a vigil" or "watch held over the body of a dead person prior to burial and sometimes accompanied by festivity." An older child might understand this obtuse definition, but a younger one would find it too complex and abstract.

p. 53 According to a federal law enacted following World War II . . . : I obtained this information from an interview I conducted with Dennis Daulton, a licensed funeral director, 23 July 1997.

p. 55 Bewildered, I waited for his explanation . . . : Regarding the biblical reference to dust, Genesis: 3:19 Revised Standard Edition.

p. 55 *Preschoolers* (ages three to five) take all explanations . . . : Fox, *Good Grief*, 7–12; Peter Stillman, *Answers to a Child's Questions about Death* (Madison, Ala.: Guideline Publications, 1996). You can procure this booklet from Guideline Publications, P.O. Box 1141, Madison, AL 35758 or call 800-552-1076.

p. 55 *Latency-age children* (ages six to eight) have a real curiosity about dead people . . . : Ibid.

p. 56 *Preadolescents* (ages nine to twelve) are typically inter-ested . . . : Ibid.

p. 56 *Adolescents* (ages thirteen to adulthood) might have . . . : Ibid.

p. 61 An autopsy refers to a medical examination . . . : I have obtained this definition from "Autopsy," Microsoft Encarta CD-ROM, copyright 1994 Microsoft Corporation and copyright 1994 Funk & Wagnall's Corporation.

p. 61 If your child is interested in the detailed procedure . . . : The Pathology Laboratory for Medical Education has a website on the Internet as well as links to other sites. Its URL is http://telpath2.med.utah.edu.

p. 62   In 1996, there were 34,550 people waiting for kidney donations . . . : Statistics for waiting recipients come from the United Network for Organ Sharing. This network's hotline, available twenty-four hours a day, seven days a week at 800-24-DONOR, provides general information on transplants and gives all transplant centers. You can also contact its Internet website at http://www.unos.org. The American Council on Transplantation provides information on organ donation at 800-ACT-GIVE. The council's address is P.O. Box 1709, Alexandria, VA 22313.

p. 62   How do we explain organ harvesting . . . : Channing L. Bete Company publishes free scriptographic booklets that explain to children organ donation. Titles include *About Organ and Tissue Donation* and *Let's Learn About Organ and Tissue Donation.* You can call the company at 888–834–6640.

p. 62   The doctor would run a series of brain tests . . . : *Understanding Brain Death* (New York: National Kidney Foundation, 1996); *For Those Who Give and Grieve,* 2d ed. (New York: National Kidney Foundation, 1993). You can write to the National Kidney Foundation at 30 E. 33d Street, New York, NY 10016 or call 800-622-9010. The foundation's Internet website is http://www.kidney.org.

p. 62   The National Donor Family Council . . . : For a copy of the "Bill of Rights for Families" and a subscription to the free newsletter, *For Those Who Give and Grieve*, contact the National Kidney Foundation.

p. 63   There is also a National Donor Family quilt project . . . : For information concerning the quilt and *Stories from the Quilt,* contact the National Kidney Foundation.

p. 63   Many older kids would be interested to know that cremation . . . : The Cremation Association of North America provides a history of cremation through the following Internet website: http://www.cremationinfo.com/cope/history.html. The association's address is 401 North Michigan Avenue, Chicago, IL 60611, and phone number is 312-644-6610.

p. 64 I asked Dennis Daulton, a licensed funeral director . . . : Personal communication, 23 July 1997.

p. 64 The body is enclosed in a wooden or cardboard container . . . : The Cremation Association of North America publishes many brochures about cremation. Some include "Explaining Cremation to a Child," "The Cremation Process: Step by Step," and "Cremation Explained." I obtained these brochures through the courtesy of Debbie Dodge and Dennis Daulton of Dodge Laboratories, Cambridge, MA 02140.

p. 65 It can be a very delicate situation for funeral professionals . . . : Dennis Daulton, personal communication, 23 July 1997.

p. 65 Many kids think of Egyptian mummies . . . : For a history of embalming, see "Embalming" Microsoft Encarta CD-ROM, copyright 1994 Microsoft Corporation and copyright 1994 Funk & Wagnall's Corporation.

p. 65 Dennis Daulton told me that some youngsters . . . : Personal communication, 23 July 1997.

CHAPTER 5

p. 67 *Going on involves a transformation* . . . : Claude L. Normand, Phyllis Silverman, and Steven L. Nickman, "Bereaved Children's Changing Relationships with the Deceased," in *Continuing Bonds: New Understanding of Grief*, ed. Dennis Klass (Washington, D.C.: Taylor & Francis, 1996), 109.

p. 68 More recently, bereavement specialists have learned . . . : Kirsten Tyson-Rawson, "Relationship and Heritage: Manifestation of Ongoing Attachment Following Father Deaths," in *Continuing Bonds: New Understanding of Grief*, ed. Dennis Klass (Washington, D.C.: Taylor & Francis, 1996), 134–43.

p. 68 This sort of representational attachment . . . : Normand, Silverman, and Nickman, "Bereaved Children's Changing Relationships," 110.

p. 68 Along with her colleagues, Phyllis Silverman . . . : Ibid., 88.

p. 69 Some children conceive of their deceased parent . . . : Ibid., 88–90.

p. 69 If he doesn't work through the mourning process . . . : Ibid., 107.

p. 69 Judy was *emotionally detached* from her mother . . . : Tyson-Rawson, "Relationship and Heritage," 140.

p. 70 Those who envision a deceased parent . . . : Normand, Silverman, and Nickman, "Bereaved Children's Changing Relationships," 90.

p. 70 Mom had become a frightening ghost . . . : Ibid., 88; Tyson-Rawson, "Relationship and Heritage," 138.

p. 71 Their connection centers around their memories . . . : Normand, Silverman, and Nickman, "Bereaved Children's Changing Relationships," 90–91.

p. 71 In this way, Annie began her mourning process . . . : Ibid., 96.

p. 72 They believe that this parent is in heaven . . . : Ibid., 91.

p. 73 These qualities were a *legacy* from her dad . . . : Ibid., 93.

p. 74 Although Kathy has positive feelings . . . : Tyson-Rawson, "Relationship and Heritage," 139–40.

p. 74 She realizes that her dad . . . : Ibid., 136–38.

p. 77 The story of James Barrie . . . : *Peter Pan*, rev. ed. (New York: Bantam Books, 1994).

p. 81 Margaret Wise Brown wrote a poignant children's book . . . : *The Dead Bird* (New York: Dell, 1939).

Chapter 6

p. 85 When he created the main characters . . . : William Styron, *Lie Down in Darkness* (New York: Vintage Books, 1992); *Sophie's Choice* (New York: Vintage Books, 1992).

p. 85 Since Styron discovered that he suffers with depression . . . : William Styron's memoir is *Darkness Visible: A Memoir of*

Madness (New York: Random House, 1990); the quote is from "A Conversation with William Styron," a workshop conducted at the Boston Center for Adult Education, 17–18 October 1997.

p. 93–94 Always terminal, ALS . . . : The medical term for Lou Gehrig's disease is amyotrophic lateral sclerosis, or ALS. A brief explanation of this disease can be found in *Taber's Cyclopedic Medical Dictionary* (Philadelphia: F. A. Davis, 1988), 77.

CHAPTER 7

p. 110 Jessica, Josie's youngest granddaughter . . . : A brief explanation of senile dementia can be found in *Taber's Cyclopedic Medical Dictionary* (Philadelphia: F. A. Davis, 1988), 434–35.

CHAPTER 8

p. 115 Dominant among these issues are . . . : In "Stress and Coping in Children (Part I)," *Young Children* (May 1996): 42, Alice Sterling Honig has outlined a few issues that children and families face with a sibling loss.

p. 116 Support and care outside the home . . . : Alice Sterling Honig, "Stress and Coping in Children (Part II): Interpersonal Relationships," *Young Children* (July 1996): 55–57.

p. 129 Over 100,000 youngsters . . . : National Center for Health Statistics, "Annual Summary of Births, Marriages, Divorces, and Deaths: United States, 1994," *Monthly Vital Statistics Report*, vol. 43, no. 13 (23 October 1995): 4–5, table D. This statistic includes accidents, homicides, and suicides.

CHAPTER 9

p. 132 He tackled a large project of writing a book . . . : We are gratefully indebted to Maria Rege, Joey's aunt, for her generosity in giving us permission to print an excerpt from his book. For a copy of *Joey, You've Got a Brain Tumor,* write to Maria at 36 Eastnor Road, Apt. 3, Newport, RI 02840.

p. 136 Make-A-Wish is a nonprofit, volunteer organization . . . : For more information about this foundation, contact its Internet website at http://www.maw.org.

p. 137 Some students danced and all sang . . . : We are gratefully indebted to Judi McNulty for her generosity in giving us permission to publish the song that she and her fourth graders composed.

CHAPTER 10

p. 147 The word *stigma* . . . : Mary Tasker, *How Can I Tell You?* (Bethesda, Md.: Association for the Care of Children's Health, 1992), 6.

p. 158 A big one is the responsibility . . . : Ibid., 7.

p. 158 In either case, they might bitterly resent . . . : For general information on disclosure, see ibid., 15, and National Pediatric and Family HIV Resource Center, *What's Best for You,* a thirty minute film on HIV disclosure, Newark, N.J.

p. 159 Nine-year-old Yuri wrote . . . : You can obtain Yuri Evelyn Norton's book by contacting Shirley Baldwin Waring, 11 Mitchell Lane, Hanover, NH 03755.

p. 159 The poem "The Elephant in the Room." . . . : The poem was published and is copyrighted by *Bereavement Magazine.* We are gratefully indebted to Andrea Gambill, the editor-in-chief of the magazine, for her generosity in giving us permission to reprint an excerpt from this poem. For information about the magazine, a subscription, or a list of its book and poetry publications, contact Andrea at 5125 North Union Blvd., Suite 4, Colorado Springs, CO

80918; phone 719-266-0006; fax 719-226-0012; website
http://www.bereavementmag.com.

CHAPTER 11

p. 160 On the first day following this devastating act . . . : Cited in
Marilyn Augustin, Steven Parker, Betsy McAlister Groves,
and Barry Zuckerman, "Silent Victims: Children Who Witness Violence, *Contemporary Pediatrics* (August 1995):
35–36.

p. 160 The U.S. Department of Health and Human Services . . . :
Center for Mental Health Services and American Acadamy
of Pediatrics, *Psychosocial Issues for Children and Families
in Disasters: A Guide for the Primary Care Physician*
(Washington, D.C.: U.S. Department of Health and
Human Services, 1996), 3. Read more about this publica-
tion and others at the Center for Mental Health Services
website, http://mentalhealth.org.

p. 161 The bombing of the federal building . . . : For a discussion
about natural and human-caused disasters, see ibid., 3–4.

p. 161 They had great difficulty separating from their parents . . . :
Ibid., 8; Augustin et al., "Silent Victims," 36; "A Year of
Healing," *Sesame Street Parents* (April 1996): 40–42; and
John Leach, *Survival Psychology* (New York: New York
University Press, 1994), 134–36.

p. 164 Reading a comforting and happy story . . . : Ava L.
Siegler, "Safe and Secure: How to Help Your Child Feel
Protected from Life's Uncertainties," *Child* (April 1994):
43–44.

p. 164 When children are anxious about a disaster . . . : Ibid., 43.

p. 165 Playing, writing, and drawing pictures with them . . . :
Project Heartland, "When Something Bad Happens," a
brochure that discusses ideas about how to help kids work
through their grief following disasters. You can obtain
this brochure from Project Heartland Center, 5500 N.
Western Street, Oklahoma City, OK or call 800-522-
9054.

p. 166 By the time the fourth graders wrote letters . . . : "A Year of Healing," *Sesame Street Parents,* 41–42.

p. 169 The New York Times Company polled . . . : Cited in Alice Sterling Honig, "Stress and Coping in Children (Part I)," *Young Children* (May 1996), 56.

p. 171 *Being with Mother Teresa* . . . : We are gratefully indebted to Noah John for his generosity in giving us permission to reprint his journalist report. We are also indebted to Stefan Nadzo, editor of "The Zoo Fence," for permission to reprint this report, which first appeared on his website "The Zoo Fence—A Spiritual Commentary" at http://www.zoofence.com.

CHAPTER 12

p. 174 Psychologists have found that witnesses to an act . . . : Joy D. Osfsky and Emily Fenichel, eds., *Islands of Safety: Assessing and Treating Young Victims of Violence* (Washington, D.C.: Zero to Three: National Center for Infants, Toddlers and Families, 1996), 10.

p. 175 Although controlling chaos is wise and necessary . . . : Gale D. Pitcher and Scott Poland, *Crisis Intervention in the Schools* (New York: Guilford Press, 1992), 137–38.

p. 180 The adolescents and adults employed two common defense mechanisms . . . : I. Bolton, "Beyond Surviving: Suggestions for Survivors," in *Suicide and Its Aftermath,* eds. J. Dunne, J. McIntosh, and K. Dunne-Maxim (New York: Norton), 289–90.

p. 180 Some kids and adults used denial to defend against . . . : Ibid.

p. 180 Other adolescents and adults wanted to project . . . : E. Lindemann and I. Greer, "A Study of Grief: Emotional Responses to Suicide," in *Survivors of Suicide,* ed. A. Cain (Springfield, Ill.: Charles C. Thomas, 1972), 63–69.

p. 181 Research has indicated several relevant symptoms . . . : Scott Poland, *Suicide Intervention in the Schools* (New

York: Gilford Press, 1982), 68–72.

p. 181 I provided the parents of Rudie's peers with a pamphlet . . . :
Information in this pamphlet was taken from M. Seibel and
J. Murray, "Early Prevention of Adolescent Suicide," *Educational Leadership* (March 1988): 48–51.

p. 183 Although *anger* and *sadness* are the principal feelings . . . :
Lindemann and Greer, "A Study of Grief," 63–69.

p. 184 With an intentional death, the powerlessness that survivors
feel . . . : L. Berman, "Adolescent Suicide: Clinical Consultation," *The Clinical Psychologist* (Fall 1987): 87–89.

p. 190 This situation suggests the inexact nature of treating psychiatric illness . . . : K. Smith, "Child Suicide: Issues in
Assessment and Treatment" (paper presented at "Child
Suicide: A Conference of Hope," Houston, November
1985); Rae Corelli, "Killing the Pain," *Maclean's* (29 January 1996): 54–56. *Maclean's* is a Canadian news magazine
published weekly. On p. 55 of the article, a parent whose
adolescent committed suicide said that "if people talked
more openly about the suicide of loved ones, that might
diminish the stigma and make doctors and psychiatrists
less inclined to dismiss parental concerns."

p. 190 With a traumatic loss, the media's MO seems to be . . . :
J. Ring, "Working with the Media," in *A School Approach
for the Prevention of Youth Suicide,* ed. Indiana State
Board of Health Education (Indianapolis: Indiana State
Board of Health Education, 1985).

p. 192 Rudie, we hardly knew each other . . . : We are gratefully
indebted to Rosemary Banks for her generosity in giving us
permission to publish her poem.

p. 195 The network ran . . . : "Checkpoint on Suicide" (Boston:
WCVB-TV News, 12 March 1993), feature story on
nightly news broadcast.

p. 196 I call this phenomenon the "wet cement" dynamic . . . :
Pitcher and Poland, *Crisis Intervention in the Schools,* 39–42.

CHAPTER 13

p. 198 *Bereavement overload* originally defined . . . : R. J. Kastenbaum, "Death and Bereavement in Later Life," in *Death and Bereavement*, ed. A. H. Kutscher (Springfield, Ill.: Charles C. Thomas, 1969).

p. 198 Past experiences might leave bereaved kids . . . : Therese Rando, *Grief, Dying, and Death* (Champaign, Ill.: Research Press, 1984).

CHAPTER 14

p. 219 Although parents become ex-husbands and ex-wives . . . : Neil Kalter, *Growing Up with Divorce* (New York: Ballantine Books, 1990), 13.

p. 219 As divorce has become more prevalent in our society . . . : Barry B. Frieman, "Separation and Divorce: Children Want Their Teachers to Know," *Young Children* (September 1993): 61. Frieman quotes two statistics concerning divorce in the U.S. in the 1990s: Close to one-third of the kids under eighteen can expect that their parents will be divorced, and many couples divorce during their kids' first eight years.

p. 219 Even five years following the divorce . . . : Alice Sterling Honig, "Stress and Coping in Children (Part I)," *Young Children* (May 1996): 59.

p. 219 In 90 percent of divorces . . . : Kalter, *Growing Up with Divorce*, 11–14.

p. 220 A child's adjustment to parental divorce . . . : Ibid., 5; Honig, "Stress and Coping in Children," 59–60.

p. 220 For some families, the crisis . . . : Kalter, *Growing Up with Divorce*, 5–6.

p. 220 The first phase of the divorce process . . . : Ibid., 6–12; Honig, "Stress and Coping in Children," 59.

p. 221 Kids might witness verbal . . . : Kalter, *Growing Up with Divorce*, 10.

p. 222 Contrary to what we might assume . . . : Ibid., 9.

p. 222 Parents who argue and disagree . . . : Ibid., 12–14; Honig, "Stress and Coping in Children," 59–60.

p. 222 If parents don't assume joint custody or responsibility . . . : Kalter, *Growing Up with Divorce,* 12.

p. 222 Adjusting to custody settlements can be . . . : Ibid., 13–15.

p. 223 During the transitional phase, kids also must begin . . . : Ibid., 16.

p. 223 Anger, jealousy, emotional dependency, depression . . . : Ibid., 18.

p. 224 At the same time, *remarriage,* which happens . . . : Ibid., 18–21.

p. 225 Anger, sadness, anxiety, abandonment, loneliness . . . : Frieman, "Separation and Divorce," 62.

p. 225 Parents need to observe their behavior . . . : Honig, "Stress and Coping in Children," 60.

p. 225 "If he loved me . . . :" Ibid.

p. 225 Many young school-aged kids . . . : Frieman, "Separation and Divorce," 62.

p. 225 Teachers, in turn, should be compassionate . . . : Ibid., 61.

p. 226 Both boys and girls can suffer from lack . . . : Kalter, *Growing Up with Divorce,* 15.

CHAPTER 15

p. 239 Help your children to develop relationships . . . : Neil Kalter, *Growing Up with Divorce* (New York: Ballantine Books, 1990), 21.

CHAPTER 16

p. 265 He had multiple sclerosis (MS) . . . : A brief explanation of MS can be found in *Taber's Cyclopedic Medical Dictionary* (Philadelphia: F. A. Davis, 1988), 1075.

CHAPTER 17

p. 271 The first swallow tells Mr. Rat . . . : Kenneth H. Grahame, *The Wind in the Willows*, 75th ed. (New York: Antheneum Books, 1993).

CREDITS

WE are gratefully indebted to . . .

Maria Rege, Joey's aunt, for her generosity in giving us permission to print an excerpt from his book. For a copy of *Joey, You've Got a Brain Tumor*, write to Maria at 36 Eastnor Road, Apt. 3, Newport, RI 02840.

Judy McNulty for her generosity in giving us permission to publish the song, "A Song for Ryan," that she and her fourth graders composed.

Andrea Gambill, editor-in-chief of *Bereavement Magazine*, for her generosity in giving us permission to reprint an excerpt from the poem, "The Elephant in the Room," by Terri Kettering, which is copyrighted by *Bereavement Magazine*. For information about the magazine, a subscription, or a list of its book and poetry publications, contact the magazine at 5125 North Union Blvd., Suite 4, Colorado Springs, CO 80918; phone 719-226-0006; fax 719-226-0012; website: www.bereavementmag.com.

Noah John for his generosity in giving us permission to publish his journalistic report, "Being with Mother Teresa." We are also gratefully indebted to **Stefan Nadzo,** editor of *The Zoo Fence* for permission to reprint this report that first appeared on his website:

"The Zoo Fence—A Spiritual Commentary" at http://www.zoofence.com.

Rosemary Banks for her generosity in giving us permission to publish her poem, "In Mourning."

INDEX